Mind in the Heart of Darkness

MIND IN THE HEART OF DARKNESS

Value and Self-Identity
among the Tswana of Southern Africa

Hoyt Alverson

New Haven and London
Yale University Press: 1978

Designed by Thos. Whitridge and set in IBM Theme type.
Printed in the United States of America by The Murray
Printing Company, Westford, Mass.

Published in Great Britain, Europe, Africa, and Asia (except
Japan) by Yale University Press, Ltd., London. Distributed
in Australia and New Zealand by Book & Film Services,
Artarmon, N.S.W., Australia; and in Japan by Harper & Row,
Publishers, Tokyo Office.

Library of Congress Cataloging in Publication Data

Alverson, Hoyt, 1942–
  Mind in the heart of darkness.

  Bibliography: p.
  Includes index.
  1. Tswana (Bantu tribe) 2. Self-perception.
3. Acculturation. 4. South Africa—Economic conditions.
5. Botswana—Economic conditions. I. Title.
DT797.A44   301.24'1'0968   78-4909
ISBN 0-300-02244-1

To Rre Gustav Ernst Segatlhe
and other friends among the Tswana

"Ditsala tsame, batho ba Botswana, ke nna Modise. Mo lokwalong lo, ke kwadile mafoko ya lona, dikgopolo tsa lona. Buka e ke borogo, jwa go bofa, jwa go lomaganya, mafatse a rona. Ke itumetse thata gore ke kana ka ultwatsa tuso, e lo e mpileng ka bopelonomi. Kealodumedisa, kealeboga, lona lotlhe. Ke eleletsa gore, re tlabo re bonana gape kgantelenyana."

CONTENTS

ILLUSTRATIONS

Maps, pages xiv and 20

Modern Botswana
South Africa, 1899

Photographs, following page 164

Mother and child in the courtyard
Contractees just home from the South African mines
Inspanned oxen
Horse and wagon
View of Kanye, a large Tswana village
Housing in Soweto, Johannesburg, South Africa
Women singing prayers before the meal
Traditional doctor and herbalist in Kgaphamadi
Young girls hauling water
Children in Kgaphamadi
Old men selecting an animal for slaughter
Slaughtering a goat for a feast
Rre Segatlhe "discerning" by throwing bones
Man playing the *saranguri*
Cooking hut in a Tswana homestead

PREFACE

This book describes researches carried out among the Tswana of southern Africa, in communities representing varying degrees of exposure to a colonial political economy. I made my observations first in South Africa, in five Witwatersrand (Johannesburg) industrial firms and one Orange Free State gold mine, over the course of one year, 1966–1967; and, later, in Botswana over an eighteen-month period, January 1973 to March 1974, June 1974, and December 1974 to January 1975. In describing the settings and the methods of these investigations, I have made an effort to depict accurately my own relationship to the Tswana, a departure from the tradition that assumes the ethnographer and the reader are "objective" spectators of the society under study.

The book is a philosophical meditation as much as it is a report of my observations. During the years between the two stages of my research, I wrestled with a familiar intellectual dilemma: how does one reconcile the freedom and creativity of thought and language with the material determinism of society and history? Or, in another formulation, how does one reconcile consciousness, looked on as a structure that can comprehend pure possibility, with the deterministic, probabilistic, and random processes of culture and evolution? It was my training in modern transformational linguistics that led me to see consciousness as a structure open to pure possibility, while my interpretation of the structure of culture and evolution flowed from an explicit set of neo-Marxist assumptions about human societies. The insufficiency of either of these approaches for understanding the data I was amassing motivated an intense philosophical inquiry during the first six months of my field work.

Rather by chance I had included among the books I carried into the bush two volumes which I turned to during this period of questioning: *The Phenomenology of the Social World*, by Alfred Schutz, and *The*

Phenomenology of Perception, by Maurice Merleau-Ponty. In these two writers I found not only a satisfying theoretical and intellectual synthesis of materialism and idealism, but also a program, a design, for my own research. Readers familiar with the philosophies of Schutz and Merleau-Ponty will be in a position to ferret out of my purported *description* of the Tswana the critical, that is philosophical, arguments that I am making not only concerning the Tswana but also against much of contemporary empiricist anthropology and social science in general.

While my research and writing have been largely solitary in conception and execution, I have benefited immensely from the stimulation, material assistance, and charity of others, and to them I wish to express my gratitude. Allie Dubb, director of the African Studies Institute at the University of the Witwatersrand in Johannesburg, and his wife, Erika, provided me and my family with most welcome intellectual stimulation and cordial hospitality during our stay in Johannesburg for the year 1966–67 and during our brief visits there while working in Botswana. David Hammond-Tooke, chairman of the department of social anthropology at the University of the Witwatersrand, not only provided study facilities at the university but also made available to me, at cost, camping equipment, research supplies, and a four-wheel-drive vehicle for my work in the Kalahari Desert. Indeed, the members of the department of social anthropology at "Wits" formed a most congenial academic milieu in which I spent many rewarding hours on visits to Johannesburg from Botswana. Among their number I should like especially to thank Kerileng Moloantoa, both for her rigorous and patient tutoring in Setswana and for her help in getting us settled in Botswana. My thanks go also to David and Glenda Webster for their solicitous and unstinting moral and logistic aid and companionship.

For nine of my first fifteen months in Botswana, my family and I lived in a mud and dung rondavel in a rural area, where the nearest water was over four kilometers away. About seven kilometers from us was Content Farm. Ellwyn Miller, a Peace Corps volunteer who was the farm manager, and his wife, Beverley, opened their home to us, and we visited them every three or four weeks for conversation in English, sharing of varied experiences, and for hot baths, which meant so much to us in the dusty and windblown semidesert environment. Now settled in Vermont, the Millers are still the good neighbors they were then, 8,000 miles away.

My wife, Marianne, and my children, Keith and Brian, experienced both the joys and trials of my first fifteen months in Botswana. The fact of our living together as a family and the rapport we all established with the community made my presence and my work far more meaningful both to me and to the Tswana than it would have been had I been alone.

Several dozen Tswana opened their lives to me, making possible all that follows in these pages. To them, and in particular to Rre Gustav Ernst Segatlhe, my "Father" in Kgaphamadi, the book is dedicated.

A number of friends and colleagues have read portions of this text, expending considerable time and effort to provide me with constructive criticism. My thanks go to William Foltz, Stanley Greenberg, Harold Scheffler, and Leonard Thompson, all of Yale University, and to Gwendolen Carter of the African studies department at Indiana University, for their assistance. My colleagues at Dartmouth, Hans Penner and Edward Yonan, have provided cogent criticism of my writing and warm encouragement of this project. My friend and colleague David Gregory gave me, very freely, days of his time to prepare and develop the photographs used here. He did his best to salvage the artistic and cultural significance from often poor or damaged negatives and badly taken pictures. Ellen Graham of Yale University Press took immediate and serious interest in the manuscript. She gave me critically important advice in revising early drafts and shepherded the manuscript through a rigorous process of review and criticism. Maureen Bushkovitch did a meticulous and masterly job not only in copyediting but in querying abstruse argumentation and helping to provide a clearer and more readable text. For their incisive criticism and their warm encouragement I am most grateful.

Apropos of writing: I have avoided using Setswana words except parenthetically and when they seemed called for in the interests of those readers who know the language. In the few cases where I have used Setswana terms, I have chosen not to encumber them with Setswana derivational and inflectional affixes. The exception is the word *Setswana,* which means "language and culture of the Tswana."

Finally, I wish to acknowledge the material support offered me by Dartmouth College in the form of a Faculty Fellowship and fifteen months leave, and receipt of a grant from the National Institutes of Health (RO1MH22010-A1), without which this work could never have been undertaken. Needless to say, the findings and conclusions it contains are mine alone and do not necessarily reflect the opinions or policies either of Dartmouth College or of the National Institutes of Health.

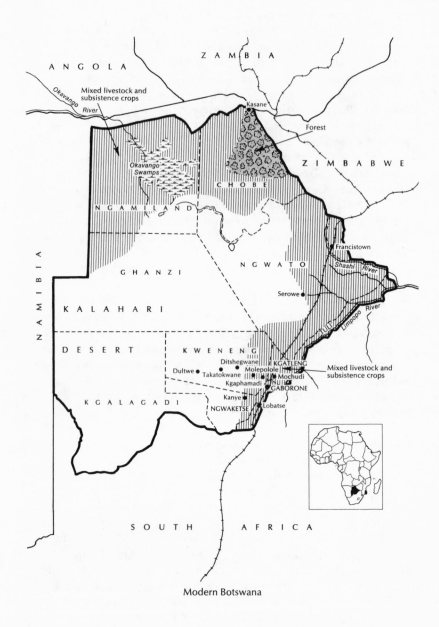

Modern Botswana

I THE MAJOR QUESTIONS

An ambitious and timely question in the human sciences asks how social institutions shape an individual's beliefs about who and what he is. In other words, how do the institutions of which an individual is part affect his conscious self-identity? A narrower question following from this wider one asks how rigid systems of colonial control affect the conscious self-identities of peoples whose existence is for the most part lived out in the lowlands of colonial domination.

In the social sciences, in psychiatry, in the novels and poetry of Third World writers, the well-articulated answer—almost the consensus—is that the denigration inherent in modern colonialism, called here "the heart of darkness," produces deep and lasting psychic scars in the peoples subjected to such systems. According to this view, colonial institutions shape, indelibly and ineluctably, the most central beliefs an individual holds about his own being—his conscious self-identity. While the rulers as well as the ruled are shaped by the institutional fabric of the heart of darkness, it is the bondaged and not their masters who are said to bear the scars of domination.

Three contemporary Third World writers—Richard Wright, E. D. Morel, and Frantz Fanon—provide compelling formulations of this "scars of bondage" thesis.

> Frog perspectives: someone looking from below upward. . . . a sense of someone who feels himself lower than others. A certain degree of hate combined with love . . . is always involved in this looking . . . and the object against which the subject is measuring himself undergoes a constant change. He loves the object because he would like to resemble it. He hates it because his chances of resembling it are remote. . . . The core of reality today for hundreds of millions resides in how unlike the West they are and how much and how quickly they must [come to] resemble the West. . . . This "frog perspective" prevails not

1

only among Asians and Africans who live under colonial conditions, but among American Negroes as well. [Wright 1964, pp. 5-7]

For three centuries the white man seized and enslaved millions of Africans. . . . But what the partial occupation of the soil by the white man has failed to do, what the maxim and the rifle have failed to do, what the slave gang, labour in the bowels of the earth, and the lash have failed to do, . . . the power of modern capitalistic exploitation . . . may yet succeed in accomplishing. From the evils of the latter . . . there is no escape for the African. Its destructive effects are permanent. It kills not the body merely, but the soul. . . . The African in the tropics is capable of tremendous physical labours. But he cannot accommodate himself to the Europeans' system of monotonous, uninterrupted labour with its long and regular hours, involving . . . severance from natural surroundings. . . . When the system is forced on him, the tropical African droops and dies. [Morel 1969, p. 8]

I came into the world imbued with the will to find meaning in things . . . , and then I found I was an object in the midst of other objects, sealed in that crushing objecthood. . . . I am overdetermined from without. I am the slave not of an idea that others have of me, but of my own appearance. [Fanon 1970, p. 82]

Western social science and psychology have added their diagnostic epithets to the painful cries of Third World elites. "Dissociative reactions," "self-hate," "inconsistent self-image," and "regression" are some of the suggested outcomes of discrimination in a colonial mode. "Culture of poverty," "backward society," and "culture of repression" are social science categories subsuming whole communities within the range of effects stemming from colonialism.

To argue fairly and cogently that the conclusions of these and numerous other writers are false or substantially in error would require a considerable digression at this point. While some criticism of these claims has been made (Valentine 1968; Leacock 1971; Alverson in press), I believe that the materials presented in this book will show the necessity for a serious rethinking of what has been cited as a "majority view" on the "scars of bondage" thesis.

To motivate concern for the wider question of the correspondences between the content of conscious self-identity and the institutions of society, we will enter the world of a people called the *Tswana*, who live in southern Africa. They live in places where the indignities we call colonialism—the heart of darkness—have been a central fact of life for over a hundred years. But there has been much more there as well: tradition, change, survival, struggle, movement, coping, adaptation. There is much we can learn from the Tswana which bears directly on our major questions. But to learn from a people so distant and seemingly so different from ourselves as the Tswana, we cannot simply travel, tourist-like, through their communities and their lives, taking superficial, cross-sectional pictures of the action. For the important lessons are to be found not so much in the surface features of social behavior as at the deeper levels of meaning and experience. In no human society are the deeply held beliefs that comprise self-identity reliably signaled or designated by overt behavior—the surface of social life. If we are to understand the correspondences between the Tswana's institutional structures and their authentic beliefs, we must of necessity enter their interior lives. Our principal tool will be language; our principal strategy will be our reflection on and analysis of their forms of language-use. But before we can undertake this task we must define certain concepts, so that we may observe and reflect with precision and clarity. As Alfred North Whitehead has said, "Thought precedes observation." We must know before we can see.

Conscious Self-Identity: Some Preliminaries

The following is a useful and reasonably precise definition of conscious self-identity: Self-identity consists of those authentic beliefs a person holds about the *who-and-what-he-is* which resist variations in the outside forces that impel his various social actions. Despite the metaphoric qualities of this definition, it captures four important considerations. First, the words *who* and *what* tell us that the beliefs have as their object some essential core of features, attributes, propositions, feelings, and so forth, which are not accidental or variable but *necessary* to the experience of the self. Second, the word *resist* implies something more than a mere "common denominator" of the experience of self or of behavior. It suggests, rather, an active striving against forces which, were it not for this striving, might alter those beliefs about the self. Third, the phrasing of the definition implies that the person himself is conscious of what he believes. While not everything one is lies within consciousness, much of it does. This conscious component consists in particular of the beliefs one holds about the essential *what-I-am.*

Finally, this definition concedes that while an individual's social behavior may be impelled (by habit, sanction, and so forth), what a person believes himself essentially to be is *not* merely the sum of his accumulated behaviors or actions. Rather, it is a construction, an object of belief which resists the shaping and molding of social forces. His self-image resists, and therefore is not a simple function of the patterned and predictable actions he performs in acquiescence to society.

What are some of the properties of consciousness that must be assumed in an attempt to understand the Tswana? There are two important conflicting views on this subject in philosophy and the human sciences. The first or *empiricist* account argues that mind or consciousness as such is fairly simple: thought and belief are possible because the rich and varied environment of the organism is slowly "interiorized" via experience (learning); the "sensed" environment becomes, over time, the content of the interior of the organism—its mind.

Mind or consciousness, in this view, is basically the way in which sense impressions and behavior patterns are recorded and remembered. Through the behavior of the organism—impelled by simple drives, guided by sensory capabilities, reinforced or punished through contact with the external world—responses are learned and stored in memory. By these means consciousness, including self-consciousness, is slowly constituted. The content of mind, self, thought, or belief has its origin in the individual's biography of overt, behavioral experience. Appeals to an a priori structure of mind or consciousness are considered either pointless or spurious. The structure of the environment and a few mechanistic assumptions about "states" of the organism: drives, sensory capacities, random movement, memory, and so forth, are sufficient to account for the organism's skills, abilities, habits, and beliefs.

The second and contrasting philosophical tradition in the study of consciousness and its contents is called *rationalist*. In this tradition mind or consciousness is assumed to have a highly complex structure that is not learned or acquired, but innate, making an active contribution to experience. The environment, or sensory engagement with it, is considered relatively less important in accounting for thought, skills, and beliefs. In this view, "direct" contact with the environment is only one factor in the learning enterprise; it sets in motion the inborn structures of the mind, which can then manifest themselves in language, belief, and behavior. No amount of mere contact or acquaintance with the external environment can possibly account for the content of mind.

As the rationalist position maintains that consciousness is not simply a correlate of overt behavior, so it holds that human *freedom* and *will* play an equal role, along with the determinism of history and material circumstance, in the making of culture and in our being human; and that through the limitless capacity of language and the language-user to create universes of symbolic experience, meaning becomes as much the domain of the possible as of the actual.

In relation to our major questions, the differences between a rationalist and an empiricist account become very clear. The empiricist observes the colonial scene and posits its phenomenal qualities from his own, "objective" viewpoint. He does the same with the behavior of the subject: he observes his behavior "objectively" and describes its phenomenal qualities. The empiricist's task is then one of discovering the correspondences between the colonial system (the input) and the behavior of the colonized (the output). Relatively few assumptions are made concerning the way in which processes of thought, consciousness, meaning, or belief intervene in these correspondences. Hence the relation between input and output is presumed to be direct and causal.

On a rationalist account, the colonial environment is seen as only *one* of the factors contributing to the behavior or belief of an individual. His consciousness is thought of as a complex structure, capable of creating meanings and projecting these meanings onto environments and events. Therefore consciousness and self-identity are not simply parallel to the person's environment nor are they determined by it. Behavior and belief can only be related to the colonial experience by means of a complex model of human consciousness. Neither colonial domination nor any other empirical circumstance can directly determine the content of belief or action, including beliefs concerning self-identity. In other words, a rationalist would argue that colonial experience itself is principally to be found in the subjective world of consciousness.

Merleau-Ponty provides a persuasive rationalist formulation of a person's relation to himself in consciousness—a view I shall adopt in interpreting the self-experience of the Tswana: "It is clear that no causal relationship is conceivable between the subject and his body. . . . For myself, I am neither jealous, nor inquisitive, nor hunch-backed, nor a civil-servant. Consciousness can never objectify itself into 'invalid-consciousness,' or 'cripple consciousness' . . . in the heart of his own consciousness, each one of us feels beyond his [external] limitations" (Merleau-Ponty 1962, p. 434). No human being is simply the sum of the "objective" characterizations that others have created. The experience of self results only in part from taking on the views of the others. Our knowledge of others may be based on analogy with what we know of ourselves; but our knowledge of ourselves cannot be based simply on what we imagine others know of us.

The *self* must exist in part by virtue of the freedom or power of the individual to create meaning in the world. And it is this ability to bestow meaning and hence to help constitute the nature of the environment that is the privilege of consciousness and distinguishes it from a mere thing. As Merleau-Ponty says: "In order to be determined . . . by an external factor, it is necessary that I should be a thing. . . . If, *per impossibile*, I had once succeeded in making myself into a thing, how should I subsequently reconvert myself to consciousness?" (Merleau-Ponty 1962, pp. 434–35).

Self-identity, self-image, or self-concept, as I shall define it in this investigation, is a structure containing beliefs pertaining to a unique province of meaning, in that the meanings and beliefs that flow from consciousness refer directly back to consciousness itself. This "self-reflexive" quality of consciousness makes it unique. The capacity of consciousness to invest meaning extends to the self as well as to events and the environment. Hence, a person's central beliefs entail—more or less prominently—an awareness of oneself as the one who believes. In the course of a normal day everyone has reason to make hundreds of "predications" upon an "inchoate I," the foundation of self-identity. I'm a ____ ; that sure was ____ of me; she really feels good about having ____. But despite the fact that everyone daily makes or hears numerous, important predications upon the "I," few ask the fundamental question, "What is that 'I' which exists *prior* to such predications, yet which changes through time as a consequence of them?" Most people in most societies do not ask such questions. But all peoples do ask questions or make statements which bear directly on these issues. It is universal of human experience that the believer, the actor, exercises his capacity to move from awareness of the public meaning of thoughts, actions, and beliefs back to the agent, the self who acts, thinks, and believes. This is not to suggest that all humans, or even many, are philosophers. It is to say that common sense and the stock of beliefs contained in culture reflect man's now explicit, now tacit, curiosity about the self.

Now inquiry into something as abstract and arcane as *self-identity* poses a serious problem. How does one ask pertinent questions without "leading the witness"? How does one avoid suggesting ideas that may never have occurred to a respondent? How does one know that the subject's thinking is not a product of the researcher's particular queries? A possible solution is the empiricist one: do not inquire directly into the construct under inquiry, but instead infer—by means of "psychological" formulas—the nature of the construct from responses to seemingly unrelated, innocuous questions or observations. What the research subject believes concerning the topic of inquiry is in this view an impediment to obtaining "scientifically" valid data. A consequence of this supposition is that researchers generally do not tell subjects much about what information is actually being sought. Behind this approach lies the conviction that conscious beliefs—whether they belong to common sense or to cultural knowledge—are generally erroneous and ill-founded. Hence, to remove the "contaminating" or "confounding" effects of conscious knowledge, the researcher must pose only those questions whose intended meaning for research the naive subject cannot discover or interpret. Likewise, the meaning imputed to the responses usually bears little relation to the meaning the subject intended to communicate.

The work reported here is based on the contrary premise that a person's conscious and sincerely held beliefs about self-identity as such and himself in particular are important and valid indicators of—or even the basis for—what he objectively is. Further, this fundamental concept of the self (or some closely related meaning structure) profoundly affects the way an individual interprets a wide range of experiences that *affect* self-identity. In short, *a concept of self-identity is itself part of self-identity.* Hence any study of self-identity must come to grips with people's own beliefs about it. This view suggests the pertinence of a direct or "phenomenological" approach, the methods for which are described in succeeding chapters.

From this understanding of what constitutes consciousness of self flows a premise that informs my whole endeavor to interpret the correspondences between the material incorporation of the individual into society's institutions and the content of his conscious self-identity. A *belief in one's power to invest the world with meaning* (the "will to believe") and a *belief in the adequacy of one's knowledge for understanding and acting on personal experience* are essential features of all human self-identity. I assume in this study that these are to some degree universal and innate properties of human Being. The belief in one's power to create meaning and the belief in the adequacy of one's knowledge for understanding and acting on personal experience are influenced by two considerations in the case of the Tswana: (1) the material conditions of the individual's self-sufficiency or dependency and (2) his pursuit of specific goals or *life-projects* through command over central cultural resources. Consciousness is always free and creative, but freedom and creativity are not limitless. We all live within the constraints and limitations of a material and institutionalized world, which presumably exists in some way independent of our beliefs and our knowledge of it. The goal of this book is to describe both the material, institutional context of Tswana life and the subjective meaning or experience of that life as it bears on the content of the conscious self-identities of the people. I will include in this discussion questions arising from the claims of the "scars of bondage" literature: for example, do there exist specific material, institutional conditions (viz. in a colonial political economy) which can effectively destroy a person's power to create meaning and hence to understand the "facts" of his experience in life? Does any aggregate of Tswana exist under material conditions which present the individual with such inexplicable facts of experience that he is overwhelmed and comes to question his very human worth?

The organization of this book directly reflects the concerns expressed in this introduction. Chapter 2 is a broad general introduction to the Tswana and to southern Africa. It attempts to fill out the abstract questions just posed by reference to the history, political economy, culture, and community life of the Tswana. Chapters 3 and 4 offer a detailed description of the material, institutional aspect of the Tswana world. These chapters describe the relationships that exist among various indigenous Tswana communities and institutions and the surrounding colonial political economy of southern Africa, whose center is of course that industrial colossus, the Republic of South Africa. Chapters 5 through 8 describe, primarily in the language of the people themselves, the meaning and significance the Tswana give to their own social world as well as to the colonial industrial order within which, in varying degrees, their lives are circumscribed. The final chapter suggests some of the implications of this study for the ambitious questions asked in this brief introduction.

2 SOCIAL AND HISTORICAL BACKGROUND OF THE TSWANA

To discover the correspondences between the institutions of Tswana and southern African society on the one hand, and the "self-identity" of various Tswana individuals and groups on the other, we must be aware of the major social forces, historical and contemporary, that have affected their world. Many studies—those in the "scars of bondage" genre, for example—fail to take into account the rich and complex meanings that the important events take on in the lives of the people studied.

I will begin with a brief sketch of the recent history and broad institutional horizons of Tswana society, with special reference to the ways in which local communities are systematically linked to the political and economic institutions of nation states and the regional economies of which they are a part.

The Sotho-Tswana: A Background Sketch

By 1600 the Sotho and Tswana already occupied approximately their modern habitats. There is some evidence to suggest that eastern South Africa was settled by groups possibly ancestral to the Sotho and Tswana as early as 1100 A.D. (Inskeep 1969, p. 39). The Sotho and Tswana constituted one of the main components of the great prehistoric "Bantu" migrations from the Great Lakes of the Rift Valley into southern Africa.

The Tswana are a linguistically and genealogically defined subgroup of the Sotho peoples, who have over the past four or five hundred years become ecologically and culturally differentiated from the other southern Bantu-speaking peoples with whom they share a common heritage and origin. Today the Tswana peoples are found throughout Botswana, the western Transvaal, and northeastern Cape Province. Small enclaves are also found in southwestern Zimbabwe (Rhodesia), Namibia (South-West Africa), and the northwestern Orange Free State. Throughout this vast region the Tswana coexist with other Bantu-speaking peoples. There is some variation in dialect and other components of culture but in the main the Tswana are culturally "homogeneous." Tswana political units are based on a putative kinship principle which serves to divide the society into discrete groups. Most of these groups constitute chiefdoms, where centralized authority resides in a single ruler or chief, his council, and his kin or others whose loyalty and allegiance is given directly to him. In modern times the underpinnings of these groupings have been profoundly altered by the existence of nation states and colonial regimes. Hence the concept of chiefdom and the distinctions based on it are more and more confined to "memory culture": ceremony, oral history, and anthropologists' observations.

Today there are over two million people who call themselves "Tswana," or agree that such a label applies to them. One-third live in Botswana, the other two-thirds in the Republic of South Africa. In "pre-contact" times these numbers were much smaller. Traditionally the Tswana were a self-subsistent agricultural and pastoral people. Since aboriginal times they have practiced hoe agriculture with rotating fallow. During the nineteenth century they adopted plow agriculture, using their own oxen as draft power. Food production was, and in Botswana still is, mixed and eclectic. Agricultural practice is limited more by resource availability than by "inertia" or lack of ideas.

Water was and still is the single most important variable in determining the scope, scale, and mix of various food-production strategies. The climate in this "platteland," or upland savanna, is rather uniform, except for rainfall. The westernmost Tswana area, the Namibia-Botswana border, is desert, with 250 millimeters of rain or less per annum. Agriculture there is confined to animal husbandry and kitchen gardens where ground water is available. As one moves east, the desert continues for some five hundred linear kilometers and gradually gives way to mixed scrub, associated with greater mean annual rainfall. In the area about one hundred kilometers west of the modern rail line through Botswana, the desert ends and veld or savanna commences. Here the rainfall varies from around five hundred millimeters to about eight hundred millimeters per annum in the central Transvaal.

The rain falls in a single season, November through March. Arable agriculture is pretty much confined to this period. Since frost is light even in the dead of winter, it is only the lack of water that prevents year-round agriculture. The principal indigenous crops grown are sorghum, millet, and, since contact with the Europeans, maize. These are supplemented by varieties of melons and squashes, in addition to wild berries and tubers.

Animal husbandry is valued equally with arable agriculture by the Tswana, although its nutritional importance is much less. Goats, sheep, cattle, and pigs are kept, as well as chickens. Dogs and, since contact, donkeys, mules, and horses are nonfood animals used in a variety of ways. Roughly speaking, livestock represent in Tswana culture what the "investment portfolio" represents in ours. One keeps stock for a variety of goals, long- and short-term, some practical, others symbolic or expressive. In all cases animals are a central measure of one's worth, self-esteem, and peace of mind. Animals were not traditionally grown for sale, in the sense we think of in our own beef-hungry society of universal salability. Hunting is important to all Tswana, and every Tswana loves a guinea fowl or rabbit in the pot, even if today it is hunted by running it down in a pickup truck. In pre-contact times hunting of large game was a collective, "age-set" endeavor and was done with spears, axes, and clubs. Today systematic hunting is not typical of the Tswana, except in some Kalahari communities where arable agriculture is not possible because of a shortage of water.

The Tswana, both today and aboriginally, derive a very high proportion of their total caloric and protein intake from a beer called *bojalwa*—a light, chalky beverage made from sorghum or millet, a culture of bacteria, and now malt. While diet is varied and fairly rich in protein by African standards, improper nourishment (or even what by our criteria counts as malnutrition) is an important factor in the epidemiology of disease.

Both traditionally and today, many of the Tswana maintain a complex pattern of residence. Typically each Tswana has three residences, although only one is officially "home." Each Tswana lives, first, in a home village. Villages are "nucleated" settlements composed of wards or sections that are, ideally, territorial groupings of kin by descent and marriage. Villages can vary in population from a few hundred to several thousand. The modern "tribal capitals" of Serowe, Mochudi, Molepolole, Kanye, and Ramoutswa range from ten thousand to twenty thousand inhabitants. It is in a village that the Tswana usually maintains a permanent residence and here he lives when he is not working on the agricultural lands, which are in some instances many kilometers from the village. At the "lands" he often maintains a second residence, whose quality, size, and elaborateness reflect the amount of time he chooses to live there. Generally he will live there during the rainy season, when plowing, planting, and harvesting are taking place. Cattle are kept (at least for a good part of the year) at a third location, called the "cattle posts." Here the accommodations are rudimentary, and those staying there are typically adolescents or others whose labor is cheap. These are ideally areas with a rich natural grass cover and a water supply, though when cattle are moved it is most often in search of water.

The household usually contains a core of a husband and his wife or wives, children, perhaps the parents of the husband or wife and the children of certain sons, and typically (in older days) daughters whose "bride wealth" had not been received. The division of labor by sex and age is less rigid—that is to say, less mutually exclusive—now than in times past, though sex constitutes by our standards a very rigid, vertical, caste-like cleavage affecting every aspect of human relations. Men and women see each other as members of different "groupings" and in many social activities one's sex may be a more important criterion for association than ties such as marriage and kinship.

Men have had and still do have enormous power over the disposition of a wife's labor. Generally men dominate women psychologically. Women were in past times, with few exceptions, legal minors dependent on some man or men. There is no real folk conception of an illegitimate inequality between men and women. The relations between the sexes are seen as based on a *proper* inequality (like the relationships between adults and minors in our own society).

Tswana society puts great emphasis on kinship as the basis on which the political, juridical, economic, and religious aspects of society are organized. Sedimented in the terminology of the kinship system are the most important principles for recruitment to social roles: sex, age of one individual relative to that of another (senior versus junior), and lineage membership. These are the three main criteria that determine entitlement to most of the other roles an individual will occupy in his lifetime—roles which are "elaborations" of these basic entitlements. Most important in the history of the Tswana peoples has been the founding of autonomous chiefdoms based upon the breaking up of royal lineages, often under the leadership of dissident members or heirs to statuses or chattles. Tswana chiefdoms (there are fifty distinct ones named by the Tswana) are in fact political communities based upon the tracing of descent or affiliation to the chief, who traces his descent to the founding ancestor of the tribe. Even the distinct chieftainships base their kinship to one another on putative genealogical connections among their founding ancestors. Now, to be sure, the actual membership of any given chiefdom is not made up of definite or even fictive descendants of a common ancestor. Yet, conceiving of the political community in terms of royal lineage with several "attached" or common lineages, all of whose members are kin, is a powerful factor in Tswana society.

The most important kinsfolk of any individual are naturally those most "closely" related. But the principle of lineage makes closeness relative to the *kinship system* rather than to some genetic principle. One's lineal ancestors and descendants traced through men on one's father's side of the family are the most important, as they constitute a corporate landholding, wealth-controlling group. One's mother's kinsmen (especially the mother's brother) stand in a special relationship too. This can also be said of the parents and grandparents of one's wife. The wife's patrilineage and the husband's patrilineage achieve an alliance through the marriage of the "children" of their lineage.

Establishment of residence and most other social undertakings take place within important constraints and opportunities provided by the kinship system. Villages and lands are generally divided into hamlets or sections within which the heads of households will typically be patrilineally related kinsmen. One's closest associates throughout life are likely to be kinsfolk by blood or marriage.

Age is an important ranking criterion in Tswana society. Generally speaking, any senior of the same sex is one's superior and any junior of the same sex one's subordinate. These echelon-type entitlements of age are contravened only in certain cases, for instance in the relations among the chiefly and the commoners, where age may be subordinated to descent as a ranking principle. Ranking by age is further elaborated in a complex system of age-sets or age-regiments. Among almost all the Bantu-speaking peoples of southern Africa these age-sets are based upon tribe-wide groupings of men and women who come to maturity at about the same time. Periodically, male and female adolescents are separately initiated into sexually segregated sets in elaborate ceremonial and educational rites de passage. A person remains in his or her age-set throughout life. He owes deference to age-sets of his seniors, can expect the same from junior age-sets. Typically one of the tribal chief's younger children or nephews (or nieces) would be appointed as the age-set leader. While the set is tribe-wide and therefore cuts across the local and vertical cleavages created by the reckoning of descent, it is still organized on a local community basis for many of its activities, such as warfare, public works, hunting, policing of executive decrees, entertainment, and so forth.

Wealth differences in preindustrial societies differ in kind and degree from those that appear in industrial societies. In general, the less "complex" the society is and the less the "social-economic surplus" produced, the smaller wealth differences will be. By our standards the Tswana are a most egalitarian society. From the point of view of the Tswana themselves their society exhibits enormous differences in individual wealth. The major index or marker of wealth, as well as the chief form of wealth itself, is cattle, which are a source of draft power, of cash, of advantageous loans and alliances, of clients bound to one's favor, and of women (i.e., wives and the children they bear, over whom one exercises power). Wealth differentials, however, are subject to redistribution. In former times wealth carried with it the heavy burden of generosity. This was a requirement that had teeth, for the loss of services due to stinginess could impoverish an individual despite his temporary cushion of stock and fields. The burdens of having wealth in Tswana society led to much more and more certain redistribution than is accomplished by our own allegedly progressive income tax. Communal life is necessarily antithetical to a ruinous individualistic freedom to hoard, accumulate, or otherwise control scarce resources against the interests of all other members of the community.

The governance of Tswana life everywhere has been profoundly altered by the advent of Europeans and their governments. The actual working effectiveness of tribal-chiefly government varies considerably from group to group in modern Botswana, and it is a ceremonial and social control agency of the state in South Africa. At the village level there are still in most places courts of the traditional sort competent to try certain offenses against certain communal laws, if committed by certain parties (i.e., both parties are under the jurisdiction of the court for that offense category). Chiefs and their subchiefs command informal respect by virtue of personal generosity and wise counsel. But their capacity to make or find law, either in the settlement of disputes or in their actions as legislators in the traditional councils, has been tightly circumscribed by the administrations in both Botswana and South Africa.

What we call the *supernatural* or sacred is a very important part of daily life for almost all Tswana. The distinction between the known and the unknown or the sacred and the profane (that is to say, what we verify or falsify versus what we accept on faith) has no analogy in Tswana society. The world is the world; life is life; and people living or dead are people somewhere carrying out their human work. The Tswana speak of the "created order." This includes stones and witches alike. God is autonomous but *definitely a part of creation as much a creator.* Evil is committed by incarnate and nonincarnate agencies, all of which are part of the *natural* or "created" order. God is very much alive for believers, present but hardly active for most, and maybe dead for a sizable minority. Less than half the Tswana I met in Botswana professed any religion, in the sense of affiliation with a church or other organized body of believers.

The belief that there exist animate and intelligent nonanimal beings. who may be benign or malevolent, is nearly universal, from the ministries of the national government to the most remote rural villages. These are the kind of living forms we call ghosts, spirits, witches and so forth. In addition to these nonanimal living forms there exist *certain modes of human intending* which cause effects directly, *independent* of any overt action of those intending. For example, sorcery can affect the victim's life and welfare. Even envy and jealousy can bring about illness in those who are its objects. *Motives,* or modes of intending, *can pollute or cleanse the world just as do the "spirits."*

The Tswana believe in what we call rational explanation. In their system of knowing there is the unknown but there are few "mysteries." The unknown remains unknown because of inadequate methods and too little time to use even these. The world is orderly and that is why knowledge is orderly. As far as I can tell, there is nothing for the Tswana that is inherently irreducible to a rational system of belief. Even such "unknowns" as eclipses, behavior of animals, human fickleness, and strange epidemic illness are assumed to have causes which are in principle like those of well-understood phenomena. European medicine, for example, is considered better in treating certain illnesses than is traditional medicine. But no Tswana believes that European medicine works in mysterious ways. The Tswana—like all of us—accept things on faith, because there is every reason to believe that things accepted on faith can ultimately be known, and will not hold any great surprises when they are. Like humans, supernatural beings have wily ways, but Tswana medicine is powerful and one can deal effectively with witches, sorcerers, ghosts, and so on. A person need only be prudent and timely in his countermeasures. Death, a mystery for some of us, is for the Tswana a logical, necessary progression which is no more mysterious than other boundaries in life, space, and time.

Southern Africa: Dramatis Personae

The Beginnings
The aboriginal inhabitants of southern Africa were not Bantu-speaking peoples nor Europeans, but rather the San (popularly called "Bush-men") and the Khoikhoi (popularly called "Hottentot"). The San have been displaced by Europeans and Bantu-speakers, and they now occupy limited areas of the Kalahari Desert, a fraction of their former habitat. The Khoikhoi have been genetically amalgamated with the Dutch immigrants and the descendants of slaves they imported from Southeast Asia, Madagascar, and tropical Africa and (with the assistance of various segregation laws) have formed a heterogeneous hybrid population known collectively today as "Cape Coloured." The Khoikhoi were incorporated by European settlers as farm labor and occasionally as soldiers. The San have been made clients in the pastoral economies of the Kalahari by the Tswana and other Bantu-speaking peoples. Both these groups are peripheral to our study.

The modern principals in the southern African scene, the Bantu-speakers and the Europeans, are both comparatively recent arrivals to the territory south of the Limpopo River. The Bantu-speakers came no more than fifteen hundred years ago, while the Europeans have been there as settlers for little more than four hundred years.

The beginnings of white hegemony over southern Africa are traced by many historians to the establishment of a refreshment station at Table Bay in 1652 by Jan van Riebeck on behalf of the United Netherlands Chartered East India Company. This station constituted the beginnings of Cape Town and of the gardens that were to grow food to supply the company ships that plied the waters east around the Cape of Good Hope. To maintain this station at Cape Town, a small colony capable of producing a surplus of food as well as its own subsistence was required. The labor for this task was to come principally from free farmers (Boers) who emigrated from Holland, Germany, and other parts of northwestern Europe to Cape Town. These people, along with some Huguenot immigrants who came after 1685 and English settlers after 1800, comprised the vanguard of the white conquest of southern Africa.

The first 125 years of this white settlement did not bring the European immigrants into intimate contact or conflict with the main population of the Bantu-speaking peoples. The settlers in this period, migrating both northeastward (toward the Orange River), and eastward (toward the Indian Ocean) were moving in territory occupied mainly by San and Khoikhoi, whom these trekkers rather effectively displaced, killed, or assimilated as an underclass in the frontier society. The Bantu-speaking peoples were to be found in the eastern areas of what is now the Cape Province, in Natal, and in the high central plateau known as the "highveld." The settlers did not make significant intrusions into these regions until the last quarter of the eighteenth century.

During the 125-year period from the founding of Cape Town to the beginnings of warfare between the white settlers and the Bantu-speaking peoples, the basic economy and culture of European life in southern Africa were established (Katzen 1969, p. 184). The settlers who migrated away from the commercial center at Cape Town were essentially agricultural and pastoral peoples. Living in isolation from the intellectual, economic, and technological changes that took place in Europe from the seventeenth to the twentieth century, they established and sustained the values and institutions of a frontier society, basing them on ideas of religion, labor-practice (including slavery and indentured servitude), and political independence that drew inspiration from pre-Enlightenment Europe. These values and institutions the settler (or "Afrikaner") immigrants fought to uphold against the contrary interests of the indigenous Africans, against the policies of the Dutch East India Company, and, after 1806, against the British. The Afrikaner disaffection with company policy and the crowding of land near Cape Town led many Afrikaners to trek away from this center, inland and along the coast, in search of new territory, greater personal autonomy, and indentured or enslaved labor. This movement proceeded without interference from the Bantu-speaking peoples until the third quarter of the eighteenth century. At that time the two peoples, both expanding in search of land, cattle, and game, confronted one another in the general area of the Fish River. The next hundred years would witness a protracted and bloody struggle between the Afrikaners and the Bantu-speaking peoples, including the Tswana. The result of this struggle would be the subjugation of all the African peoples by the Afrikaners and their incorporation as an underclass into the agricultural and, later, industrial economy of South Africa.

The Invasion of the Tswana World

> No one who wishes to understand the history of South Africa . . .
> can ignore the *platteland*, for the platteland was the cradle of Afri-
> kaner life and nationalism. Indeed, it was the place where most of the
> groups for which South Africa was home had had their formative
> experience. . . . It was in the platteland that there evolved . . . the
> pattern of relationships between Black and White that was to imprint
> itself indelibly upon the country's political, social, and economic
> structure. [Francis Wilson, 1971, p. 104]

Two events provided the foundation of platteland history. First there
were the violent interethnic wars waged by the Zulu chief Shaka and
his successors. Spawned by combinations of population pressures,
technological innovations, and megalomania, these wars affected
virtually all of southern Africa. The second event was the migratory
expansion of the Afrikaners from the coastal regions of Cape Province
and from Natal to the interior platteland. Both of these events took
place during the brief period between 1823 and about 1840.

The indigenous upheavals begun by Shaka in the second decade of the
nineteenth century are known in Zulu as *mfecane* and in Sotho or
Tswana as *difaqane*, which means in both languages "the time of great
troubles." The origin of this spread of conquest societies was Zulu-
land, where the Zulu under Shaka developed a new form of military
organization based on the same economic surplus as in the older societies. Shaka's exploits occasioned the appearance of similar organizations among other Nguni-speaking groups, such as the Swazi and
Ndebele (Matebele). In 1823 this latter group, under Mzilikazi, one of
Shaka's client lieutenants, penetrated deeply into the platteland occupied by the Sotho and Tswana. This invasion of the Sotho-Tswana
world by the Matebele led to profound population movements, including the migrations of the Sotho into the hills of modern Lesotho and of
the Tswana into the western Transvaal and modern Botswana. These
movements precipitated many changes in the structure of the older
societies. Continuous warfare and a search for territorial security added
to the extent of these social changes. As more and more groups began
to gain their own economic surplus by means of predatory warfare and
fewer and fewer by their own indigenous agriculture, total agricultural
production in the region declined dramatically. Reduced total production necessitated increased interethnic predation as a means of gaining
a livelihood. Thus the necessity either of waging war or of defending

oneself against invaders became a cardinal consideration in the organiz-
tion of society.

One of the most important social changes among both the Nguni and
the Sotho-Tswana was the adaptation of the age-regiments to largely
military purposes. As mentioned above, the age-set organizations
grouped individuals on the basis of a society-wide initiation of adolescents. These individuals remained in the same group throughout their
lives. Sets of varying seniority represented ranks with specific obligations to society. With the increased importance of military activity, the
age-set principle came to overshadow the lineage principle in the organization of collective effort and in the distribution of power. Age-sets
became military age-regiments directly under leaders appointed by the
chief. In short, what were once fraternities of men united by common
age, yet divided by varied kinship ties, became private armies. In the
days before the *difaqane* the age-sets had competed with the lineages
in the exercise of power. Now they became a power unto themselves
under the direct command of the chief or, significantly, under that of
his appointed deputies. By means of the age-based regiments, different
communities were organized into larger and larger units whose sole
raison d'être was armed combat.

The use of leaders who were not necessarily relatives of the chief yet
were appointed by him to command the age-regiment activities created
new opportunities for rebellion and division within these societies. No
longer were the age-grades hedged in by kinship restrictions and the
power held by royalty. With each appointed bureaucrat having a
standing army at his disposal, the temptations and opportunities of
rebellion and revolution were greatly increased. This opportunity is
illustrated by the appearance of various renegade groups that hived off
from what had up till then been unitary societies.

In 1806 the British wrested control of the entire Cape Province from
the Afrikaners, control which in 1843 was extended to Natal. The
advent of the British constituted one of the major causes of the Afrikaner migration from the coastal regions into the platteland. British
settlers had arrived in the Cape and after 1849 in Natal and had begun
to compete with the Dutch in the local agricultural and commercial
economy. In time the British began to impose certain conditions on
the Afrikaner settlers. First, in 1812 the British established a series of
circuit courts to hear, inter alia, charges of brutality in the Afrikaners'
treatment of African laborers. Second, in 1828 the British abolished
most of the Afrikaner-inspired "vagrancy laws," violation of which was

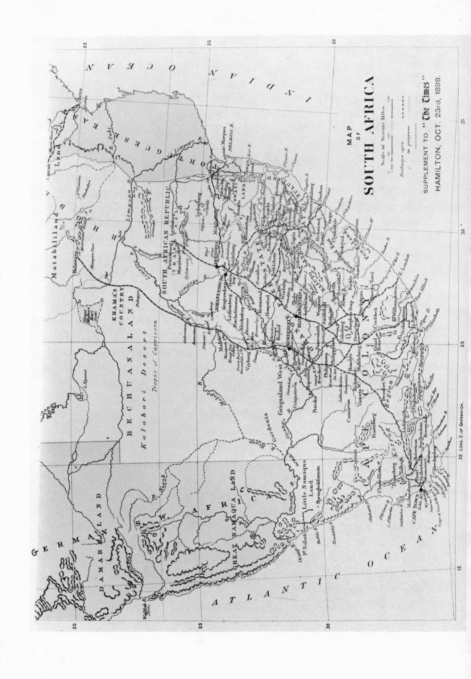

MAP
OF
SOUTH AFRICA

Scale of Statute Miles

Railways open
in progress

SUPPLEMENT TO "The Times"
HAMILTON, OCT. 23rd, 1899.

the pretext used to secure indentured African labor. Third, in 1834 the institution of slavery was abolished throughout the British Empire. In the Afrikaner view these events threatened their survival in Africa. In 1836 some of the Afrikaners, in search of new lands and a haven from British administration, began massive treks into Natal and north beyond the Orange River. Within two years of entering Natal, the Afrikaners had conquered the Zulu, one of the great battles being the one at the Blood River in 1838. This defeat of the Zulu (under Dingane, Shaka's successor) facilitated the rise of less prominent imitators of the Zulu chief. For reasons too complicated to go into here, many of these trekkers were frustrated in their efforts to settle in Natal, despite the vanquishing of the Zulu (cf. Thompson 1969a, pp. 364–73). Large numbers of Afrikaners then crossed the Drakensberg Mountains and settled in Vaal-Orange river basin. Meanwhile, beginning in 1836, large numbers of Afrikaners in the Cape Province, fed up with direct British interference in their lives, sold their property and trekked off to areas north of the Orange River (Thompson 1969b, pp. 405–06). This Afrikaner "invasion" of the highveld of course disrupted—indeed, in some cases, devastated—Sotho-Tswana groups there.

The Afrikaner settlements, also called "republics," gave the Sotho-Tswana peoples of the platteland their first significant contact with white *settler* colonization. Even though the Dutch population north of the Orange River at mid-century was less than forty thousand, while the African population was in the millions, the Dutch were able to incorporate the Africans into a system of peonage, thus providing the labor necessary for Afrikaner pastoral and farming business.

The Matebele meanwhile continued to prey upon certain Sotho and Tswana groups and upon the Afrikaners as well. But in 1837 the Dutch themselves colonized the highveld and defeated the Matebele decisively, chasing them across the Limpopo River into Zimbabwe, where their descendants remain to this day.

In sum, a three-pronged invasion of the Tswana world took place in the first half of the nineteenth century. Afrikaners, missionaries, and various indigenous military conquerors, in particular the Matebele, all converged on the platteland—the home of the Tswana—at about the same time. The major adaptive problem faced by the Tswana and their Sotho neighbors to the east was to find a territorial and cultural modus vivendi with these mutually hostile forces.

While the British controlled the Cape Province and Natal, their entry into the platteland added yet another important dimension to the historical and cultural background of the Tswana peoples. In 1852 and again in 1854 the British formalized their conflict with the Afrikaners by recognizing the various Boer republics which had been established in the platteland. The most famous of these republics were the Orange Free State and the South African Republic (the Transvaal). Each of these Boer republics established a body of law concerned mainly with securing a steady, plentiful, and cheap supply of farm labor. This was the prime meaning of Afrikaner colonization to the indigenous peoples of the platteland. Between 1836 and the 1870s most of the Tswana became serf-like subjects of the Dutch farmers. Expropriation of land forced the Tswana (and others) to occupy a much smaller territory than before the white conquest. This meant that many Tswana had to settle as squatters on farms, earning their living by offering their labor in exchange for the right to use land taken from them only a few years earlier.

In the thirty years after 1852, Afrikaner interests in the land to the west (now Botswana) increased, as did the contrary British interest in preventing them from blocking the (Botswana) road to the north. The Tswana tribes in the west, namely the Kwena, Kgatla, Ngwato, and Ngwakgetse, remained intact and independent of extensive intrusion by the Afrikaners until the discovery of minerals: gold in Tati (northeastern Botswana) in 1866, diamonds at Kimberley in 1867, and gold on the Witwatersrand in 1886.

After the establishment of the Afrikaner republics in the highveld, commercial agriculture rapidly rose in importance: sheep in the highveld interior and sugar in Natal. Wheat, maize, butter, and beef were all in demand in the growing urban centers on the coast, especially Cape Town. This increase in agricultural commerce led the Afrikaners to expand their territorial holdings at the expense of already conquered or recalcitrant Tswana and to impress more and more of them into agricultural labor. The Afrikaners became plantation owners rather than farmers. In each of the republics many "laws" were enacted that were in fact pretexts for securing farm labor. The rapid incorporation of Africans as squatters (for a consideration) precluded any successful regrouping of displaced Tswana or Sotho peoples into the tribal political communities from which they had been extirpated during the "time of great troubles" (*difaqane*). Only the westernmost Tswana remained outside the increasing control of the Afrikaners and their forced labor regimes. But the less fortunate of the Orange Free State and Transvaal people had been completely conquered and "pacified" by the last third of the century. Tribal life became a shrinking domain of social practice and more and more a memory, a cherished recollection of things past, as the realpolitik of the white colonists transformed the people into a rural peasantry.

The labor-recruiting system of the Boer republics was integrally related to their criminal law. For an African *not to be working* for the Afrikaners constituted a liability for criminal prosecution and summary justice, which would result in contractual servitude to the landowning class. Breach of this contractual servitude was informally an injury to the farmer and formally an assault on the state. Corvée labor (provided by docile chiefs) was a part of the public service to be rendered to the state by each tribe or lineage. Cattle were taxed, thus forcing their sale to Afrikaners at favorable prices. Forced residence on reserves too small to support the population compelled Tswana to live on squatter sections of farms, where so many days of labor per year were required as "rent." Africans were permitted "legally" to leave their reservations only if they were ready to work on farms under the conditions set down by the Afrikaners. In the South African Republic (Transvaal) an apprenticeship labor system was adopted, wherein children captured in various skirmishes with Africans could be kept as labor pawns for specified periods until they earned their freedom. Destitute parents could even sell their children into pawn in order to get the cash necessary to buy food or other goods. These purchases probably put the money right back into the hands of the Afrikaners, as they were the main purveyors of goods.

Many missionaries who had entered the platteland from the southwest, shocked and outraged, were prepared to act against the Afrikaners for their treatment of the African population. The missionaries were in something of a bargaining position with the British government, since the latter saw the missionaries as useful agents of social control in the interior. The missionaries would presumably "pacify" the Africans on the side of the British, occasionally supply guns to them for use against the Afrikaners, and keep the interior open to British and Cape Province interests.

Once again the Afrikaners found their access to land and labor obstructed by the British, this time by their missionary work. The Afrikaners' expanding population and wasteful farming practices necessitated a continuous search for new lands. No sooner was the ink dry on the Sand River Convention in 1852 than the Afrikaners decided that the land in what is now Botswana was fair game. In this convention no mention was made of the *western* boundaries of the Transvaal Republic. In 1853 a commando of Boers trekked off to the west, sacked Molepolole (the tribal capital of one of the Tswana groups), and burned David Livingstone's nearby house. Livingstone, away at the time, escaped harm and appealed to the British in Cape Town to help get the Afrikaners out of Tswana territory. The British did not respond. For the next two dozen years the Afrikaners continued to expand westward and northward into Tswana territory, checked only occasionally by the armed resistance offered by some Tswana groups. During this time Britain gave up even its halfhearted efforts to contain Afrikaner expansion and its alleged protection of African interests as the missionaries represented them.

The discovery of gold in 1866 in extreme northeastern Botswana, while short-lived, attracted many to parts of Tswana territory that had until then been spared white occupation. In 1867 diamonds were discovered at Kimberley in territory that was soon incorporated into the Cape Colony. Once again Afrikaner and other prospectors and settlers were attracted to the diggings, where they settled and generally disrupted indigenous Tswana life.

Continuous pleas from Africans to the British to intervene on their behalf and protect them from settler aggrandizement fell on deaf ears. In 1868 the Orange Free State came so close to toppling the southern Sotho leader, Moshoeshoe, that the British reluctantly declared Basutoland a colony. The same appeals from the Tswana in the west to declare a protectorate were ignored.

The diamond discoveries at Kimberley did, however, prompt the British in Cape Province to take measures to prevent the Afrikaner republics from annexing this mineral-rich territory. The British government even went so far as to try to annex the Transvaal in 1877, but it relinquished that control after a military defeat in 1880. As part of the treaty restoring the independence of the Transvaal, the western boundaries were fixed roughly where they are today. Still the Afrikaners continued to stream westward across the established frontier into western Tswana territory. Despite the appeals of such chiefs as Sechele and Khama, Britain remained unmoved by their pleas for protection against the Afrikaners.

For two important reasons Britain abruptly changed its policy in 1885. First, Britain (or at least its agents) was persuaded that extensive mineral wealth lay in the African interior and therefore wished to preserve access to the region. As long as the Tswana could keep the settlers from completely dominating the "road to the north," Britain believed that its caretaker mission of protecting its access to the interior was being fulfilled. Second, in 1884 Germany declared a protectorate over the entirety of South-West Africa, and at the same time the Transvaal declared a protectorate over the Boer mini-republics of Stellaland and Goshen. With Germany entrenched in east Africa (now Tanzania), staking its claim to South-West Africa, and quite capable of making alliances with the Afrikaners, Britain saw clearly that Germany was capable of establishing a coast-to-coast colonial presence in Africa. This coast-to-coast German preserve would effectively block Britain's access to the interior and the fabled wealth it contained. In 1885, on the pretext of protecting the Tswana from Afrikaner incursions, Britain declared all the territory between South-West Africa in the west and the Transvaal in the east to be the Bechuanaland Protectorate.

For a time it seemed as if the western Tswana (of the Bechuanaland Protectorate) had succeeded in ridding themselves of the white man's domination. This seclusion and territorial integrity were short-lived, however. Political boundaries may have limited Afrikaner military incursions, but they encouraged and facilitated economic transactions, especially the flow of labor. In 1886, one year after the declaration of the Bechuanaland Protectorate, gold was discovered on the Witwatersrand, in the heart of the southern Transvaal. Within twenty-five years most of the Tswana, both those from the Transvaal and those from the Bechuanaland Protectorate, would form a giant industrial reserve-army to mine the gold.

The Tswana and Modern Political Economy

Gold and Mine Labor

The extraction of gold and its sale on world markets has been the sine qua non of modern society in southern Africa and the basis for much of the polity of South Africa and the adjacent states. The recruitment of large quantities of very cheap labor was a necessary condition for the profitable extraction of gold. While the pastoral and agricultural economy of the Afrikaners had led to the disposition of white and black under one set of conditions, labor recruitment and organization for purposes of large-scale mining exposed the Africans to European institutions of a radically different kind. Afrikaner pastoralists had competed with Tswana pastoralists over mutually valued resources: land, cattle, and farm labor. But the African laborers sought by the British mining magnates were destined to toil in worlds never dreamed of before.

From the very first days of gold and diamond mining, the prospectors and fortune hunters had one central problem: how to secure an ever-increasing supply of labor that would work at subsubsistence wages. Subsistence was very expensive in the mushrooming urban centers that grew up around the mines at Kimberley and Johannesburg.

The labor-intensive agriculture of the Afrikaners could not adjust quickly to the enormous demands for food made by the population of nonfarmers required by the mining industry. This meant, of course, that prices for food soared as it fell into short supply. The railroads that reached Kimberley in the 1870s and Johannesburg in the 1880s further stimulated the demand for agricultural goods. Food production actually fell, in part because much African labor was enticed away from the farms to the mines.

It was through mine-labor recruitment agencies that African populations, among them the Tswana, experienced their first contact with industrialism. The obstacles to attaining African labor were many. First, white farmers competed with the mines for African labor. Second, most miners worked with specific goals in mind, goals that could be given a monetary value. As soon as the miners earned the amount they needed, they ceased to work and returned home.

But the principal obstacle to massive labor recruitment was that the majority of Africans, who could still subsist by traditional means, had no desire to become wage laborers in the mines. The conditions which ultimately forced the Africans into mine labor were British- and Boer-arranged rural impoverishment and taxes. The Afrikaner republics of the highveld had forced the rapidly expanding African population on to "native reserves" much smaller than the territory they occupied aboriginally. Taxes on "head" and "hut," which had to be paid in cash, were levied by various governments. While the sale of cattle and other goods was a way some Africans could raise the necessary money, for many migration to the mines was the only choice.

In the thirteen-year period from 1886 to 1899 the African labor force on the Witwatersrand gold mines alone grew from 1,500 to over 96,000 (Francis Wilson, 1972, p. 4; Doxey 1961, p. 51). In 1893 the owners of the different gold mines had successfully established a central mine-labor recruiting agency. The necessity of this organization can be readily seen, for without the millions of Africans who worked the mines, the gold could not have been profitably extracted (Doxey 1961, p. 60). The value of the gold was largely, then, a function of the unrenumerated work of the black labor force. Labor received only a tiny fraction of the revenues—that is, the exchange value—derived from the sale of the gold in Europe. Cheap African labor turned an unrealized possibility into the fountainhead of industrial growth in southern Africa.

But we are getting ahead of the story. How did this massive recruitment of labor affect the rural, African populations, especially the Tswana? I will give only a sketch now; a more complete answer is to be found in the remainder of the book.

Early in the operation of the diamond mines at Kimberley many important patterns of work organization that were uniquely suited to the exploitation of African labor were developed. There was from the beginning a disparity in the numbers of black and white workers. By 1877 black miners at Kimberley outnumbered white miners two to one. The initial differences in skills between black and white exacerbated the rigid, caste-like cleavage between Europeans and Africans. Enormous wage differential accompanied this division. All of these factors prevented the emergence of any class consciousness common to both black and white wage workers. The privileged white artisans and mine management consciously acted to forestall the appearance of a white proletariat.

Another pattern of work organization grew up from efforts to control illicit diamond-buying (Doxey 1961, p. 24 ff.). Management developed a "compound system" for housing African labor. This system involved a rigid, closed military-like barracks and commissariat. By controlling the miners' lives almost every minute of the working day, the opportunities for smuggling diamonds to the outside world and the black market were minimized.

As we will see in subsequent chapters, it is an enormous culture shock for a young rural-born African to be thrown into such a life. The burdens of mine work itself and the authoritarian regimentation of the compound meant that few Africans "willingly" embraced the mine as a place to earn a living.

Despite prodigious efforts to recruit African workers to the mines, a critical labor shortage remained in all sectors of the South African economy. It has been claimed that even the substantial rise in mine wages in the last years of the nineteenth century, though to some extent it increased the availability of labor, led to a "backward sloping labor-supply curve." This means that African miners presumably quit sooner when paid higher wages per time unit, since they were working for specific cash targets.

By far the most important pattern of work organization to develop in the mines was the circulatory migration of Africans from rural homes to the mines on contract for specified periods of time. The Tswana, both in the Transvaal and in the Bechuanaland Protectorate, became extensively involved in this labor migration.

The Bechuanaland Protectorate was supposed to insure that the western Tswana would have control over their land and their lives. In particular, they would be free of the domination of European interests. We can easily see that this was an illusory goal. The lack of any "development" of that territory, plus the uninhibited recruitment of mine labor, meant that thousands of Tswana had to leave their "protectorate" and pursue lives in South Africa on terms laid down by the whites. By 1895 even this tenuous security based on local sovereignty was being threatened by commercial interests. Cecil Rhodes, the industrial and mining magnate who controlled the diamond mines at Kimberley and much of the gold mining on the Witwatersrand, founded the British South Africa Company in 1889. This company was granted charter rights to explore for and extract mineral wealth in Bechuanaland and other territories to the north of the Cape Colony. Rhodes envisaged a continuous Britannic fiefdom stretching from Cape Town to Cairo. To insure unfettered access to riches farther north, he wanted to have personal control of Bechuanaland. He made representations to Britain to grant the British South Africa Company rights to govern the protectorate as a private chattel.

Predictably, the Tswana were horrified at the thought of their land becoming a piece of corporation property. In 1895 three Tswana chiefs, Bathoen, Sechele, and Khama, went to Britain to plead their case against Rhodes's petition before Queen Victoria. The compromise agreement reached between Rhodes and the Tswana chiefs was to grant Rhodes an easement for a rail line that would connect Kimberley with Bulawayo. This narrow strip of land would run through eastern Botswana from north to south. Rhodes was to have no other control within the territory.

Boers versus Britain: Time Out for War
The Tswana were not the only ones who feared the incursion of outside interests. By the mid-1890s there were several gold mining companies

on the Witwatersrand. They had employed thousands of foreign, white miners in addition to Africans. The processes of urban growth, industrialization, and the immigration of thousands of foreign whites created fears among the Afrikaners of the Transvaal that their country was being overrun by alien forces and interests. Almost entirely farmers, they feared the demise of their rural society. Indeed, by the end of the century they saw that they would soon be outnumbered by other whites who worked in the mines and in the cities.

The parliament of the Transvaal (at that time the South African Republic) passed various laws restricting the franchise to long-resident Transvaalers, which effectively meant Afrikaners only. The parochialism and inefficiency of the South African Republic's government under Paul Kruger became more and more intolerable to the British mining magnates. The mining companies saw, for example, the capricious imposition of various transport and custom taxes as onerous impediments to the making of profits. Another irritant to the British was the pretense made by Germany of assisting the Transvaal in maintaining its autonomy from British control. Cecil Rhodes wanted to get rid of Kruger and hatched a plot in collusion with the mine management to overthrow the government of the Transvaal. In 1896 a motley group were sent to seize Johannesburg, but they were ignominiously defeated by Afrikaner commandos.

By 1899 commercial and capitalist interests had made the case in Britain that the "disenfranchised (white) foreigners" were living under tyrannical repression. More important, the mining companies wanted to have a government congenial to their goals and methods of operation. On October 11, 1899, the government of the Transvaal declared war on Britain, knowing that the British were about to declare war on them. The Boer War had begun.

While this three-year war was a critical point in southern African history, it is not crucial for understanding the incorporation of the Africans into a capitalist political economy. It was a war between two imperial interests, both of which had similar plans for the Africans. Hence the war and its outcome did not materially affect the lot of the indigenous Africans.

Black Africans and Native Policy

In all of this commercial and imperial maneuvering, the black Africans were not to play a central role. Only after the war, and with the establishment of the Union of South Africa, could the reunited white capitalists (the British) and the white landed gentry (the Afrikaners) turn their attention back to the quest for the good life as subsidized by a rigorously controlled black population working in the service of white development.

The basic problem for the Europeans in this quest came to be formulated as "native policy." Under this heading falls the body of law and the institutional arrangements that have circumscribed the existence of nonwhite people in the Union of South Africa from its founding to the present day.

The labor needs of South Africa were gargantuan and still growing. Now the requirements for communal survival in nonindustrial rural African societies are such that only a small fraction of the total population can absent itself at any one time without completely destroying the social fabric. Thus a specific goal of native policy was to preserve the indigenous rural communities as catchment areas for discarded African labor and as reservoirs for fresh labor as well. The survival of "tribal society," even the *creation* of "tribal society," was an important aim in the formulation of Union policy toward Africans. Equally important, if labor in the mines was to be kept cheap and readily controlled, the emergence of an urban proletariat had to be prevented. The creation and maintenance of tribal society furthered these goals. To this end, labor recruitment had to expand all over the subcontinent, even as far north as the Congo (Zaire), to obtain sufficient labor for the mines while maintaining rural communities at a semi-subsistence level.

If the necessary labor was to be provided at minimal cost two obstacles had to be overcome: the first arose from the short-term interest each mine had in attracting labor by bidding higher wages for the scarce available supply; the second was the problem of how to increase the absolute supply of labor by recruiting Africans who would work in the mines at minimum wages and under wretched living conditions. By 1900 the mining companies had developed jointly a system for monopolistic buying of contract labor, which was put into effect by two organizations: the Native Recruiting Corporation and the Witwatersrand Native Labour Association. The mines agreed among themselves, as a condition of labor recruitment, not to bid up the price of labor through direct competition. Rather, scarcity of labor was to be dealt with by two other means: rationing (allocation of labor according to the "needs" of the mines) and financing of more and more extensive efforts by the recruiting cartel to obtain cheap, naive, docile labor from surrounding territories. By agreement among the mining companies, wages for Africans were fixed, and even wage differentials associated with incentive schemes (e.g., piece work) were to be held within very strict tolerances. Any mine whose rate of pay was found to exceed certain "maximum averages" permitted under the intercompany agreement would be heavily fined.

This system of monopolistic recruiting, coupled with the crude, unhealthy, and oppressive living conditions in the compounds and mines, allowed the mining companies to maintain constant real wages for Africans during most of the twentieth century. Only in the last five years or so has there been any significant upgrading of African wages. With the continuous increase in the demand for gold and its sale at ever higher prices, the exploitation of African labor has brought great benefits to the white ruling class, not least the large surplus value in profits and wages for the whites.

As stated above, the mines have always claimed that they experienced "labor shortages." Sheila van der Horst (1971, pp. 167–72) has asked whether this is economically plausible. Why would mines have a built-in "surplus" technical capacity which is always used at less than optimum levels due to labor shortage? She speculates that pleading "labor shortage" may have been a ruse of the mining companies to secure a greater share of the workers rationed by the labor cartel.

"Liberal" economists, sociologists, and others frequently say that the system of labor recruitment and allocation used in South Africa, especially in the mines, is "irrational." That is, it works at higher costs or lower efficiency than would be the case if pure market forces operated. Thus if wages were raised for Africans and the industrial color bar dropped, more labor and more productive labor would enter the market. But this view ignores two important facts. First, radical increases in African wages would have to come in large measure from reductions in the wages of elite white labor or from profits realized by capital. Second, if Africans entered industry or the mines in terms of the marketplace, this would imply greatly increased power, including, surely, the power to unionize and strike for even higher wages. This would spell the end of the nearly inelastic labor supply. Under such conditions the gold would never come out of the mines, as it could not be sold at a price that would allow capital to recover its costs either in wages or advanced capital.

The plan of replacing such labor with machine capital is conceivable but in my view totally impracticable under current conditions. No other combination of capital, labor, and skill could get the gold out of the ground and yield such high profits, least of all a combination called up by some imaginary market principle that has never been allowed to function anyway. Of course, the question of how long the current system of labor exploitation will be *tolerated* is quite different from the question whether or not it is *efficient*.

The wages of Africans in the mines are very low compared to the wages paid in industry and commerce, where African labor must be attracted without the aid of recruitment cartels working abroad. In 1964 average African wages in the mines were 152 Rand per annum, while in manufacturing they were R422 (Institute of Race Relations 1964, p. 251). (One Rand equals 1.15 U.S. dollars, 1977.) In 1973 the figures were: R360 in mining and R840 in manufacturing. This represents a marginal increase of about 8 percent in mine wages in relation to those in manufacturing (Institute of Race Relations, 1973, p. 238). The relatively greater economic opportunity found in industry and the towns, coupled with continuing rural poverty, has resulted in an absolute and proportional increase in the number of Africans employed in urban-based industry.

These observations seem to be demanded by the following statistics quoted by Dubb (1974, p. 442). In 1911 there were 677,000 whites and 524,000 Africans in urban areas. In 1960 there were 2.6 million whites and 3.6 million blacks in urban areas. (Note, however, that no African in South Africa today may own property in an urban area, and few Africans have the perpetual right to live there.)

Urbanism among Africans implies the "urban location"—another aspect of political economy that touches directly on the life world of Africans. Urban-location life, like mining life, is characterized by poverty. There are enormous wealth differentials between black and white, perceived by the vast majority of Africans to be totally illegitimate.

The average African family residing in town in South Africa today does not and cannot earn sufficient money to maintain the minimum standard of living *white* South Africans deem necessary for a decent life. In 1970 over 25 percent of the white population earned more than 2,000 Rand per annum (Institute of Race Relations 1973, p. 201), while less than 1 percent of Africans had such an income. As of 1972 the minimum income required for what is locally defined (Johannesburg) as a decent life for a family of five must be about 106 Rand per month (Institute of Race Relations 1972, pp. 231–33). In 1970 the University of South Africa's Bureau of Market Research found that the average Johannesburg African household contained 5.4 people and had an average income of 87 Rand (Institute of Race Relations 1972, p. 233)—a shortfall of nearly 20 Rand per month from the minimum income required for a decent life. This situation is, however, a great improvement over the earlier years, when poverty was even more stark than it is today.

The growth of towns and the availability of Africans to work in them—in industry, domestic service, and elsewhere—is intimately connected to mine-labor recruitment. Any attempt by the mines to recruit labor by raising wages necessarily cut into the supplies of labor for farm work and of migrants coming to town to sell their labor on the streets to the dragoons of industry. The decision by the mines to recruit widely outside the boundaries of South Africa (e.g., in Botswana) permitted mine wages to remain low and in turn allowed industry to retain its own reserve army at wages much lower than would have been possible had the mining interests created a labor shortage by offering direct competition.

To summarize: eight facts about the institutional arrangements in South Africa describe those aspects of the political economy that most directly shape the lives of the Tswana in both South Africa and Botswana:

1. Tswana (African) residence in rural areas which are to varying degrees *impoverished*—i.e., incapable of producing the material resources necessary to the biological and social survival of communities situated there
2. Various factors that lead the Tswana (or others) to seek wage work in the "money sector"—principally, rural poverty and taxes payable in money only; secondarily, the desire to escape from troubles and beliefs of the Tswana concerning the use-values of money earned
3. Commercial farming controlled by a white gentry: (a) African squatting on such farms necessitated by overcrowding of reserved (African) rural areas; (b) labor extracted from the Tswana and other African groups as the price for squatting
4. A mining industry with monopolistic recruitment of African labor and creation of conditions of an "inelastic supply" of African labor
5. Urban growth, expansion of secondary industry, and concomitant growth of peri-urban African locations
6. Police power for control of African movement and residence; in particular, obligatory residence for Africans in rural reserves

except to seek and obtain work in (3), (4), or (5)

7. Labor migration between rural homes, mines, or towns; and state authority for controlling allocation of Africans to their work and defining its conditions

8. Expropriation of the surpluses created by African labor by the white ruling class and their redistribution as wages and profits for that class

Different communities of Tswana are differentially affected by this political economy, though all are dependent upon its needs and hence shaped by its forces. Capitalism is compatible with a variety of forms of labor recruitment, and the system employed in southern Africa is highly rational given the premises of capitalism—the goal of profits through labor exploitation. The political power and authority added to the purely economic factors of the southern African political economy make "the world of employer and employee, the world of black and white, and the world of town and country in fact a single world" (Rex 1973, p. 275). This dependency upon the ecologic niche defined by a colonial political economy has played a key role in creating African society and communal life as it exists today. Indeed, "what happens to (the black labor force) and what it does is determined not by its separate culture, but by the needs of the economic system. . . . What is true for the workers themselves extends to their dependents in the (rural) reserves as well as (to those) in the towns. Natives form a separate class, a class both in-itself and for-itself" (Rex 1973, p. 280). This latter claim may seem contentious or unwarranted, but I shall outline materials evidencing its pertinence.

Botswana: Linkages to South Africa

At this point in our discussion of labor migration and the South African political economy a question arises. Since the present research concerns the Tswana of Botswana and not the Tswana who live as "citizens" within the boundaries of South Africa, I must establish the degree to which Tswana there are incorporated within the colonial political economy I have outlined. Let me clarify this point right now.

The Tswana from Botswana (formerly Bechuanaland) have always been very much sought after as mine workers. From the early recruitment efforts in Bechuanaland grew up a pattern of labor migration to South Africa on mine contracts that persists to this day. The Tswana, along with other African populations, comprised a reserve army of potential labor—that is, labor that it was hoped would exist in inelastic

supply and cost industry nothing at all when not being used. Bechuanaland and the rural, native reserves in South Africa itself were, and from
the capitalist viewpoint still are, social security systems that keep labor
alive until such time as it is in demand by the money sector.

Britain's complicity with South Africa in the formulation of policy
for Bechuanaland has been well documented: "Lord Hailey . . . could
report 'it was not until 1927 that the imperial government began to
give any sign of a practical interest in the means necessary to improve
the local economic and social services' " (Halpern 1965, p. 108). The
British followed a policy of "parallel rule" in Bechuanaland. They
allowed a modified form of traditional chieftainship, which controlled
some internal matters, but the colonial administration collected taxes
in money and controlled all external affairs. The guiding principle followed by the administration was that the High Commission Territories
existed ,to supply the requirements of the Union's labor market. British
imposition of taxes to be paid in money coupled with their systematic
design not to provide any of the large-scale instrumentalities of a cash
economy forced the Tswana to go outside the country in search of cash
wages (Halpern 1965, p. 111).

Many profound changes in the communal life of the Tswana resulted
from this necessary search for work. While the requirement to pay taxes
in cash fell universally on adult, male Tswana, other conditions that
led to migration for work varied from one community to another, both
within South Africa and in Bechuanaland.

Botswana today has, according to the *National Development Plan*
(Government of Botswana 1970, p. 12), a potential labor force of
about 160,000 males (ages fifteen to sixty-five) out of a total population of less than two-thirds of a million. Of these, over 24,000 are
gainfully employed in Botswana, while 42,000 are said to be workers in
South Africa. Another 3,000 are self-employed or employed in
domestic service. This leaves about 92,000 potentially employable
males with no wage labor. Smit (1970, p. 75) estimates that expatriate
Tswana working in South Africa currently number around 55,000.
Given a current job situation in Botswana where wage laborers working
in South Africa outnumber those working in Botswana itself by more
than two to one, it can readily be seen why there is such a need for the
South African labor market and why the country of Botswana as a
whole depends on the exportation of labor.

The annual per capita income of rural Botswana (1968) is about 52
dollars (Government of Botswana 1970, p. 13). This figure does not

include remittances from workers employed in South Africa. According to Smit (1970, p. 125) the total value of remittances in cash and kind sent to Botswana, plus deferred payments, in 1969 alone was 3.5 million Rand. This income derives from about 51,000 individuals whose total earnings in South Africa are estimated to be 13.7 million Rand. One must conclude from this that a substantial part of the disposable cash available in rural areas of Botswana is derived ultimately from wages earned abroad—that is to say, in South Africa—and remitted home. Later I will show that in years of poor crops and harvest a high percentage of this money is used to buy food. Hence for many people part of the motive for migration is dire necessity.

While the Tswana of Botswana enjoy and consciously value the political freedom and personal security that come from living in Botswana, through their dependency upon wage labor abroad they are incorporated into the institutions of the South African political economy in the very same way as black South African nationals (Monica Wilson 1971, pp. 102-03). It should be remembered that Botswana (earlier Bechuanaland) was clearly intended to be a rural labor reserve on a par with other "native reserves" found within the boundaries of South Africa itself. By 1900 Bechuanaland had been divided into eight tribal reserves, within each of which a semblance of traditional polity was practiced. But no indigenous economic infrastructure involving wage labor was permitted or encouraged by the British. Subsubsistence usufruct from the land made functional proletarians of the Bechuanaland Tswana, who had to sell their labor on terms laid down by South African capitalist interests. This parallel between the British dependencies in southern Africa and the "rural reserves" of South Africa itself is reflected in the fact that per capita income in the South African native reserves (now called "Bantustans") is about the same as in Botswana. South Africa is a very rich country—one quite capable of rapid rural development for all its citizens. Yet it has quite predictably and consciously chosen to maintain its reserves as impoverished catchment areas for discarded labor and as a pool for fresh labor. Britain—its commercial interests and those of South Africa being identical—did not until after World War II begin to make any substantial financial grants-in-aid to Botswana to develop the rudiments of internal social services. Britain saw the future of the Bechuanaland Protectorate as allied to the political economy of South Africa in much the same way as are the contemporary "Bantustans" within South Africa's borders.

Botswana: The Nation Today

Botswana lies landlocked in the center of southern Africa, more than eight hundred kilometers from the coast to the west, south, and east. With over six hundred thousand square kilometers and less than three-quarters of a million people, the population density is among the lowest in the world. The country is semiarid, and small but critical variations in rainfall have a major influence on animal and arable agriculture. Botswana is poor but with promise for growth based on enormous mineral wealth only recently discovered: nickel, copper, coal, diamonds. Remittances to Botswana of wages earned in South Africa are, as stated, a major source of personal income and national revenue. Sale of cattle to the government abattoir is another, as is the penny capitalism of village economies. The income from mineral sales has not been distributed in large amounts to the population in any form: cash, services, or public works. From the standpoint of the majority of rural or village-dwelling people, the economy of Botswana is based on agriculture, livestock, labor migration, some cottage industry, and some wage labor in commerce or the civil service.

Politically, the land of Botswana is divided approximately in half: one part under "tribal" auspices, and the other under state or central-government control. A small percentage is held in freehold by private companies and individuals. The vast majority of Tswana hold land in tribal areas—land to which they are entitled by birth and citizenship in the tribe. With the independence of Botswana in 1966, the system of land tenure has changed in such a way as to *reduce* the authority of tribal leaders and councils to allocate land or adjudicate competing claims for land.

There are eight recognized landholding "tribes" in Botswana, with great variations in population and territory size, and hence in the ecologic conditions of life. The largest tribe, the Bamangwato, have a population of about 200,000 and live in an area of 115,000 square kilometers, while the Batlokwa have a population of about 4,000 and live in an area of 170 square kilometers. I carried out the research reported in this book among the Bakwena, who live in an area of about 40,000 square kilometers in the east central part of modern Botswana and have a population of about 73,000. It must be noted that only about 10 percent of Botswana land is suitable for intensive agriculture under current technological conditions. Furthermore, most of the population resides in the eastern third of the country.

The 1971 census shows Botswana's population to be 630,379 (Government of Botswana 1972a, p. 95). This population has five very important features that bear directly on the problem we are investigating here: (1) its youthful character (over half the population is under fifteen years of age); (2) its mobility (internal and external movement are very high); (3) its imbalanced sex ratios in specific localities (men outnumber women in many places; in other places the contrary prevails); (4) its rapid rate of growth (over 3 percent per annum); and (5) its concentration in the eastern third of the country (along the rail line). These five demographic features are part of a pattern of interaction between demography and economy; the figures reflect facts of the environment that are themselves dependent on antecedent environmental conditions.

I mentioned above that the Tswana traditionally had three sites of occupation: village, lands, and cattle posts. There is a definite tendency for the former nomadic movement among these to give way to more permanent settlement either in the village or on the lands. The settlement of people in land areas is giving rise to an increased number of dispersed settlements, which are permanent yet small (under 1,000 people). At the same time the de facto populations of the larger villages are decreasing, while their official populations remain the same. According to the census published in 1972, the proportion of the population living in settlements of 1,000 or more was 37.1 percent (213,113); in settlements of 500 to 1,000 persons, 10.45 percent (60,001); and in settlements of less than 500 persons, 52.4 percent (300,980) (Government of Botswana 1972a, p. 98). In short, *Botswana is very much a rural society of people living in small dispersed settlements.* If one counts all the people who claim to be citizens of one of the seven largest villages, the total large-village population is 139,607. But the sum of the actual populations enumerated there at the time of the 1971 census gives the much smaller figure of 72,440.

Regional sex ratios reflect the high rate of sex-specific migration internally and externally. The national sex ratio (males per 100 females) is 84. In mining centers like Selibi-Pikwe it is 188.4; in urban areas it is 80; and at the lands, 90 (Government of Botswana 1972a, p. 93). Migration is common for both sexes; only the termini are sex-specific. In the eleven administrative districts enumerated in the 1971 census, of persons absent from the district the proportion resident elsewhere in Botswana was the same as the proportion outside the country (an average of about 14 percent were absent from the district, with about

7 percent elsewhere in Botswana and 7 percent outside the country). As we shall see, women are much more prevalent in the former group.

Economic opportunity affects mortality and fertility as well as being affected by them. The infant mortality rate is fairly low by African standards. Of every 1,000 live births, 126 die before reaching age two (Government of Botswana 1972a, p. 163). On the average, Tswana women at the time of the census were bearing between five and six children live during their productive years (under age 55). The rate of natural increase at the present time is 30.8 per thousand population per annum. Current projections for population growth, under varying assumptions of fertility, mortality, and emigration, yield a population in twenty-five years of between 1 and 1.65 million people—double the present population (Government of Botswana 1972a, pp. 187, 192).

Botswana began its nationhood under many severe handicaps, principally the benign neglect of eighty years of British suzerainty. This neglect may have had some advantages—for example, the country was not pillaged by land- and mineral-hungry tycoons or turned into a settler estate for overseas European colonists. Internal development and the consequent reduction of dependence on overseas economies became the central task of Botswana's first political leadership.

To characterize the goals claimed by this leadership, one cannot do better than quote directly:

> The basic political principles which have determined the policies and objectives described in the Five Year Plan (1970-1975) [are]: . . . firstly, we wish to strive for social justice; secondly, we are concerned to provide wherever possible equality of opportunity; thirdly we intend to use persuasion rather than compulsion in order to achieve change in a democratic and constructive way. . . . Thus, economic and technical arguments strongly favor land reform. But reform must be accompanied by popular consensus and social justtice. . . . And the reforms which are implemented must not favor the wealthy and deprive the poor. [Government of Botswana 1970, Introduction (n. p.)]

The economic goals of Botswana, in brief, are:

(i) To secure the fastest possible rate of economic growth in a manner designed to raise the living standards of the great mass of the inhabitants of Botswana; (ii) to achieve budgetary self-sufficiency in the shortest possible time consistent with rapid economic growth;

(iii) to maximize the number of new job opportunities; (iv) to promote an equitable distribution of income, in particular, by reducing income differentials between the urban and the rural sectors through rural development." [Government of Botswana 1970, Introduction (n.p.)]

This last point underscores one of the principal means the government is using to make an impact on the social and economic structures of rural communities. This impact has not been uniform throughout Botswana. Both ecologic and economic factors have necessitated a section-by-section approach to rural development. But though the practical impact of government policy has differed from region to region, one can safely say that institutions of the nation state are now intruding into rural communal life to the extent that they form a significant part of the ecology—the effective environment to which local communities must adapt or respond in some way. As capitalist political economy forms, ineluctably, a central feature in the ecology of the Tswana life world, so the nation state Botswana, its agencies and assigns, now does too.

Domestic rural income in Botswana for 1968 was estimated to be R16,985,000 or about R35 per capita. The distribution of this income is a much more salient fact. "Some 13% of the rural population (62,000) appear to depend entirely upon remittances or the charity of others. Approximately a further 21% (100,000) are members of agricultural holdings possessing no cattle whatsoever. . . . On the other hand, 4% of the agricultural holders own some 30% of all the cattle" (Government of Botswana 1970, p.6). As cattle are not only a principal index of wealth and a major source of draft power in agriculture, but also in hard times the major goods a person can sell to raise cash for purchase of other necessities, their distribution is a critical factor in determining the self-sufficiency of a communal or household unit.

According to the *National Development Plan* (Government of Botswana 1970, p. 33), approximately half the national herd is owned by about 10% of the farmers; over 25% of farmers have no cattle at all. Control of cattle is of course correlated with ability to do extensive plowing and is also associated with ownership of small stock: pigs, goats, and sheep.

Those who are gainfully employed in the cash-wage sector of Botswana are typically large holders of stock. There is a direct relation between stock ownership and wage employment. While there are many large stock holders not earning wages, there are very few wage-earning Tswana who are not large stock holders. Wage employment, then, does not typically serve as an *alternative* for those who lack herds. Rather, the opportunity to acquire herds is enhanced by means of wage labor, savings from which are typically invested in stock. Increasing wage employment is positively associated with a growing asymmetry in the distribution of livestock ownership.

Land distribution has perhaps been more significantly affected by new legislation than has cattle distribution. Access to land was traditionally a right of citizenship. One could have access to land adequate to one's needs or commensurate with one's ability to plow, plant, and cultivate it. Traditionally land was inherited by the sons of a man in accordance with their station and need. But the chief of a tribe was a trustee for the whole tribe in holding the right to allocate and reallocate land in the manner he deemed to be in the public interest. He held reversionary rights in land unused or uninheritable. However, segmentation due to alienation of land among multiple heirs has tended, along with population growth, to reduce the size of holdings and, recently, to create a real land shortage, exacerbated by the current conditions of agriculture. A major change in land tenure was made in 1968, when all of the former chiefly prerogatives in land allocation were transferred to government agencies known as "Tribal Land Boards." I do not have access to data that permit me to infer whether their criteria for allocating land or adjudicating among claimants for land differ from those used by traditional chiefs. In any case they have been active for only the last few years.

For those few Tswana who manage to get into the "education stream," work-seeking in South Africa is both less frequent and usually not a dire necessity. The proportion of Tswana in this stream is very small. According to Botswana sources (Smit 1970, p. 75), three-quarters of the Botswana population is illiterate. From my own sampling in the Kweneng District, I should say this is an optimistic estimate or one based on a very generous criterion for defining literacy. While the educational system is expanding, at present only about 50 percent of school-age children go to school at all. Only a handful completing primary grades go on to secondary school. According to the 1971 Botswana *Statistical Abstract* (Government of Botswana 1971, table 12), 83,000 children were enrolled in primary school in 1970, among a school-age population of 198,000 (ages five to nineteen years).

The demand for labor with primary level training is not growing nearly as fast as the demand for labor with advanced technical skills. Botswana's external trade in commodities parallels that in human labor. When one considers that Botswana is primarily an agricultural country, it is all the more surprising that in recent years from one-fifth to one-third of its annual imports are foodstuffs. Smit (1970, p. 113) reports that the overall trade deficit in 1968 was 15.74 million Rand (approximately 18 million dollars). While foreign dependency is something that the government of Botswana is seeking to decrease, it should be noted that the bulk of capital investment in Botswana is foreign and much of that investment is channeled through subsidiaries and other conduits in South Africa.

These figures reflect the historical fact I alluded to above: namely, Botswana's dependency on South Africa. Predictably, inequality is not confined to asymmetric economic transactions between Botswana and South Africa. Within Botswana itself, gross inequalities exist. According to the Botswana *Statistical Abstract* (Government of Botswana 1971, table 21), the average monthly wages paid to citizens of Botswana in mining and manufacturing was 33.5 Rand per month (approximately 39 dollars). For noncitizens working in Botswana in this same sector, the average monthly wage was 350 Rand per month (approximately 403 dollars). It must be realized that over 95 percent of Tswana citizens are nonwhite and over 95 percent of expatriate workers are white. Thus whites as a class in effect earn over ten times the amount earned by blacks as a class. This superficial statistic reflects the way elite, largely expatriate personnel and their families live side by side with a rural peasantry and proletariat. Differences in amenities, health care, education, and style of life are a function of the incredible wage differentials presumably based on skill, but correlated closely with race. Racial inequality in the industrial and mining sector is as salient in Botswana as it is in South Africa. That the wealth differences are merely de facto in Botswana but de jure in South Africa is a legal subtlety absent from the consciousness of most Tswana.

Village life, especially small-village and lands life, has to date been little affected by the programs and national institutions of Botswana society. But changes have been made, and they will become more significant in the future. Community development—especially rural community development programs—is just being inaugurated. They will inevitably form a part of the total resources that go to make up village ecology and economy. But as to ties to the regional southern African economy: I am doubtful that development policies will result, in the near future, in economic structures that decrease the everyday dependency of rural people on labor migration and trade in commodities that come from outside the country. In fact, if population projections are correct, the picture for the next twenty-five or so years will be one of increasing demand from South Africa and the world for meat, men, and minerals, together with an increasing need within Botswana for export of those commodities. Thus, *the next twenty-five years will witness an increasing dependency of Botswana on world market conditions.* If the population were to remain constant, it would be possible perhaps for the country to make significant gains in its agricultural self-sufficiency. But with the prospect of a doubled population in twenty-five years, to stay at parity will be a monumental achievement.

3 THE ECOLOGY OF VALUES
IN THREE TSWANA COMMUNITIES

Research Design and Settings

Botswana is a large country with a dispersed population. Ecologic variation from district to district is significant. More important, the economies of various districts differ markedly—in terms of degree of self-sufficiency; principal goods produced; closeness of linkages to, or intrusions from, the "outside" world; extent of labor migration; and intactness and efficacy of traditional communal institutions (particularly village and "tribal" government). All of these sources of variation in demography, economy, and ecology mean that generalizations made for the country as a whole will be more or less inaccurate if applied to specific regions and tribal groups. Since this study is concerned with the life world—the world of a person's experience—I must necessarily restrict the focus to units much smaller than the nation state. In doing so, I hope to offset what is lost in generality of findings by a depth of penetration that will illuminate, at a theoretically useful level, elements of Tswana life worlds that are quite disguised by surface averages and variances. Different groupings of Tswana have very different experiences of colonial domination, despite the many constant features it manifests to all Tswana. In part these differences in experience can be traced to correlative variations in the material conditions in which various Tswana live. These conditions I shall call *ecology* and *economy*. Ecology is the study of the adaptation of human communities to their material environment. Economy refers to those institutional arrangements of production and distribution in a community that are most directly concerned with adaptation to, and exploitation of, the material environment. Ecology and economy are two aspects of one unitary phenomenon. One's economy—its productive forces and their social

organization—define to a high degree one's ecologic niche; one's ecologic niche defines to a high degree the institutional and technological
possibilities.

The aspects of ecology-economy in the Tswana world which most
directly affect the problem we are investigating are: (1) the colonial
political economy of southern Africa; (2) the economy and ecology of
the rural homes and communities of the Tswana; and (3) the social and
physical organization of work and town life.

These three material dimensions of the Tswana world affect—albeit
in different ways—the Tswana consciousness of self. They are related
dialectically to form a grid or matrix with which the individual Tswana
must cope by working out a life-project.

Variations in the material conditions of the world affect the content
of one's beliefs, including those about the self. One good way to discover how material and social conditions affect belief is to conduct
inquiry among groups of people whose material and social conditions
of life differ in determinate ways. These differences, must, of course, be
isolated in advance and be deducible from a theory that describes and
relates them in some clear and significant fashion. The task then is to
relate variation in the content of belief with variation in the social and
material conditions of life of the individuals who assert these beliefs.
Material conditions of life differ among the Tswana principally in the
degree to which a group must cope with and adapt to *incorporation
into the colonial political economy of the surrounding industrial
society*, whose principal social forms have been described above. As I
will try to show, the nature of colonial domination (that is, the necessary dependency of Tswana communities on colonial institutions)
comprises a central yet *variable* aspect of the ecology of Tswana communities.

For the purposes of this study I have distinguished between "objective" domination and "subjective" domination. In this chapter we are
concerned with *objective domination* (or dependency) only. As I shall
show in the following chapters, the extent or character of objective
domination (or dependency) does not determine beliefs about, that is
to say, the subjective meaning of, domination or dependency.

Objective domination or dependency is defined here in ecologic and
economic terms, that is, in terms of the institutions and technology
that define a community's command over material resources. Necessary objective dependency on the "outside" colonial political economy
is obviously a function of a community's own capacity for controlling

the relevant material resources. In short, *a community's material autonomy is the inverse of its necessary dependency.* In other words, the degree of control over one's own resources together with the extent to which necessary resources are uniquely or principally controlled by the colonial system jointly determine the degree of any given community's objective dependency on the outside world (the colonial political economy). One of the major questions of the present study asks what effect this objective domination by external powers has on a person's self-identity—his experience of himself?

The variety of material conditions of a life world that could affect one's beliefs about oneself or beliefs comprising the experience of colonial inequality is indefinitely large. Practically any institution could conceivably make an impression on an individual's self-identity: child rearing, nutrition and diet, education, religious belief, the legal system, distribution of wealth, ruling class, and so forth. It would be a hopeless task to state what causes self-identity to be what it is in an individual's life. Hence, what I shall do here is try to show that the life worlds of the Tswana have properties in common and distinguishing features. Since the common elements (e.g., Tswana culture, history, and relative poverty) are preponderant and, conversely, the variable features comparatively few, this permits the hypothesis that the *variations* in beliefs concerning self and beliefs concerning colonial inequality—*insofar as they are a function of the material and social conditions of life*—are traceable to this small number of variable features of the material conditions.

These considerations led me to select as sites for this research the following three settings: (1) the Eastern Kweneng District, (2) the Central Kweneng District (Kalahari Desert), and (3) the capital of Botswana, Gaborone. The first two of these settings are discussed in this chapter; the third, the town and the mines, is discussed in chapter 4.

The eastern half of the Kweneng District, within an east-west distance of under two hundred kilometers, exhibits such great variations in rainfall, soil cover, surface, and groundwater availability that it ranges from true desert to temperate, comparatively well watered savanna. Within this district significant new opportunities of wage employment for rural-dwelling people have appeared—employment that can be engaged in without the necessity of migration from one's rural home. These factors—urbanization, rural wage employment, and differential agricultural self-sufficiency associated with marked climatic contrasts—are all to be found in this fairly small region. They are directly associated with the degree to which the various communities of Tswana are dependent upon—that is to say, their life chances dominated by—the political colonial economy of southern Africa. While other factors, such as religion, cultural pride, kinship reciprocities, philosophical knowledge, and so forth, are also crucially important, in this section I shall emphasize description of the *material* conditions that affect the Tswana life world.

The Kwena are one of the nine major Tswana tribes located in Botswana. The Kweneng Tribal District, now also a national administrative district, consists entirely of tribal lands. There is no freehold tenure. The district is located in the southeastern portion of Botswana, covers 38,122 square kilometers, and has a total population of 72,093, of whom almost all are Tswana, in particular Bakwena and Bakgalagadi. As is the case for Botswana as a whole, over half the district's population live in villages or other settlements of under 500. The remainder live in villages ranging in size from 500 to a de facto population of about 10,000 in the largest village and tribal capital, Molepolole. The vast majority of the population is concentrated in the southeast corner of the district between Molepolole and Gaborone. The remainder of the district, particularly the part to the west of the tribal capital, has a low population density (about 4 persons per square kilometer and less). The densities in Molepolole and east are over 39 persons per square kilometer.

The three sites selected for this study (Eastern Kweneng, Central Kweneng, and Gaborone) have taken advantage of most of the demographic, geographic, climatologic, and economic variance that this district has to offer. The principal area—where I spent eight months in residence and with which I kept in almost daily contact for another three months—is a fairly rich lands area called Kgaphamadi, which has a settled, year-round population, most of whom come from one of the nearby villages: Kopong, Mogoditshane, Mmopane, Mankgodi, and Gabane. Kgaphamadi is just eighteen kilometers by dirt road from Gaborone. It is a rural farming area where some cattle are kept. Somewhat unusual is the nearby location (just some five kilometers away at Sebele) of a thousand-hectare government agricultural-research farm which employs a number of local people living in Kgaphamadi and other nearby areas. This opportunity for some to live in the rural home and yet undertake wage labor is quite unusual in Botswana as a whole. In addition, a few of the residents of Kgaphamadi find casual wage labor in Gaborone, working as day laborers.

The second site of my research was three small villages in the Central

Kweneng: Ditshegwane, Takatokwane, and Dultwe. These are located on a track that runs west from Molepolole into the Kalahari Desert all the way to Kang in the west and then north to Ganzi and Maun. These three villages, each with a de facto population of less than 500, are located in true desert, where agriculture in recent times has been at best an intermittent activity, and where the principal source of wealth, even subsistence, is remittances from employment undertaken elsewhere, especially in the mines and farms of South Africa.

The third site for research was Gaborone, in particular the so-called traditional settlement area, "Old Naledi," the established residential area called "Bontleng," and finally the backyards of a number of Gaborone's bourgeoisie, in which live domestic servants. Many of the people living in Gaborone are squatters—escapees to town life from rural areas. Some have found rather steady work there. Yet it must be noted that while Gaborone has a de facto population of about twenty thousand, its official population is less than six hundred. The principal reason for this is that Gaborone was built only in the last fifteen years and the vast majority of people now working there claim allegiance to home villages in other parts of Botswana. A detailed description of Gaborone and of the gold mines of South Africa is given in the next chapter.

While variation in dependency on wage labor, especially labor in the mines, was the principal initial criterion for selecting Tswana communities for study, I soon discovered that one other condition profoundly affected that set of beliefs I call self-identity. That was a person's cultural "age." While a full discussion of the Tswana concepts of time and age is given in chapter 7, I should indicate here that age in Tswana culture is only very grossly correlated with our concept of natal age. Age for the Tswana is principally the attainment of certain social positions. Thus an individual who has accumulated sufficient resources to pay his "bride wealth," who has a wife and children, who has established himself in farming in sufficient measure to avoid continuous labor migration, is said to be an accomplished or proper person irrespective of natal age. I call this cohort "old" for convenience. A person who is unmarried, or who has not settled down to a legitimate marriage with custody of his children, who is not able to support himself by farming, and who takes contracts to the mines regularly, is a youngster no matter what his natal age; the Tswana would call him *lekolwane*. I call members of this cohort "young" for convenience. Control of cultural resources, life experiences, and place within social structure all meld in the Tswana conception of age. Unless a person is experiencing events, time does not exist; likewise with age. One cannot age except through experience. Aging is creating time through experience and through the attainment of crucial, social positions made possible by the command of relevant cultural resources.

Thus, the design of research entailed sampling three communities or ecologic niches, each divided into two contextually meaningful age-cohorts, *young* and *old*. Subsequent research showed that this division correlated in important ways with variations in many aspects of Tswana self-identity. Hence, this stratification of the population has been retained throughout the analysis of data to be presented here. The total number of *men* intensively interviewed in terms of these community and cohort memberships is shown in the accompanying table.

TABLE 1
NUMBER OF MEN INTERVIEWED

	Gaborone	Kgaphamadi	Kalahari	Totals
"Young"	11	10	5	26
"Old"	6	15	6	27
Totals	17	25	11	53

While many more than fifty-three men were interviewed in the eighteen months of field research, this number represents a sample of individuals with whom I conducted ten to twelve intensive interviews in addition to maintaining extensive informal contact. They form the core of the people I got to know as individuals and whose lives became more or less open to me. While fifty-three people do not constitute a statistically adequate sample of the population of southern Botswana or of the Kweneng and Gaborone for *all* purposes, they are fully representative for many others. Moreover, I had to probe in depth for much of my material, and a sample of fifty-three is in the upper tenth percentile of sample sizes for ethnographies conducted in non-Western communities on the basis of such intensive methods.

The Tswana are typical of southern Bantu-speaking peoples in having a rigidly segregated and hierarchically stratified society in terms of sex. Traditionally women were the legal minors of either their parents or their husbands. The man is the head of the household (the "root' of the household, as the Tswana say). Women have far fewer direct personal encounters with the world outside the traditional community than men do. An exception is those who have migrated to towns to work as domestic servants. Women in Botswana (among the nonliterate) have seldom obtained wage labor in South Africa. They have never worked in mines. I have taken great care to include women and their perspectives in my research (a total of twenty-seven women were intensively interviewed). In this particular report I am going to concentrate on my findings concerning men. I shall, however, make observations on sexual differences in self-identity from time to time. The study of women's identity, in fairness to women, should be treated in a separate book, as their position in Tswana society itself is radically different from that of men.

Kgaphamadi and the Southeastern Kweneng District: An Overview

Physical Environment

In the following descriptions I shall confine my remarks to those aspects of demography, ecology, and economy which (1) are most general throughout the Kweneng District or which (2) are quite variable and are exemplified by the three particular sites most intensively studied. We will begin with the rather densely settled lands area at Kgaphamadi, as this ecologic niche is most representative of those in which the vast majority of Tswana now live.

Kgaphamadi shares most of the ecologic and economic features that characterize the densely and in general permanently settled lands areas of the Eastern Kweneng District and other parts of eastern Botswana. A brief description of these conditions was given in the previous chapter. Over half of all Tswana live under conditions not unlike those I shall describe for Kgaphamadi. The two unusual features of this area are its opportunitites, albeit limited, for rural wage employment and its proximity to the growing urban center Gaborone.

The ground surface in the area is characterized by ferruginous soil, with considerable sand—typical subdesert soil. The porosity of the surface means high water penetration. The dry air promotes high evaporation and transpiration rates. The soil, while not particularly fertile, does respond (as do most such subdesert soils) to such kinds of fertilization as manuring. The intense, year-round sunlight obviates the need for the rich soil required to grow most crops in climates with extensive cloud cover.

The pasture land is endowed with a variety of sweet grasses, but it is prone to rapid dessication under conditions of intensive grazing. Trees are typically thorny scrub types. A great variety of edible wild greens, berries, tubors, and legumes are to be found, and under the fickle conditions of agriculture are an important supplement to the diet, especially in years of low yield. The available data indicate that on the average one year in four is a drought year (rainfall under 330 mms.). This severely reduces the agricultural yield, and makes gathering capability extremely important in the local ecology.

Local hunting is confined to snaring of birds, rabbits, and small antelope. Children especially are gifted in trapping and shooting these animals. In fact, domestic cats are eaten by young people. The larvae of a large moth known as "mopane worm" is a favorite snacking-food. There is much that could be eaten that is not deemed edible: canine and reptile are tabooed generally. Fish are available only in a few streams. Two naturally available forms of wildlife considered to be delicacies are guinea fowl and rabbit.

There are literally hundreds of plants used not only as food but also prophylactically against certain illnesses and in the treatment of the same. The Tswana pharmacopoeia is large and effective. Herbalists are specialists in the Tswana community and a definite part of their trade is their extensive and precise botanical knowledge of the area.

Large-game hunting locally is almost nonexistent, as these animals have been decimated due to the widespread use of firearms. A few Tswana go west in the winter to hunt large grazing animals, in particular blue wildebeest.

In sum, the land at this point is capable of providing a natural abundance of food forms, which are critically important to the Tswana, especially in years of bad harvest. The population, however, is too great to live off hunting and gathering either exclusively or principally, even when supplemented by the practice of agriculture as it now is.

Population and Settlement Pattern
The population of the Kgaphamadi lands area and parts of immediately adjacent areas numbers about six hundred people, in an area of about twenty-five square kilometers, giving an average density of about twenty-three people per square kilometer. Over 90 percent of the households in Kgaphamadi and the immediately surrounding lands areas are occupied year round by all or some part of the families owning them. Water is available year round, but some of the families in

this area live over three kilometers from permanent water sources (boreholes). A few individuals have created dams which block up springs, and one "wealthy" resident has a borehole with a diesel-run pump.

The settlement pattern is typical for Tswana lands areas. A compound with two or more rondavels of mud and dung with grass roofs is located adjacent to the cultivated fields. There will usually be a kraal made from trees and thorn bushes in which will be kept small stock. Cattle are typically not corralled at night, a result of which is much midnight foraging by stray cattle. The compounds, being permanent, year-round residences, are well kept and are occupied by various members of the immediate family as well as grandparents, in-laws, and other kin. The distances between compounds vary, but typically within four hundred meters of any compound there will be two or three others. The compounds tend to be clustered socially by reference to kinship ties among the resident families. The community is not composed exclusively of closely related kin, but most of the people will have several kinsfolk living in the area. There exists the nominal outline of wards, kin-based aggregations of compounds, but population movement in and out has made the ward purely nominal, not a kin-based societal grouping.

In the *Kweneng Resource Survey* (Government of Botswana 1972b), an omnibus demographic-economic study of the region between Mole-polole and the Southeastern District boundary, a census of the entire resident population was undertaken. While this census did not include Kgaphamadi, it did include villages and lands within eleven kilometers of it. These areas are quite similar to Kgaphamadi, as the sample of the Kgaphamadi population among whom I lived and worked showed. Hence it is probable that the observations drawn from this survey apply to the Kgaphamadi lands with only small discrepancies. I did not make a census of Kgaphamadi lands, in part because this other census material was already available and seemed to apply to Kgaphamadi quite closely.

The number of people temporarily or permanently away from the region covered by the *Survey* was 3,614 of a total enumerated population of 28,598 (13 percent). Of those away, 2,759 were males, and of those males over one-third were young men in their twenties. Sixty per-cent of the young men in their twenties reported to be members of enumerated households were not resident there during the time of the population census (Government of Botswana 1972b, p. 20).

This high percentage of young men away makes the sex ratio heavily imbalanced, especially in the age grades where female fertility is highest. Of 4,994 mothers enumerated, some 1,405 were not married (Government of Botswana 1972, p. 20). To be sure, this does not imply that there was no responsible father, genitor, or other person supporting the mother and children. Marriage in Tswana society is only fully consummated with the conveyance of "bride wealth" from the husband's father's family to the wife's father's family. Nevertheless, a number of so-called unmarried women were without a male to support them if my evidence from Kgaphamadi holds for the entire surveyed area.

Of all children born to women under the age of thirty, 51 percent are born to unmarried mothers; and 63.6 percent of mothers under age thirty are unwed (Government of Botswana 1972b, p. 23).

Among the 2,398 households enumerated, 1,897 had male heads and 501 had female heads. Most unmarried women were living either in a male kin-headed household or with the man who would be recognized as a husband when bride wealth was conveyed. A majority of household heads (76 percent) were residing at the lands at the time of enumeration (Government of Botswana 1972b, p. 27). In Kgaphamadi the percentage was even higher (if my sample error is small), with 85 percent of household heads residing at the lands most of the year.

Household heads tend not to have received any education. Only 5.6 percent of female heads of household and 2.1 percent of male heads had had any schooling whatsoever (Government of Botswana 1972b, p. 27). This is lower than in my sample in Kgaphamadi, where 15 percent had received some schooling.

Local Economy

The basis of local economy is the quest for food. The social organization built around the practices of production and distribution of food supply have persisted into the present day with greater tenacity than any other set of customs and usages, save perhaps those associated with traditional medicine and certain beliefs regarding the "supernatural."

The availability of water has been shown in a general way to be crucial to agricultural productivity. One of the economic aspects of this availability in Kgaphamadi and elsewhere in the region is private ownership of permanent water supplies. This implies the right to charge a fee for use of water. In both Kgaphamadi and several areas covered by the Kweneng Survey, many individuals must pay a fee in cash or goods for water both for personal use and for livestock.

The fact that water is very often quite distant from the home means that one must cart water continuously and, necessarily, in small amounts at a time. The scarcity of water precludes the successful cultivation of small kitchen gardens near the compound and other "customary" agricultural practices. Water availability or lack affects most Tswana regardless of their wealth. True the wealthier can buy water for their stock, but they cannot irrigate fields nor can their cattle—starving for lack of fodder—pull a plow. Ownership of cattle, on the other hand, shows marked variation among the Tswana in Kgaphamadi and elsewhere. Control of cattle is an important factor in production in arable agriculture, and like all capital equipment its ownership has important implications for social relations and the generating of wealth.

The distribution of wealth, especially animal wealth, in rural Botswana is quite varied. There exists a wide disparity between the "rich" and the "poor," though we would count all but the very richest as very poor by our standards. In the *Kweneng Resource Survey* (Government of Botswana 1972b, p. 31), 2.9 percent of enumerated households had no visible means of support; 5.1 percent held no land, though they may have "borrowed" land to plant on. The number of households possessing all of the locally important capital resources—cattle, small stock, and land (and nowadays at least one wage earner, usually abroad) —was only 30.5 percent of the total (Government of Botswana 1972b, p. 31). Another survey, conducted in Molepolole, the capital of the Kweneng, reported the number of households with cattle, small stock, and land to be 23 percent of the total (Eding 1972, p. 106). In this same area, 3.4 percent of the households owned 32.7 percent of the cattle, while almost half the households owned no cattle at all. In Kgaphamadi about one-third of the households had no cattle, another half owned between one and nine cattle, and one-sixth owned more than nine head.

Arable agriculture is the other half of the basic production of foodstuffs, along with animal husbandry. But the two are not separate or unrelated activities. Control of stock is positively associated with agricultural productivity. Sorghum is by far the most intensively cultivated crop and the one with the highest success rate under the social, technological, and physiographic conditions of the Southeastern Kweneng, including Kgaphamadi. The number of bags (90 kgs. each) of sorghum harvested varies positively with the three critical factors of production— labor, cattle, and rainfall—which have additive effects on total yield per household.

The most important aspect of food production is its sufficiency.

Because of the vagueness of the term *sufficiency*, however, survey data are likely to be in error in reflecting this kind of information. The *Kweneng Resource Survey* (Government of Botswana 1972b, p. 46) reported that in the regions closest to Kgaphamadi, only 13.7 percent of enumerated households said they "usually produced sufficient food" for their own consumption. For the area of Kgaphamadi itself, that same question asked among my sample showed that 25 percent said "usually," but almost all the respondents said that the variation was so great from year to year that they could not really give an answer to the question. While these statistics show that there is a considerable dependency on wages to purchase food supplements, relative to the Kalahari this area produces a substantial proportion of its subsistence requirements. In the event of an insufficient harvest the most common means for coping are: (1) sale of stock to raise money to purchase food; 31.9 percent cited this; (2) remittances from family members working in the mines (31.7 percent). Other means reported indicate the importance of wage labor in the subsistence sector; 17 percent reported that a family member would send money (place earned not specified), and 14.5 percent borrowed money from relatives (Government of Botswana 1972b, p. 46).

Labor Migration
Labor migration is not new to the Tswana, as we have seen; and the people of the Southeastern Kweneng District, including Kgaphamadi, are no exception. By 1880 there were 2,135 Tswana at the diamond diggings in Kimberley, most of them Kgatla, Ngwato, and Kwena (Schapera 1947, p. 26). The resident commissioner for Bechuanaland complained in 1899 that the protectorate was being flooded with labor recruiters whose actions were seriously disrupting communal life (Schapera 1947, p. 26). Beginning in 1903 there occurred limited but important European settlement in parts of eastern Botswana for the purpose of farming. Large tracts of nontribal land were set aside for European occupation under freehold title. Naturally these Europeans, mostly Boer and British, employed local Tswana in farming on the very same basis as in South Africa. World wars I and II created heavy demands for African labor both in industry and in the military. Tswana responded in ever increasing numbers to the appeals to leave the rural home in pursuit of cash wages abroad. The trend has been, until very recently, toward an increasing rate of out-migration with a decreasing rate of return home. This implies longer and longer

periods of voluntary absence from Botswana on the part of many migrants.

The Kweneng District as a whole is, absolutely and relative to its total population, a larger reservoir of labor for the South African mines and industries than most other areas of Botswana. Some of the reasons for this are: (1) proximity of the population to centers of mine recruitment, and (2) vagaries of climate greater than are found in other comparably sized regions of Botswana. The figures presented in table 1 give evidence of this. The populations given are approximations of the de facto figures; 1970 was a good agricultural year, the other two drought years.

TABLE 2
MINE LABORERS RECRUITED FROM TRIBAL CAPITALS

	Kanye (pop. 10,500)	Mochudi (pop. 7,000)	Molepolole (pop. 9,500)
1967	1,394	850	3,516
1970	553	329	1,892
1973	2,025	921	4,636

Source: Mine Labour Organization 1974.

Part of the reason for Molepolole's high rate of output lies in the fact that many of the recruits from the desert areas of the Western Kweneng sign up for mine work at the Molepolole office of the Mine Labour Organization. But this is not the sole reason; the population of the town itself is less well off materially than are the populations of the other two tribal capitals. This contributes significantly to migration propensity.

The *Kweneng Resource Survey* (Government of Botswana 1972b, p. 74) reports for the two enumeration areas closest to Kgaphamadi—both within fifteen kilometers—and most like it economically and ecologically, that of the total population enumerated, 13 percent were temporarily or permanently away (645 out of 4,785). While I have no census data for the lands area, Kgaphamadi, the figures from the region as a whole are fairly close to my sample figures for Kgaphamadi. Of the households in the surveyed region, 1,722 out of 3,745 had at least one nonagricultural worker (Government of Botswana 1972b, p. 34). This meant a total of 2,934 wage laborers, of whom more than two-thirds were employed in the mining sector of South

Africa. The remaining less than one-third were employed within Botswana, almost all somewhere other than the village or lands where the household resided. Hence internal and external migration in search of wage work must be considered a central institution in Tswana communal life.

How much of earned income from the mines is repatriated? In 1973 (a bad agricultural year) 4,636 mine contract workers from the village of Molepolole alone voluntarily had 495,856 Rand withheld from their pay and deferred collection of it until they had returned to Molepolole. Moreover, those same 4,636 workers made 5,796 remittances to Molepolole of pay collected while on contract, for a total amount of 167,960 Rand (Mine Labour Organization 1974). In a year in which the crop failures were enormous and nearly universal in the area, there is no question but that food was the first item bought with these funds.

Returning to Kgaphamadi, the sample of individuals I worked with reveals another dimension to the picture of labor migration. Of the twenty-five adult males I intensively interviewed, twenty-one had been to the mines. Their mean age was, in 1973, forty-nine years. They had completed an average of 6.24 nine-month or one-year contracts and had spent an average of 10.65 years in South Africa in some kind of wage employment.

The lack of education is intimately associated with labor migration. Within the adult male population of Kgaphamadi who had received *less than* three years of schooling, all but one had been to the mines. This brings us back to a point made earlier. Those who are fortunate enough to get into the "education stream" generally never go to the mines. The Botswana bourgeoisie gives evidence of this. For example, at a lecture I gave in Gaborone at the University of Botswana, Lesotho, and Swaziland, attended by over a hundred Batswana, I asked how many had ever been on a mine contract. Only two claimed they had. Of the people I interviewed in Kgaphamadi who had *more than* three years education none had been to the mines, or even out of Botswana, in search of work.

The fact that some 71.1 percent of Botswana males and 64.5 percent of females have *never* attended schools means that the majority of Botswana are in the labor-migrant class. It is for this reason that the samples of people interviewed in all the parts of the Kweneng in which I worked were confined largely to the noneducated.

Another important fact about absence from villages for mine labor is that very few migrants acquire any significant experience living in urban centers. This is slowly changing with the advent of small towns in Botswana. But among the Kgaphamadi population, of thirty-seven interviewees, male and female, only five had ever resided in a town for any length of time. A corollary to this is that five or fewer of the Kgaphamadi sample of thirty-seven had ever worked in industry, which is usually urban-based. This absence of experience in town is associated with a lack of experience in coping with the world of Europeans. The knowledge to be acquired about Western social life is very different in a town and in a mine compound, as I shall point out in succeeding sections. While I have no national or regional census data, the population of Kgaphamadi as a whole had had very little experience living in towns.

Other Aspects of the Local Economy

From what has been said concerning the remittance of money to Botswana by migrants, a question immediately arises. What kinds of demand does this money make possible? Effectively, how does the spending take place? This in turn leads us to the issues of how a local village or lands area, like Kgaphamadi, responds to (1) an increasingly "monetized" expression of wants, and (2) exchange through money in a market-like setting. Indeed the advent of the use of money and exchange in accordance with market-like principles has adumbrated considerable change in local village economies and in central beliefs concerning wealth, power, value, and self-identity.

In certain areas of the Southeastern Kweneng, money has not been simply and exclusively a substitute means of acquiring food, but in some years has represented a "surplus"—an excess over and above what the local economy produced before the advent of wage labor. But this point must not be overstated. I think Schapera does this when he asserts that the accumulation of European material goods represents an increase in the "natives' " standard of living (1947, pp. 6-8, 157-63). In fact, much of what rural Tswana accumulate in European goods is a replacement of indigenous commodities whose use fell out, and only in part is it because the Western goods are in some sense superior. Many of the traditional crafts atrophied because of migration itself. There simply were not the people available to sustain the traditional crafts. The craftsmen too had to migrate to seek wages. Hence the purchase of those commodities whose local manufacture had ceased becomes almost necessary.

The Tswana generally have proven to be quite receptive to Western technology and the idea of a market in commodities and labor. In part

THE ECOLOGY OF VALUES

this acceptance has been forced on them. They have simply had no choice. Many innovative (i.e., new) adaptations to the presence of monetized exchange have been made over the past hundred years; however, most of these are concerned manifestly with the circulation of commodities and other wealth.

One of the most interesting economic practices of the rural Tswana is the institution of "stockfair" and the selling of beer. Both function to redistribute money in the community from its chance concentration in a few hands to others. Stockfair is basically simply rotating credit. Each person in a group contributes a fixed sum of money—say one Rand—to a certain group member. With this money the individual buys ingredients for beer and brews it. This beer is then sold on a weekend. The person who has received the cash advance gets to keep all the earnings, or he may pay it out as dividends to all the contributors. Both arrangements are common. This results in a fairly large profit for the individual. The following week or month another member of the group is the recipient of the advances—the "shares" in the beer. He then is the recipient of the revenue derived from the sales. By this means, every person in the group is able to obtain on credit enough cash with which to buy the ingredients and labor necessary to make the beer. Few individuals on their own could afford the outlay of fifteen to twenty Rand that it costs to brew four hundred liters of traditional beer. By means of the stockfair association, the local people get beer at .05 Rand a "scale" (a scale is about one liter) every weekend, and one person per week realizes a "profit" on his sales. This "profit," however, is subject to redistribution—either as dividend to members or as credit advanced to others.

Another important practice in the local village economy is "breaking bulk." Many commodities—such as tobacco, tea, or sugar—are only available from shops in villages, where they are often sold in quantities so small that many local people have sufficient disposable income on hand to buy them. But their unit price is staggering in comparison with bulk price. This situation lends itself to the appearance of an entrepreneur who can raise sufficient cash to make a trip to a larger town, buy a commodity in bulk, bring the commodity back to his village, break the bulk, and sell the small parcels to the local people at an absolutely low but relatively high price. Industrially brewed sorghum beer, tobacco, sugar, and tea are commonly purveyed in this way.

At the time of a harvest or slaughter, many households will hold "parties." Parties are a time for eating and also an occasion for entertainment

and relaxation, announced by the blaring, droning rhythms of a bat-
tery-run gramophone. But the beer and edibles are for sale. The earnings
accrue to the household member who "owned" the capital—the grain
or the meat.

This last account raises the question of agricultural surplus. Since I
cannot discuss the concept of "surplus" in detail here, I shall take the
liberty of defining it in terms of an "excess of the local, culturally
defined minimum which is necessary to maintain the biological and
social survival of the community in question."

That beer made from locally harvested grain is sold would seem to
imply an agricultural surplus, that is to say, something produced for
sale and not needed by its producer for his own subsistence. But this
is not necessarily the case. The amount of food produced seldom shows
a surplus. African beer is in reality a central part of the diet and is quite
nutritious. It is often drunk *in lieu of* eating. Further, much of the
money earned by the sale of beer will be saved and used to buy food
when the stores of grain are exhausted. Only a small fraction of the
money earned by selling beer will go to the purchase of goods other
than those necessary to biological survival. Hence only to a small degree
does the sale of grain, meat, and so forth, represent a true surplus.
Botswana—especially certain of the drier parts—seldom produces even
an annual surplus. And if one considers longer time spans—say de-
cades—no part of Botswana in the subsistence sector produces a true
surplus, I should venture to guess. The money spent in years of famine
or poor harvest exceeds any money earned by the sale of putative
annual surpluses harvested in good years. What we see in the sale of
beer or *Kgadi* (another favorite alcoholic beverage among the Kwena)
is the circulation or storage of wealth, not the expansion of the economy by means of a surplus.

The local sale of labor is now becoming quite common, though
traditionally this was unheard of. Wages are very low, but the "opportunity cost" of forgoing a day's activity to work for someone else may
be zero in certain seasons. Only the physical pain of hard labor is the
perceived cost to many a person who stands ready to plow, plant, milk,
or thrash.

A person who owns a scarce piece of consumer capital, like a grinding
mill, a large iron kettle, or a cow, can lend it out for a consideration.
Cattle were traditionally sent out by fairly well off Tswana to be kept
by others less fortunate in return for rights to the fruits of cattle:
milk, calves, dung, and so forth. Nowadays many capital goods are

bought, often with the intention of leasing rights of access to them. A person for example may buy a grinding mill, and charge one bucket of ground grain for each use of the mill.

New crafts have appeared to supplant the old. These new crafts are products of cottage industry; an individual produces them in his home with a minimum of special equipment. A craftsman may use his own children as his apprentices and his spouse as a sales agent. In Kgaphamadi the most popular crafts were sewing, woodwork, pottery, and house construction. The crafts or skills made may be sold locally, usually for money but also in exchange for other goods like food. In the towns, where a wider range of partially processed raw materials is available, a wider range of crafts will be found. A common example is metal work—pots and pans, tubs, buckets, and so on, are typically made in the larger towns using imported raw materials.

The advent of tourists and expatriate residents has created the demand for trinkets, gadgets, and sundry objets d'art. Most children are now learning to carve, knowing there is some market for these wares in the tourist centers.

In these statements about the local economy I have begged the question of the division of labor and the significance of this local production in the total economy. First, the advent of the freer exchange made possible by money has both reduced the number of older trades and given rise to new ones. In the process it has made the division of labor more flexible. In particular it has afforded women a control over means of earning that they did not formerly have. Women, as in West Africa, tend to thrive in the marketplace. Women who brew beer control the earnings of that beer quite independent of their husbands. In fact, I was quite surprised to find, in this society of legendary male dominance, how many prerogatives and liberties for control of resources women exercised in the area of local economic production and exchange.

Pigs and chickens tend to be cared for and controlled by women, while men control sheep, goats, and cows. In many households, it is possible to find certain stock that belong to the woman, not to the husband. A good measure of the increasing assertiveness of women in Tswana society is found in their uncontested rights to purvey commodities in the nascent money economy and control the disposition of revenues derived from those activities.

There still exist varieties of peonage that have been practiced since pre-European times. Attachment of destitute individuals to the households of the wealthier is not uncommon. Labor will be rendered in return for food and shelter. Children are still pawned by destitute parents. A poverty-stricken mother may enter a contract with a man (or woman) whereby her son will herd the person's cattle for a year in return for a few goats or 90kg. of meal payable upon successful completion of the service by the child. Such arrangements have abetted the practice of children running away from the cattle posts to town to escape the drudgery of serfdom.

Today the household is the principal unit of production and consumption. In former times the ward (*kgoro*) was an active unit of cooperation in almost all economic undertakings. Today the wards have very little economic importance. There are new interdependencies among households growing up on the principal of market exchange where formerly there were reciprocities prescribed by the bonds—the rights and duties—of kinship. But the importance of cottage industry, breaking bulk, rotating credit, child peonage, or selling beer must not be overemphasized. None of these activities generates much "new" wealth in a community. True, a woman who walks twenty kilometers to Gaborone, sells her pottery, and returns with hard cash has brought "new" money into the community. But this is exceptional. Most "commerce" in the local villages simply *circulates* commodities and money. There is a finite supply of cash and hence a finite demand. Further, there is only so much free time available for nonprimary production. The major source of "new wealth" (very small at that) for most people lies in the remittance of money earned by individuals who for some period completely forgo their roles as local producers to engage in wage labor. These are the providers of new wealth, yet they do it at a definite social cost. They are lost to the community as citizens, husbands, fathers, judges, sons—in short as *producers*—so long as they are away. Yet it is their earnings that are circulated by means of stockfair, breaking bulk, craft sales, sale of animals, and so forth.

This raises the question of "underemployment" of labor in the rural sector. I will offer the flat judgment that Western-trained economists have a simplistic view of underemployment. Granted, there may exist at a given moment more bodies than are needed or required to perform certain socially necessary labor. But social life is far more than what we define economy to be. The absence of men at the mines has not been achieved by creaming a surplus of men from communities that did not need them anyway. These communities, like Kgaphamadi, were profoundly altered in permitting the absence of such multitudes. In many ways some rural Tswana communities have become quasi-societies and quasi-economies, for the absence of men and women abroad has virtually destroyed institutional life and replaced it with nothing except cash.

For example, reciprocal kinship obligations, which were sanctioned by elaborate symbolic, ritual, and ceremonial practices as well as by a utilitarian order, have been shattered by labor migration. This in turn has meant that many of the institutional practices by means of which young people raise capital have been cut off. Many of the redistributive mechanisms of the traditional economy which linked the better-off older generations with the aspiring but less-well-off younger ones no longer work. They no longer can work. This in turn has forced many young people to seek wage labor in order to get the cash to *hire* cattle to plow, to *hire* people to help thatch, to *hire* people to do this and that. A young man, being absent, could not sustain and maintain his customary obligations to kin, which would in turn oblige them to help him. He, having necessarily abandoned his traditional duties, released many of his kinsmen from their duties toward him. The only other help available to him then lies in the nexus he makes with cash.

The desiccation of groups organized to carry on economic production and of kinship obligations has been proximally caused by labor migration. This has created a communal dependency on cash, the only nexus that could replace even a fraction of the reciprocal connections that existed previously. Cash means many things are exchanged now that were not formerly exchanged. But it also means many things are not now exchanged that formerly were. The chief no longer directs communal storage of grain against bad years. There is no central collection based on individual good fortune for redistribution on the basis of individual bad fortune. The chief gets a salary. Much of the collective security of communal obligation has been supplanted by a system that has made some much richer and many much poorer than they were before. Wealth used to carry the onus of generosity. Today it does not. An individualism that never existed under communal aegis has emerged as Tswana rural society achieves the dubious goal of universal salability.

The central message in this discussion of village economy is the following: the very strategies that Tswana communities have devised to cope with the advent of the market in commodities, labor, and money have created conditions that depend even more heavily on money. This evolving specialization of Tswana society has created a dependency on the ecologic niche we call the market. This in turn *requires* of a society with no indigenous means for generating new wealth a constant replenishment of the cash upon which many of its institutions now depend. Labor migration both to the mines and to urban centers in Botswana is the preponderant form the quest for wealth takes.

Were an agricultural surplus possible, sale of foodstuffs could obviate the need for much of this search for work. Were the local herds both larger and much more equitably distributed, the sale of stock could generate "new" wealth. But since most of the population do not have herds large enough to be regularly slaughtered for sale this possibility is closed. As we will see in later sections, one of the principal goals for many young migrants is to earn the money to start a herd. Unfortunately, the earnings from migrants and others has barely been sufficient to act as a social replacement fund—that fund of wealth needed to replace depreciating capital and serve as a subvention to agriculture in bad years. Little substantial expansion and no redistribution of the national herd can be seen to result from migrant labor.

There have been attempts in some villages to inaugurate various cottage industries with a fairly heavy capital endowment. In a village just twenty-five kilometers from Kgaphamadi an enterprising Swiss had established a textile-weaving operation, specializing in hand weaving of tourist garments for mass sale in towns and abroad. The best managed of these cottage-industry schemes can do a lot to raise funds for both the workers and the communities. They have the advantage of not fracturing communal life by dragooning off the local population. Further, they can be run so as to complement and not conflict with other necessary labor performed in the round of village life. To date these schemes have just begun to appear. Their success rates vary considerably, as do the motives and competence of their organizers.

The organization of community young people into brigades to engage collectively in various "development" tasks is also an aspect of local economy that has produced a few show-window results. But in the main, the contributions from cottage industry and the activities of youth or worker brigades must be deemed marginal in the overall picture. Their aims are hindered by the absence of basic reform, namely the restructuring of rural organization, which Botswana is not about to embark upon, and which would in any case require massive outside assistance and considerable local coercion.

Most rural Tswana store and invest a large part of their wealth in livestock. Most migrants place part of their earnings in stock—principally sheep and goats, but also cattle. As we shall see in the later chapters, a strong value still attaches to the accumulation of herds. Sales are made very circumspectly, and usually only in time of dire need. This means the beasts sold are often the oldest and most decrepit. Hence their sale realizes less cash than it would if they were sold in their prime (by Western standards).

Beliefs concerning value in rural Tswana communities have been only partly eroded by awareness of the concept of price as determined in a market. Many Tswana will, for example, compute what their cash needs are, select a beast for sale, and ask a price for the beast that equals their need for cash. This could result in the price being absurdly low or absurdly high in reference to the market price that the cow or ox would fetch. I have had long discussions with many Tswana who could not be persuaded of the plausibility of a price-making market establishing the exchange value of a cow. In former times this practice of asking the amount one needed operated quite frequently. And from what informants tell me, it worked well. In effect the exchange of animals for rates that were set by needs brought the entire community into a nexus of exchange where the excess or shortfall of exchange value was complemented by a redistribution according to use-value as determined by social necessity. In this arrangement, the exchange of the beast was in fact a ceremonial or token expression of a redistribution among the partners to the exchange according to needs, not according to exchange value.

Today, rural people who attempt this gambit are ridiculed by the young and others who have been inculcated with the market mentality. But very often the market-mentality types will fall back on the same line of argument when complaining that the wages paid them for hard labor do not compensate them for the pain and fatigue of hard work and are insufficient to buy the goods and services they need. Value of labor, value of use, and value in exchange remain to varying degrees discrete, autonomous concepts in the Tswana economy.

Child Rearing and Education
No discussion of beliefs concerning self-identity could begin without an understanding of the method of child rearing. We have emphasized "economy" because this affects the way children are raised—what they are taught and the tasks they perform in their daily lives. As with my observations on economy and ecology, I shall describe prevalent practices, usages, and customs as they now exist in small villages and rural lands areas of the Southeastern Kweneng. It happens that these customs are very widespread throughout Botswana, indeed throughout much of

southern Africa. Patterns of child rearing, including instruction in matters of propriety, morality, and character, are remarkably invariant in rural and village areas in this part of the world, at least among the noneducated majority. Despite important differences in economy between the Eastern and Western Kweneng (the latter to be discussed below), patterns of child rearing are not noticeably different. This fact permits me to conclude that insofar as personality and identity are a function of early learning experiences—experiences flowing from development of erogenous zones and patterned relations with significant others—there is a substantial commonality between the Eastern and Western Kweneng. The pattern of child rearing in the modern towns is quite a different matter, as we shall see in the discussion of the underlife of Gaborone.

Isaac Schapera (1940) has written a fairly comprehensive and most readable account of married life among the Kgatla, one of the eight principal tribes found in modern Botswana. His materials, based on several stints of field research from 1929-34, are not only still valid today for the Kgatla but in the main apply to most of the Tswana of eastern Botswana, including the Kwena. In the fifteen months I spent in various communities of the Kweneng district I found very little to controvert any of Schapera's findings regarding family life. This is most fortunate, for the common practices of child rearing, education, and family life among widely different Tswana communities eliminate one of the principal sources of variation in the genesis of adult personality. Were child-rearing practices quite different from community to community in the Kweneng, we could hardly state with any confidence that variation in one's self-identity is traceable to the degree of dependency upon labor migration, as this factor would be totally conflated with child rearing.

It would be pointless to summarize Schapera's observations. I shall instead confine my remarks to certain aspects of the child's environment and the practices of child rearing and child training, focusing on what I think will be most useful as background to our discussion of conscious self-identity and the responses of individual Tswana to their experiences in enclaves of Western control. In the following comments I shall draw on Schapera's materials, but where my own observations and his are discordant I shall so indicate.

The advent of Europeans and the incorporation of the Tswana into the colonial political economy has wrought substantial changes in both the structure and the content of daily family life. To talk about the "indigenous" traditional Tswana family is to talk about what only a handful of the oldest living Tswana can remember. Besides, memory is a creative and constitutive psychological faculty. The brash, rebellious, deviant youths of Schapera's field research are the old people of my research, lamenting the decline of "pure Tswana" family ways.

A Tswana infant is born into an indulgent, solicitous, carefree world. The fathers, as well as other senior men, abandon their hauteur regarding household duties to play with, admire, and help the young infant. The primary responsibility for the nurture and care of the infant lies, never-theless, with the mother. For two or more years the mother gives the child attention on demand. Breast feeding is done on demand. The child is cradled and cuddled and amused when it shows any sign of being upset. Children are the only asset whose value and prestige exceed that of the herd in the Tswana conception of wealth. The young infant is truly cherished.

About the time the mother becomes pregnant again, perhaps two or so years after the previous birth, she will wean the child. Weaning is abrupt and constitutes the child's first real encounter with the system of negative sanctions that pervade the Tswana conception of child train-ing. The child will be refused the breast completely. He will perhaps be removed to live with another relative in the hope he will forget the breast; snuff may be sprinkled on the mother's nipple to condition the child away from the breast. The child may be told by the mother or others that the nipple is a worm and no good.

After weaning the child is more and more looked after by older, usually female, siblings, not by the mother. While the mother will still attend to the child, much of the minute-by-minute care is turned over to a child some five to eight years older, who will carry the child around strapped to her back.

Toilet training begins in the period before weaning and lasts as long as is required to achieve the desired results. Toilet training is not a major problem technically as children wear only a small cloth—around the waist in the case of girls and over the front pubic area in the case of boys. It is quite easy for a baby to learn to urinate and defecate without soil-ing its *tshega* or *lekgabe*—the two garments mentioned. As children do not have to learn about toilets, they can defecate any place they want, so long as it is not in the hut, courtyard, or near where people pass or congregate. Incentives to train take the form of instruction by the mother or another older female, coupled with very mild switching if the child "regresses" in its behavior after having been duly instructed.

With weaning and toilet training out of the way the child leaves the somewhat indulgent fold of parents or grandparents and has to make his way in the rough-and-tumble yet authoritarian hierarchy of children and childhood. In Tswana society generally, age carries with it many prerogatives. Childhood is no exception. Older children dominate younger children in many ways: delegating chores, making peremptory demands, subjecting them to idle bullying, confiscating delicacies found in the bush. While children within the same age-grade play amicably and uninhibitedly together, the presence of an older youth generally signals a time for orders to be given and unquestionably obeyed.

Much of child training consists in imparting the etiquette that an older individual (doing the instructing) feels should govern how a junior person acts toward a senior person. Basically this is training in deference. Kinsmen of various statuses will be introduced and talked about. The child learns his duties toward others in positions senior to his. From this he quickly infers his reciprocal prerogatives regarding his juniors. The Tswana are rigid and authoritarian disciplinarians who enjoy teaching legalistic dos and don'ts in manners of public decorum, etiquette, and role obligations. Despite the child's being hedged in by the "law," he has enormous freedoms when he is playing on his own, free of duties, and momentarily out of earshot of adults. When their chores are done, children may at a very early age begin staying up all night romping in the bush with their peers. Many young children go to parties attended by the senior siblings and neighbors and learn to imitate the groovy, with-it braggadocio and bravura of their teenage seniors.

Children at the early age of five to ten begin sexual play privately and together. This is regarded as quite normal by parents, and very little tutoring in the facts of life precedes puberty. At that time girls will be warned of the risks of pregnancy and boys will be dissuaded or discouraged from being crassly lecherous. Today most of this advice falls on deaf ears. Both young boys and girls are very open and candid about liking sex play and there are few inhibitions for either sex. There are penalties for bearing children out of wedlock or for impregnating a girl who is not one's spouse. In practice, however, establishing paternity is difficult and many households accept the fact that girls will bear children before they are married.

Child training is directed toward producing a mannerly, conforming, and industrious person. The Tswana, as we shall see, want the child to learn the behavior requisite to melding with the conjugal and communal economy. To be able to do for oneself, to obey legitimate instructions and requests, to follow the canons of decorum and etiquette (especially to suffer frustration and pain stoically), and to learn the duties and rights of one's station in life are the principal goals to which childhood training is directed. There is no conception, like that currently in vogue in the Anglo-Saxon world, of developing "the whole personality" by means of self-discovery, that is to say, of rewarding exploratory or innovative behavior even if it is absurd to adults. To this end the Tswana do not value entrepreneurial approaches to life. Innovation and a "critical attitude" are actively discouraged by the rigid, rote-learning approach to child training. A child who disobeys is never, in my experience, allowed to make excuses. He will be lectured on why what he did is wrong and he will be punished. Punishment often means a thrashing.

The formal education now available in public primary schools is, in its manner of approach, a perfect analogue of Tswana patterns of child training. The child learns by rote and is punished for mistakes, delinquencies, errors, or incompetence. The teachers set themselves up as authority figures and use their authority unstintingly to exact not only scholastic performance but all kinds of extracurricular favors from their pupils.

As the Tswana are naturally preadapted to this kind of educational system, so too are they to the life beyond the schools, which is based on a system of rigid deference and decorum. Propriety in Tswana society cannot be a pawn to critical thought. Radical criticism coming from people not entitled by office to proffer criticism is rudeness at least, and probably insufferable insubordination. Docility and submissiveness vis-à-vis seniors, egalitarian fraternal and sororal freedom vis-à-vis peers, and authoritarian domination of juniors is a not unfair, if stylized, summation of the role patterns inculcated by child training, formal schooling, and the established organizations of the society. (Incidentally, one of the most common complaints I have heard American Peace Corps volunteers make, especially those who teach in the various schools of Botswana, is that they are repelled by the authoritarian and doctrinaire approach to teaching of their Tswana colleagues. A corollary complaint is their stated inability to get the students to "think critically and independently." Many young PCVs go to Botswana imbued with a Summerhill-type world view in which their goal is to help the Tswana "find themselves" and discover the rich experiences of creative self-expression. This hope of Peace Corps teachers is quickly

shattered by both the structure of the educational system and the response of most Tswana pupils, who want clear instructions as to what is
expected of them and clear standards against which they must perform (Alverson 1977).

There is a chink in this system. The authority of the father nowadays
is eclipsed after the child reaches puberty. The father has lost his role
as the link between the family on earth and the paternal ancestors
whose wishes strongly affect the life-chances of the living. Ancestor
worship is dead. The ancestors traditionally punished all kinds of
earthly misfeasances, misdemeanors, and breaches of good order and
governance. The loss of this sanction, coupled with new opportunities
for the child to escape the oftimes onerous whims of the father, has led
to a diminution in what labors a father can readily exact from his children. Many adults lament that children are beginning "to do and think
as they please." While this is hyperbolical, they do often contravene
their parents' wishes and instructions.

Any physically-fit youth who appears age eighteen or over can go to
the mines. The advent of commercial and administrative towns in Botswana with their petit bourgeois high-life side by side with the squatter
underlife affords new opportunities for youngsters of very young age to
run off to town and learn to live by their wits. It is not uncommon to
see dozens of little children aged ten, twelve, or fourteen hanging
around the parking lots and shopping areas of Gaborone waiting to
"pull a caper" to get some money for bread. Many of these youngsters
have run away from the cattle posts, and their roles as labor pawns, or
they have escaped various "supernatural" evils prevalent in the family
factionalism of Tswana rural communities. This opportunity for independence means the father cannot hold the "inheritance" over the children as a means of securing service or obedience.

In most communities where severe economic scarcity is a fact of daily
existence, invidious envy can be a recurrent problem. Where one's good
and bad fortune or gains made at the expense of another are open to
public view and where one must daily face enemies or competitors, the
motives of envy and resentment loom large. This invidious envy is
called *dikgaba*. Schapera has described it as a curse that ancestors can
place on an individual for transgression of moral or other canons of
conduct. My informants referred to *dikgaba* not so much as the curse of
envy itself as the evil (or "curse") one man wishes on another because
the former envies or resents the latter's attainments. *Dikgaba* or fear of
it causes many Tswana, including children, to fear conspicuous success

in the context of their rural homes. Conspicuous display of the fruits of good fortune—education, job, money, or consumer goods—can give rise to envy in others. Often youngsters who are privileged to be sent to school—leaving other siblings behind—will rationalize their scholastic difficulties by saying they have been bewitched by those left at home.

In rural areas and small villages, typically only a few of a family's children can be spared to attend school. The costs of schooling are very high given the disposable cash income of most Tswana. Uniforms—to my mind an anachronism—are required and are more expensive than school fees. Frequently the oldest children will go to school, leaving the younger at the kraal and the cattle post.

In former times the eldest male could expect a certain priority in inheritance of the father's estate. This is still true to some degree. But the estate is now often tended by the junior siblings, who do not stand to get as much of the inheritance as the eldest child, even though it is they who are working hardest to husband the father's resources. Such siblings left behind will frequently resent their double jeopardy—no school on the one hand and a less than equal share in the inheritance on the other. Very often it is these younger children who in frustration and disgust may escape—run away from home to make their grubstake in the mines or in the towns of Botswana.

Many youngsters every year leave their home communities permanently and choose to find a life elsewhere. These people are called by the charming appellation *makgwelwa*, which comes from the word for being revolted by the breast after one has been successfully weaned. People who run away from home to town and stay are said to have rejected the breast of the home. They stay away and become accustomed to new ways. Upon returning home to the village, perhaps with fond thoughts of settling down there, they find that what was the breast of home (before weaning) has now become alien, unpleasant, intolerable—it is like the breast after weaning. Hence they return to the life of towns to which they have become inured.

The Governance of Villages and Local Life

The efficacy and importance of tribal government, village government, and the local institutions of the national government vary considerably from district to district and from village to village. Several of my friends and acquaintances in Botswana tell me that traditional tribal government in, for example, the Central District (Ngwato) is moribund. This is certainly not the case in the Kweneng District or the Kgatleng District just to the north. In fact in most of the smaller villages and lands areas of the Kweneng District it appears that the national government of Botswana, not the tribal government, is moribund. Most of the non-educated (i.e., the vast majority) have almost no conception of the meaning of national government or of the nation state, Botswana. I have spoken to hundreds of rural Tswana concerning their views on the national government and the typical reaction is one of contemptuous indifference. The government is perceived to be a body that proposes and promulgates changes, which most rural people find offensive or at least irrelevant. More seriously they see the agents of the government as rude, ignorant "big-stomachs"—people living the good life in town who have lost touch with rural life, rural people, and the values and culture of the Tswana. In all of my rather extensive interviewing I found only a few people who had any kind words to say about the national government.

Everyone, especially the men, quite readily asserts that life in Botswana is infinitely superior to life in South Africa. Here they enjoy freedom, personal security, and human dignity that they say and know perfectly well is absent "on the other side." But this desirable state of affairs in Botswana is traced by them to the "absence of Boers" rather than to government policy as such.

In the larger villages, where government agencies are at least visible, even if torpid in the view of the local people, there is greater consciousness of the concept of nationhood and national government. But most Tswana do not live in large villages. While local, "tribal" government now "interacts" with local agents of the national government in making policy decisions, I have found no evidence that many of these joint policies—whether they have to do with sinking boreholes, building grain-storage depots, or adding rooms to a school—compellingly arrest the attention of the local people.

During a debate on some mooted government proposal (e.g., where to put the water supply), people will come to debate the issues, press their viewpoints, and muster votes for their position. But this "political life" is but the tiniest fraction of rural or village life as a whole, and—as I will demonstrate later—quite peripheral to the individuals' principal concerns and ambitions. In the Kweneng at least, life is a quest for the material conditions of survival at the worst of times and a quest for some of the material prerequisites to ease the hard life at the best of times. In both of these pursuits, most rural Tswana see the national government as neither a help nor a hindrance. The fundamental unit of economy, the household, is also the fundamental unit of policy and governance. Every week in a larger village there will be issues presented before the village council (the *kgotla*)—yet this activity is no more central to the lives of most Tswana than are the daily activities of the town clerk's office to the residents of an American village.

Government, of course, links local residential areas to the larger world around. Kgaphamadi and countless other lands and villages in the Eastern Kweneng, and in eastern Botswana generally, enjoy easy access to the "outside" world by road and by rail. At Sebele—a four-or-five-kilometer walk from most parts of Kgaphamadi—is a rail siding where at least four trains a day stop to take on and discharge passengers. The train runs from Bulawayo in Rhodesia to Mafekeng in the western Transvaal, passing through Botswana for about five hundred kilometers. With first-, second-, third-, and fourth-class service, rail travel to other parts of Botswana and to South Africa is within the reach of most Tswana living in Kgaphamadi. Just in the last year the main north-south road, which runs parallel to the rail line, has begun to be tarred from Lobatse in the south to Francistown in the north. There are numerous bus and lorry services operating along the road. The national vehicle for this part of the country, however, is the bicycle. The ground is sufficiently hard to permit bicycle travel throughout the country. A network of bicycle and foot paths links practically every local village to every other. Most Tswana—even quite senior citizens—think nothing of taking off on a bike for a two-day trip to Molepolole or elsewhere. Many younger men who commute to Gaborone to work may ride fifteen to twenty kilometers each way daily on their bikes. While the total number of privately owned vehicles in Kgaphamadi and the surrounding villages is probably less than two dozen, vehicle owners make a practice of "giving" rides to all and sundry in order to help meet vehicle operating expenses.

Kgaphamadi is close to and within easy access of Gaborone and other centers where the world of commerce and business is to be found. One of the consequences of this is that it is possible to buy food and other commodities in bulk from wholesalers, who tend to be found in the larger towns and villages. This can cut household expenses and creates the opportunity for the various breaking-bulk schemes mentioned above.

The national government is beginning to make its presence felt in rural areas through its various Land Rover forays. Everything from census work to smallpox inoculations brings "big-stomachs" from town out to the countryside to deal with the local people. Hence one sees vehicles pass through Kgaphamadi several times per day.

This coming and going of people to town and the regular passage of emissaries through the villages raises the question of modernization or the degree to which Western values have been imported to these rural communities that lie so accessible to termini or enclaves of Western activity. There are three complexes of Western institutions that strike even the casual observer in rural Botswana. One is money and the marketplace; another is the church and other manifestations of Western religion; the third is the school—formal education. While the marketplace brings people to town, the church and schools have gone out to the countryside.

I do not want to undertake a discussion of Tswana beliefs regarding any of these institutions, as these will be dealt with later. I should simply like to observe that less than 10 percent of the adult population of Kgaphamadi, and of the Eastern Kweneng District generally, has ever been to school. Even the proportion of children currently of school age who have attended school is less than 50 percent for Kgaphamadi and for the Kweneng as a whole. Yet education is revered in a distinct, fascinated way by almost everyone. It is seen as the key to personal economic (i.e., career) success. The school is almost universally endorsed by Tswana as a good idea. Children hunger to learn the almost magical skills—reading, writing, and arithmetic. Those unable to get to school feel they are missing something, but they are basically resigned to their fate. Those in school feel this is a necessary step to success in the changing world where work in the money sector of the new country is the highest goal one can have.

The influence of organized religion has been much less significant in rural Botswana. In Kgaphamadi about 75 percent of the men state flatly that they are not Christians. About 20 percent state they are Christians but seldom, if ever, go to church. The remaining 5 percent are regular churchgoers. Among the women, about 15 percent are regular churchgoers, about 50 percent are believers but seldom go to church or "used to go but don't any more," and about 35 percent state flatly they are not Christians. Later we will look at some of the salient beliefs concerning self-identity in terms of this factor of religion.

Three Kalahari Villages

Most of what has been said about the Eastern Kweneng and Kgaphamadi applies to the Kalahari. There are nevertheless some very important ecologic and economic differences between the arid, Western Kweneng, and the climatically more favored eastern parts. These ecologic-economic contrasts are closely associated with the relationship between self-identity and the incorporation of individuals into systems of colonial dependency. In this brief section I should like to outline these most important contrasts. What I do not cite as a contrast you may take for granted is common to the two regions. The presence of these common features constitutes a very important "control," which shall be employed in making inferences about the effects of ecologic and economic *differentia* on self-identity.

Let me characterize the most important way in which the small villages of the Kalahari differ from their counterparts in the Eastern Kweneng by quoting from my field journal, where I recorded my first impressions and experiences in the Kalahari. By the time I made this entry I had spent over six months in Kgaphamadi; I spoke Setswana quite well and knew the rural peoples' lives quite intimately. Yet I was profoundly shocked by my first contact with these villages one hundred and fifty kilometers to the west.

We [myself, my research assistant, and Rre Segatlhe, my host] arrived in Ditshegwane about 2:00 p.m. (12 Oct. 1973). There we spent the rest of the day and night. I walked about the village and talked with the many curious people who approached me, wanting to know who we were and what we were doing. Ditshegwane revealed to me for the first time a *poverty* which I had never before experienced in my life. The village was completely segregated into Kwena and the "inferior," junior group of Tswana, the Kgalagadi. The two groups lived on opposite sides of the village, each occupying its own ward. They spoke very different dialects, which surprised me, given the closeness of at least superficial daily contact, and the small size of the village (de facto population about 400).

The answers to my questions posed about mine experiences and labor migration elicited answers quite different from those I was accustomed to hearing in Kgaphamadi. Mine labor migration is the principal means used by these people to prevent mass starvation or wholesale removal from this arid region. Agriculture is seldom practiced, said almost everyone. No planting was done by anyone this past year. Selling one or two of one's goats is the way one raises money, if one isn't recently returned from the mines or receiving remittances from someone there. With this cash one buys food in the local shops which I notice sell maize and sorghum packaged in very small units at very high prices.

Everything from the diet to the housing looks decrepit in comparison to Kgaphamadi. Several people told me, when I asked how they spend their days this time of year (before the first summer rains), "we sit in our huts and hold our stomaches." (The pain of insufficient food.) Rre Segatlhe couldn't even find a tub of beer. No beer is being brewed because there is no sorghum.

Every Kgalagadi I spoke with, and most of the Kwena in the age group 15 to 50, say mine labor is their salvation, but most surprising to me is that almost everyone says it is a "fun" experience—a good experience.

In the next two villages I visited, Takatokwane and Dultwe, farther West into the desert, this opinion about the mines was even stronger, more positive. "The mine is the place where we eat," said several young men quite independently in all three villages. When one is fed up with hunger and improvishment, said one young man age 22 who had already done four nine-month contracts on the mines, one just jumps on the MLO truck, gets a sandwich and goes off to Molepolole to sign up. When I mentioned the possibility of an alternative to mine migration, every one in each village laughed in my face. "There is no choice," they said. Yet several young men said they had taken their first mine contracts simply because they wanted to. No one was forcing them to; they could have lived on their parents' food much longer. Going to the mines under age is a common practice. While many of the younger men didn't know how old they were, several said or claimed they had been to the mines when they were 15–16 years old.

In Dultwe, I saw the most depressing sight of my life. We drove in, mid-day and stopped the truck under a tree that stood beside the *kgotla* [central courtyard of the village]. This is a desolate village at the edge of a salt pan, five hours drive from Ditshegwane. There in the middle of the village sat the residents staring collectively into space. They *were* literally holding their stomachs. The only food available in the village, said everyone who came immediately to the truck to ask if I could spare food for their children, was available in the local shop, which sold *meelies* [ground maize] at a very high price. No one had any money. Again, there was no beer, not even *Kgadi* [an alcoholic beverage made from a wild root], because no one had money enough to buy a bag of brown sugar. The mark-up commodities in local shops is incredible. The store was owned by some European who lived in Gaborone (no doubt in an air conditioned house with a swimming pool). There was no food distribution program in effect; people were completely dependent upon the shop for their staples. An odd rabbit or fowl, or the very occasional slaughter of a goat, was the only other food.

Almost no one in either Takatokwane or Ditshegwane owned cattle, the "wealthier" people owned a few small stock. Cattle, what few there were, were destroyed between 1965–1970, during a period of severe drought. There was an elementary school in each of the three

villages. But according to everyone, only a few of the younger children are attending. Very few past the age of 14 attend, as they leave
the village to find work herding cattle at posts some distance away—
cattle owned by "rich" Tswana from the East. Most others are going
off to the mines as soon as they appear old enough to pass muster.
   Another curious thing I discovered in these villages was that, despite
the extensive migration to the mines, very few of these people have
ever had contact with towns and villages even in Botswana. They go
straight from here to Gaborone, entrain and go off to Johannesburg.
Several young people said they have been around Johannesburg more
than they've been around Gaborone.

These excerpted lines from my diary convey a most important message. Research that I undertook in these villages later, where I sought
the same kinds of information as I did in Kgaphamadi, confirmed my
first impressions. The villages of the Kalahari (at least in the Kweneng)
constitute labor reserves for the mines. The annual rainfall here is less
than two-thirds that of Kgaphamadi; hence, only in the best years, one
year in about four, is a crop that the local people call "good" harvested.
Most Kalahari respondents claimed that good crops were a thing of the
past. The young who are able to enroll in schools and move out to jobs
or further education go to Molepolole or Gaborone. Those remaining
are the ones who do not enter school. They are needed at home or they
cannot afford school. The mines are their *material* salvation.
   I asked several young men whether many go to Gaborone when they
get tired of the cattle posts. The response was: "There are very few
cattle anymore, but we [Kgalagadi] dislike having to go to those parts
of the Kweneng dominated by the Kwena." There is a visible and
important measure of ethnic antagonism between the Kwena and the
Kgalagadi. The Kwena use the term *Kgalagadi* among themselves somewhat in the same way we have used the word *nigger* in our own society.
Rre Segatlhe (a Kwena) asked one young man why he couldn't speak
proper Tswana, to which the young man replied, "You oppress me into
the ground when I come to your home, but you're not going to oppress
me in my *own* home."
   I surmised, and later confirmed, that the mine experience for the
Kgalagadi is seen as an escape from Kwena domination. "At the mines,"
said one young man, "all Black people are *Kgalagadi;* so there we're
equals."
   It would be irritatingly thorough to cite the demographic statistics
which substantiate the evidence of my senses. But I wish to make this

clear: the Kalahari villages occupy an ecologic-economic niche characterized by an abject, necessary dependency upon labor migration. In
the total combined populations of the three Kalahari villages, based on
a purposive sample of sixty, only one person in fifteen of adult age
owned any cattle at all. Over half the adults interviewed had no small
stock. One in ten had planted during the past year and 40 percent of
the sample said they had not planted once in the past five years. No
one could remember a "good" harvest in the past ten years. Everyone
interviewed said that he had to buy most of his grain from the local
shops as there was not enough grown locally. Among youngsters aged
five to fifteen, only one in eight was presently going to school or had
ever gone in the past. Among all the men interviewed (forty), the mean
number of contracts taken on the mines was about twelve (double the
number for Kgaphamadi). Many had been so often they could not recall
the number of times.

Based on a sample of sixty respondents, I estimate that over two-
thirds of the de jure village population were absent during my first
survey in October 1974 and almost one-third were absent in December
1974 to January 1975, during a time when rains had fallen in abundance and planting would have been quite possible. The proportion of
the absent two-thirds who were at the mine was about 75 percent,
according to people interviewed.

I must add that these disadvantaged people of the Western Kweneng
are both absolutely and relatively a small population, even in relation
to small population sizes found in Botswana. The average population
density of the Western-Central Kweneng is about 1.5 to 3 persons per
square kilometer. The total population of the Western Kweneng is
probably less than 10,000. Recall that 80 percent of the total population of Botswana lives in the eastern corridor along the rail line. Still
these Kalahari people form part of the political economy of southern
Africa. Their significance to our major query is not diminished by their
small numbers, for in their experiences lie universal principles of human
behavior and consciousness.

The Kalahari villages are isolated from the major routes of trade and
commerce. Molepolole, the tribal capital, is a grueling three-hour ride
from Ditshegwane and seven hours from Dultwe. Probably fewer than
two vehicles per week pass through the two more remote villages. The
major means of transport is a bus service run by the Mine Labour
Organization that links Molepolole to Kang in the Kgalagadi district.
In other respects, however, these villages are much like Kgaphamadi.

Their household, ward, and village organizations are not dissimilar, except that the Kgalagadi are perceived by the Kwena as an inferior, junior aggregation of Tswana. The daily round of life, the raising of children, and many values and beliefs of these peoples are quite alike, as they are between the Eastern and Western Kweneng. The differences are primarily ones of ecology and purchase on the material means of subsistence. Yet in speaking of *local* ecology and economy I do not want to suggest that any unit is self-contained. The ecology of villages (the dependencies that exist between rural people and work) link the town and the countryside, the mines and the villages, into a single system. Rural society in Botswana is functionally a part-society; this is particularly true for the Kalahari and to a lesser degree for the Eastern Kweneng as well.

4 TOWN AND THE WORLD OF WORK

Gaborone

The town and the principal places of wage labor—the mines and industries—comprise the third niche, or type of setting, occupied by the Tswana. The main town is Gaborone. It is a new town, planned almost literally from scratch during the 1950s, whose site was picked because of the water supply. There was a small village named "Gaber-ones," which had less than six hundred people, at the present site of Gaborone. The current twenty thousand de facto residents occupy quarters built within the last dozen or so years.

Gaborone is a "town" in contrast to a village. It has paved roads, night lighting, European-owned shops offering what is for Botswana a wide range of goods and baubles. It is the seat of the national government and a nascent hub of commerce and light industry for south-eastern Botswana. Gaborone is a town of economic contrasts. It is (or can be) divided in half geographically. On the southern side are crowded some fifteen thousand Tswana and other black Africans in housing that ranges from modest two- or three-room brick and mud structures to one-room shanties made of cardboard. The northern half of the town has about five hundred new cement, iron-roofed houses and apart-ments, many air-conditioned and most with three or more bedrooms. They are electrified and have all other modern conveniences, including plenty of cheap domestic help.

In between these two zones of Gaborone are about three hundred "middle-class" dwellings, occupied mainly by Tswana but also by a few white families. On the wealthy northern side (called "little En-gland") resides the white population and a few of the new bourgeoisie among the Tswana. The local population is fully aware that the capital was planned in such a way as to create almost total de facto segregation of the races. Incredible wealth, 90 percent white, exists in the small area of less than ten square kilometers alongside poverty which is 100 percent black. An expatriate plumber or electrician from overseas lives in housing that compares with that occupied by most of the cabinet ministers of the national government. This economic disparity is fully comparable with what exists de jure in South Africa. It is a fact of which any Gaborone resident is fully conscious. While the national government tries to keep wage differentials down for its local population, it is forced in its dealings with industrial countries to pay the going wage to attract expatriate expertise.

Instead of belaboring the obvious differences in the physical properties of town and countryside, let me recount some features of Gaborone that Tswana respondents have called to my attention as in one way or another significant to the contrast between town life and "life at home."[1]

Gaborone is not a town of absentees, as we find the traditional villages to be. Of 4,828 Gaborone dwellings enumerated in the 1971 census, 4,403 were occupied. Gaborone is made up almost entirely of newcomers who define "home" as elsewhere. On Christmas Day—the day one is most likely to be *at home*—Gaborone is virtually deserted of its Tswana population.

Gaborone is also a town of "strangers"—non-Tswana. Unlike the typical villages of the Kweneng, which may have a dozen or so non-Tswana in them, Gaborone had 16,848 Tswana and 4,235 non-Tswana, out of a total enumerated population of 21,083. One half or so of the non-Tswana are "Europeans."

The town is also the show window of Botswana's efforts at social and economic development. It is a point of attraction for Botswana's educated. Fewer than half of Gaborone's population of Tswana have *never* been to school, while in the Kweneng District three-fourths of the population have never been to school. Of 18,799 Tswana enumerated in Gaborone, 3,029 are currently in school. For the Kweneng as a whole, with a Tswana population three times as large (62,552), 6,108 are in school. Gaborone has almost as many students in secondary school as does the entire Kweneng District: 458 compared to 539.

Gaborone is a center for wage employment despite its large numbers

1. All figures cited in the following section are taken from: Government of Botswana, Central Statistics Office, 1972, *Report on the Population Census* (Gaborone: Government Printer).

of unemployed. Of 6,990 males over the age of ten, 4,439 are employed in wage labor, while 2,551 are unemployed. Of 7,128 women over age ten, 2,208 are employed in wage labor while 4,920 are unemployed. The comparable figures for the Kweneng are: males age ten or over equal 15,869, of whom 1,347 are employed; females age ten or over equal 24,143, of whom 668 are employed.

Gaborone is in close touch with the "outside world." It is connected by good roads with South Africa and will soon be with Rhodesia and Zambia. Railway and bus service connect Gaborone to South Africa at a number of points. There are more radio sets in Gaborone than in all of the Kweneng; therefore more people can hear about the country and the world if they wish to.

There are over two hundred businesses, commercial organizations, and companies operating in Gaborone, including (in addition to government) community service organizations, transport services, garages, banks, various business service organizations, wholesalers, distributors, light industries, offices of mining and quarrying companies, contractors, hotels, butchers, cafes and restaurants, clothing stores, food stores, and general merchandisers (Government of Botswana 1973, pp. 177–83).

Gaborone has become a new terminus of labor migration, both circulating and one-way, within Botswana itself. Many Tswana from rural areas who have been to the mines are now seeking work in Gaborone, as are large numbers of young Tswana who have never been to the mines. Many older Tswana who had lived for years in urban centers of South Africa have preferred to take up residence in Gaborone (or other Botswana towns) rather than return to the rural life of the villages and lands.

The actual number of people found in Gaborone at any one time is bound to be far more than that given in the census. And even the former is but a small part of the total population that spends some time there over a longer period of time. Many people come for a while and then return home.

From what has been said so far, the reader can imagine that the variety of urban experience among the Tswana living in Gaborone is considerable. Experience, of course, is not to be found in the empirical characterization of things outside consciousness, and the experience of a town is no exception. Every aspect of the town is an aspect of someone's experience and hence internal to a consciousness. In looking at Gaborone we will confine our attention to the conscious experience of the nonliterate. These are the majority, even of Gaborone's population. More important, their experience of Garborone is very different from that of the educated, especially the new bourgeoisie.

The nonliterate Tswana and other Africans live in demarcated areas which have acquired place names in recent times. The most important markers of residential areas are housing types. Gaborone has, for example, an area of very low cost hostels occupied by bachelors, unattached women, and others whose roots in town are minimal— people who are temporary residents or who have recently arrived and just found work or are still job-hunting. Commonly two or more people will live together in these single-room dwellings. The crowding is horrendous. The units are not electrified and have no plumbing. They are cinderblock and iron-roof units with perhaps ten or twelve rooms to a building.

There are slightly larger single units found in an area called "White City," which contains housing provided by the Gaborone Town Council for municipal employees. These are two- or three-room cement cottages, also with no inbuilt modern conveniences. The area of *Bontleng* has some privately owned, privately built housing that shows the unmistakable refinements and care of private ownership and self-built structures. These are typically brick and cement houses with three or more rooms and a private backhouse. The area of *Old Naledi* is a squatters' section where land is simply occupied and built on with whatever means are at hand. In this area one finds no service stands (central latrines or water supplies). Water is hauled in buckets from pumps located in *New Naledi*, one of the low-cost hostel developments some one or two kilometers distant.

A number of people in Gaborone seeking housing, then, cannot be accommodated. Barring the imposition of some kind of influx control, that situation will prevail for many years. In a country of extensive rural poverty many people will exchange this lot for urban poverty, even when the city offers no increase in the "objective" possibilities of improvement.

The feature of life in Gaborone that makes the most immediate sensory impression on me and on many Tswana with whom I have spoken is its crowding. This is necessarily associated with noise and the appearance of a normless coming and going of people at all hours of the day and night. Gaborone has spawned most of the trades, services, and rackets associated with the underlife of cities. The quest for kicks and thrills leavened by beer and more potent drinks is ubiquitous. The shebeens blare *gumba-gumba* (jive) and serve beer to yelling, bump-

ing, grinding young people aged fifteen to fifty all day and most of the
night. Friday, Saturday, and Sunday nights are a circus and carnival in
most of Gaborone's African residential sections.

Town life is the life of money. In town there is a superficial veneer
of freedom and excitement which most town-dwelling Tswana describe
as better than the suffocating constraints of the statutory propriety in
force in rural areas. As we will see, many young people have come to
Gaborone to pursue a way of life away from the lands and the herds.
There is an enormous population of school-leavers who have found
work in Gaborone. Those with no schooling are also well represented.
Gaborone is becoming a place to which young boys can escape at a
much earlier age than they could when the mines and farm work for
the Europeans were the only options. A number of preadolescent
"street urchins" are appearing in Gaborone. Many of these that I have
talked with have run away from the orderly, gray, puritan life at home.
Slightly older boys, who might well have gone to the mines in earlier
years, have come to Gaborone to look for work. Many of these youngsters—boys and girls—flood into domestic service. *Garden boy* and
house girl are words known to every Tswana, even if he otherwise
speaks no English at all. For the young and uneducated, Gaborone
represents the quest for a life away from home where one hopes to
earn money, perhaps to return home, perhaps to stay for some time.
The motives (the projects-of-action) for town life vary considerably,
as I shall describe in detail.

The flood of people looking to earn cash by means of unskilled
work implies of course that wages are severely depressed. The cost of
living in Gaborone—just to keep even—easily exceeds the capacity of
all but a few. One must buy bread and milk in the stores. Even fire-
wood must be bought from vendors who collect it on their bikes from
the "bush" around town.

Gaborone life is a trap for most of the young migrants who come
there. They often leave home under a cloud and hence are not free to
return whenever they want. Many believe that they can, as in the mines,
amass some money. This seldom happens, as food, clothing, shelter,
and fuel quickly eat up most of the earnings. A "garden boy" who is
lucky enough to work full time—say a morning in one family's yard, an
afternoon in another—will earn at best fifteen Rand per month. He will
easily spend two-thirds of that on necessities, and the rest can be
swallowed by the temptations of baubles and kicks. Most garden boys
earn half that if they are lucky. A domestic servant, a "gele" (girlie),

earns twelve to twenty Rand per month working for the *haute* bourgeoisie. Many "girlie" who work for the incipient Tswana bourgeoisie earn as little as five Rand per month. On these earnings, one could work in Gaborone all one's life and never earn more than a sub-subsistence wage.

The older Tswana, who typically had extensive work and urban experience in South Africa in the days before Tswana from Botswana needed permits to live there, have become habituated to town life. The vicissitudes of agriculture often lead many to stay on resignedly in town, even if under ideal conditions they would prefer to live at the lands.

Town life is different from rural life in one respect that is central to our investigation here. It affords uneducated as well as educated Tswana the "opportunity" to see, work and live within, cope and adjust to institutions run on Western principles of organization. It gives Tswana the chance to interact face to face with white people—to get to know them, to see how they work, to hear their talk, to know their intimate routines and habits. This is something that does not, cannot, happen in either the mines or the rural areas. In town a great number of European folkways, beliefs, and other habitual modes of conduct and thought form part of the social world with which the individual Tswana must come to grips. Town is—to use voguish cant—a "learning experience," in that a Tswana can see in some detail and depth how many Western institutions and Western individuals operate vis-à-vis the Tswana.

The *experience* of being a member of an urban lumpenproletariat— a black underclass dominated in its daily personal dealings by a bourgeoisie that happens in both Botswana and South Africa to be mainly white—differs from the experience of the military-like mine compounds. The almost perfect correlation between material wealth and skin color and the perfect correlation between material wealth and political power are phenomena with which the noneducated Tswana must cope on a regular basis in his town life. The effects of ascriptive inequality on the self-identify engender active coping in the conscious mind of the Tswana, who cannot ignore the facts or brush them aside. Inequality in town has a "relevance" it lacks in the mines. I will discuss this below.

The structure of social relations in town—particularly those of family, extended kinship, and the market place—contrasts sharply to that in the rural areas. Social relationships in town involve a level of anonymity which makes them different in kind and degree from the bonds of rural life. The child in Gaborone grows up in a world where escape from the care and concern of kinfolk can readily be achieved. In a rural village a young person may leave his parents' household and live with relatives, but those relatives have almost all the rights over and duties toward the child that the parents have. Further, relatives will probably be genuinely concerned to bring up the child in the way the traditions and conventions of Tswana society dictate. In town the situation is quite different. Although very few children have actually grown up in Gaborone because it is such a young town, the children who come at age ten to twelve may stay with relatives or they may find peers living in a hostel where another can squeeze in as well. In all these cases the total amount of time the child is free of adult instruction and supervision is vastly greater than in the villages and lands. A town child is not known; he can live anonymously.

The child in town learns to cope with an environment in which there is comparatively little "recipe" knowledge on hand for dealing with problems of finding money or housing, getting along with peers, and avoiding the gangs of older youth that prey on the beggings of the younger. He must develop strategies for survival that are quite different from those sanctioned in Tswana tradition. Survival, while a considerable achievement for many town youth, is a *minimal* cultural attainment. The uneducated child does not have access—except in a marginal way—to Western institutions. He is for the most part an *onlooker*, skilled at culling the crumbs from the droppings of Western institutional life. He learns a bastard English, one that will get him nowhere. More tragically, the child does not learn the wisdom of his own parents' traditions and stock of beliefs. A most startling thing I discovered among the young males living in Gaborone is that they had been cut off, at the prepuberty level, from an awareness of their Tswana traditions, wisdom, and technical knowledge, and yet they were not acquiring any Western beliefs or skills as substitutes. At the basic level of linguistic performance, for example, many Gaborone youths could not make use of the sophisticated metaphors of either English or Setswana. They spoke rather "Setsotsi"—lexically a potpourri of English, Afrikaans, and Tswana words plugged into the morphologic and syntactic structure of Setswana.

Among the younger uneducated Tswana in town, understanding of the larger world is shrewd and efficacious only at the level of immediate survival. Unlike the mine migrants who return to have their experiences evaluated by knowledgeable oldsters and arrogant schoolboys—critics of the bravura and braggadocio of the returning heroes—the uneducated town youngster lives in an environment in which "survival" is the only selective system through which knowledge, belief, or action must pass. Discussions or exchanges of ideas have little of the philosophical depth or critical acumen found even among the younger children in the rural areas, who are privy to the counsel of adults. In town, uneducated Tswana youth do not have many dealings with educated Tswana youth. The class system segregates young people very effectively. Education serves as an entitlement to membership in circles of young people from which the uneducated are excluded.

Now to be sure there are many stable families in Gaborone among the nonliterate. There are mothers and fathers who run households in which child training is a serious business regularly attended to. But even in these cases, when the child is away from home he is not at a cattle post or hoeing in the fields; he is in patterned interaction with other people whose ideas may well be at variance with those of his parents. As the child reaches puberty and comes of age in town, he depends more and more on his own resources. He is not in school, he is on his own. The primary noneconomic activity in town becomes sex. Sex play is an important activity in the rural areas too, but in town the movement from casual union to casual union, to marriage and to divorce, is rapid and often involves only transient commitments to others. Town is not the kind of setting in which weighty moral bonds are established to substitute for those of kinship. I do not want to discuss here Tswana beliefs concerning friendship (especially in town), but I will remark that the tendency for the individual to have a wide circle of superficial friends is common, and these friendship relationships are definitely characterized by opportunism.

From the sampling I could do in town it appears that young girls are impregnated (out of wedlock) at an even higher rate than in the rural areas. Lacking access to a supportive circle of kinfolk, young girls are tied down by children in ways not found in rural areas. Of course many young girls send their babies home, but there are still many who are forced to keep them in their houses and huts in town.

One major social practice of the younger people in town is visiting clubs. Sports and "functions" (dances) are the two main activities of the clubs, especially those staffed by the younger people with some education. But among the noneducated the most important center is the neighborhood shebeen with its drinking, dancing, and sex. Otherwise life is a quest for one more shilling.

Gaborone is quite different from the rural areas in terms of the work histories of the people. There are many young people in town (adolescent to middle age) who are generally absent from the rural villages, at least among the noneducated. It is to the towns (like Gaborone) that women as well as young men go in search of work. We saw that in the rural areas male absentees far outnumbered female absentees, yet many women were gone. They are to be found in Gaborone and such places. This is reflected in the fact that the sex ratio in Gaborone is not nearly so lopsided in favor of women as in rural areas.

Among the uneducated women, the major source of employment is domestic service, either in private homes or in offices. Every day one sees young girls walking the streets of Gaborone soliciting work, asking in broken English or Setswana: "A o batla gele?" "Do you want a girl?" Wages are correspondingly depressed in this situation where supply races ahead of demand.

Among the uneducated men of Gaborone there are three clear groupings. First, there are the young men who have never been to the mines but have left home for one reason or another and come to town "to get a start in life." Their two most commonly stated motives for coming to town are: (1) to escape from home, mainly out of dissatisfaction with the physical and family environments and their demands; and (2) to earn money with which to buy stock, secure a wife, and set up a rural household. (This is grossly oversimplified, as we shall see.)

The second group are the middle-aged men (aged about twenty-five to forty) who have had many experiences working in the mines and who may have, but generally have not, lived in towns in South Africa. They have given up the rural life and abandoned agriculture as a major activity. These men may own stock and have access to land but they depend on their cash earnings in town to provide for themselves and their families.

The third group that is clearly discernible is made up of older men who almost always have extensive work experience in South Africa, including work in the mines and in industry, and who have grown quite accustomed to town or "location" life from their many years spent there. These men have become habituated to the urban setting and have become accustomed to cash as the major means to a livelihood.

The first and third groups are not frequently found in the rural areas. The old men will generally have had more work experience than the younger for obvious reasons. But there are very few older men in *rural* areas of Botswana who have had extensive *urban* experience in South

Africa. There is definitely a selective attraction to Botswana's towns for those Tswana from former Bechuanaland who have quit South Africa and come "home" to live in modern Botswana. These variations in age and in the biography of work experience are closely associated with beliefs about one's identity and beliefs about the meaning of colonial domination. This topic we shall pursue in subsequent chapters.

In Gaborone I worked intensively with a total of seventeen men representing each of these categories of people. I also worked with six women, all domestic servants. I surveyed widely, mainly by walking the streets, sitting in the shebeens, asking questions, and listening to the constant round of prattle. In the four months I spent in Gaborone among the nonliterate Tswana I became very aware of the contrasts in ecology and in belief between urban and rural life and between the people who, by choice or the force of circumstances, find themselves in the one place or the other.

The Ecology of Asylum Life:
The Mine as a Total Institution

Introduction
"A total institution may be defined as a place of residence and work where a large number of like-situated individuals cut off from the wider society for an appreciable period of time together lead an enclosed formally administered round of life" (Goffman 1961, p. xiii). In "ordinary life" (on the outside), even in nonindustrial societies, people sleep, play, and work in different places with different complements of co-participants in these basic activities and many others. "The central feature of total institutions can be described as a breakdown of the barriers ordinarily separating these spheres of life (Goffman 1961, p. 5). In total institutions all these activities are carried on in the presence of an undifferentiated batch of like others. They are administered by the same authority and are tightly scheduled on the basis of formal rulings from "above." Every activity prescribed for the inmate of an asylum is designed to fulfill in one way or the other the official aims of the total institution. To this end the major burden of the hierarchy of officials whose rulings govern the life of the total institution is not instruction or guidance, but surveillance of the inmates and the policing of their performance (Goffman 1961, p. 6). For the duration of his tenure as an inmate of an asylum, the individual carries out

all his activities within the bounds and the purview of the institution.

In very general terms Goffman's characterization of an asylum or total institution quite aptly describes the South African gold mine and other industrial firms. Many of the differences between asylum life and life on the outside that are radical in our industrial society are not nearly so dramatic in the case of the Tswana. Still, Goffman's characterization is heuristically useful. I shall draw on his discussion of total institutions in presenting the ecology of the life of African workers within the confines of the mines and the other industries that employ contract labor and require incarceration of the employee for the duration of the contract.

Perhaps the most important aspect of the ecology of the South African mine is the implicit and explicit assumptions its governing officials make about the "nature" of the Africans who are recruited as laborers. The "European" conception of the qualities of mind and body of the African is part and parcel of the way the mine orders the existence of the African employee once he enters the compound gate. As Goffman has said, the total institution "can . . . be viewed as a place for generating assumptions about identity . . . a place where the question of identity must be addressed by the participant" (Goffman 1961, pp. 186–87). To create a new identity requires, minimally, that one must create a closed universe of symbols and other experience. As I argued earlier, it is quite unwarranted to assume that because one can control the overt behavior of an "inmate," one can therefore control the universe of his experience. Yet the mines do strive to create the identity of "mine worker" in a variety of ways, from clothing and assignment of numbers to a military-like hazing called "training." While the primary adjustment of the mine worker is to the overt proscriptions and prescriptions of conduct, there are inevitably a number of secondary adjustments. These represent attempts by the worker to circumvent, dodge, deny, or ameliorate the burdens of the primary adjustments. Secondary adjustments have been called the "informal organization" of the institution. Goffman has called them the "underlife" of the institution. I shall try to illustrate briefly how the secondary adjustments form as much a part of the ecology of life in the mine or other firm as do the physical plant and formal organization of work.

The Formal Organization of Work and Compound Life
In this section I want to characterize only the physical and institutional arrangements which come to be part of the content of experience for

the mine worker. I emphasize *part* of experience, because much of that experience is a function of the beliefs the migrant brings with him to the mine or factory. As Goffman says, the entrant comes to the total institution with a "presenting culture" derived from a home world. The full meaning of being in a total institution does not exist except in relation to the special meaning of getting out, returning, or otherwise being linked to a "home" on the outside. In later chapters we will explore how *home* and *mine* are related and contrasted in the beliefs of the migrants. For now I am striving to describe "objectively" the material ecology of the compound and the mine with which the migrant must cope as a necessary condition for working there.

When the contractee arrives at the mine or other place of work, he is assigned quarters not unlike those found in a military barracks at boot camp. Upon entering the gate, he ceases to have elective, voluntary contact with the outside world, unless he does so surreptitiously. He can leave for short periods on a special permit (one or two days). But he must report back to the compound at the appointed time or he faces severe sanctions, administrative and possibly legal. Nonemployees, especially Africans, may not enter the mine or the compound without special permits, and these are issued for specific, official visits only. In short, the recruit is cut off from voluntary commerce with the world beyond the mine and compound. His world for 270 shifts (nine months) is the world of the mine and the compound.

During his first few days in the mine, especially if he has been recruited for the first time, he undergoes a rigorous and intensive training program designed to teach him basic skills in safety and first aid, in underground work and the use of mining equipment, and in how to "read" or respond to certain commands and signs in *Fanakalo*, the pidgin Zulu-English of the South African mines. His performance is constantly supervised and recorded; his various aptitudes measured and evaluated.

This straightforward set of training goals is achieved in about seven days. But the program entails far more than this. The training teaches the miner obedience to authority—unquestioned obedience. Any vestige of a sullen, slow, or otherwise reluctant compliance with rules and commands is ruthlessly punished by "BBs" (boss-boys) and by European miners. Miners are inducted as a group. They march from one class to another. When a visiting person of some authority (e.g., any European) enters an area where the miners are being trained they immediately stand, extend their arms, and salute the visitor in unison. Military discipline attempts to "dispossess" the individual of any proclivity to behave in terms of the social roles he has occupied outside. The training is an elaborate ceremony as well as a "utilitarian" instructional process. It strives to create beliefs in the individual about who and what he is.

In the mines there is much less opportunity than in secondary industry to engage in overt rebellion against the obsequies and obedience to commands that fill the miner's day. From the first day the mine imposes on the migrant its definitions and characterizations of the miner as a person, as a labor unit, and as a specialized piece of capital equipment. Attempts to deny or parry these definitions are very difficult to make and only intermittently successful, especially on the job where supervision is close and continuous. The inexorable, ineluctable awe and power of technology, replete with its capacity to crush the mind and the body, remind the migrant what potent forces have instituted the social organization of mine and compound.

The mines are hierarchically ranked in an echelon system. Until World War II almost all African migrants were treated as cheap, undifferentiated labor, good only for the most menial, back-breaking tasks. Little attempt was made to impart specialized skills. Today this is not the case to such a degree. Miners learn specialized work and are trained accordingly. Yet as a class the black workers are one: they are the bottom of the pyramid. Over them stand the boss-boys, the clerks, the black police, and all Europeans, of whatever organizational position.

The echelon system of authority implies that the African laborer is almost always under somebody's surveillance or command. This means that he is continuously caught in a cross fire of orders, requests, or remonstrations. Under such conditions the miner is unable to engage in any behavior that would show he has a mind of his own—has the power to reason or to will. As Goffman has noted, even normal discourse in giving instructions is supplanted to some degree by barking, yelling, pushing, shoving, or kicking, as if the black miner were a mule. (I will examine this issue very closely below.)

The mine is a system of very carefully arranged rewards and punishments. These are behavioristic and physical. The miner can expect promotions and little physical abuse if he performs with alacrity and exhibits no vestige of sullenness or resentment. If he masters skills, he can be promoted to better paying work. If he does well, this is recorded, and he can expect ready placement on his next contract with no loss of "time logged." If the miner "messes up" (to use Goffman's phrase), he can expect the wrath of the mine: loss of pay, physical abuse, confinement in a stockade, or repatriation (perhaps at his own cost) back home.

But the mine management knows that the psychic pain of confinement and hard work needs release. The mine organizes compound life in such a way that aggression can be expressed toward other miners, so long as it does not become a "class" action directed against the mine itself. Ample opportunities for drinking, dancing, sports competition, and movies—and even a tolerance for gambling and fighting—provide the kind of safe "releases" that make the 270 shifts a little easier to take. These safety-valve mechanisms are to be found in all compounds and constitute one of the material conditions of compound life to which the miner must make an adjustment.

Physical Conditions of Work

Mine work is very heavy, demanding, and dangerous. It is impossible to imagine any form of industrial work more unlike what is common in nonindustrial societies than underground mine labor. The work is so heavy that many Africans are rejected as unfit, and many are victims of its numerous vicissitudes during their period of employ. Temperatures underground can reach as high as 35 degrees Celsius with high humidity. The surface temperature of the rocks at 2,000 meters or more below ground level is typically around 40 degrees Celsius. Miners on their first contract, or those whose physical condition is marginally acceptable, must undergo a period of acclimatization before they are allowed to enter the mine itself. (This acclimatization has many ceremonial aspects above and beyond its physiological functions.) Miners are required to do increasingly strenuous physical exercise in steam rooms until they are accustomed to the water loss and the heat.

Most miners have previous experience. Eighty-five percent or so of the African labor force employed at any one time in the mines has had prior contract work. Ninety percent of the mine labor force is African, with somewhat higher percentages for those actually employed in underground operations.

After the period of instruction, acclimatization, and aptitude and performance testing, the new or inexperienced miner is assigned to a "gang," which engages in all of the routine work of underground mining reserved for Africans: shoveling, tramming, timbering, lashing, machine drilling, pick and spade work, and sweeping. The gangs are under the immediate charge of African boss-boys, who number one for every eight or nine gang members. It is their responsibility to train the gang and to convey the orders given by European miners.

Gold mining in southern Africa is deep mining of low-grade ores. Most of the mines mill between 80,000 and 400,000 tons of ore per month. The greatest depths are 2,000 to 4,000 meters. Under these conditions the four most striking and painful aspects of the work are heat, physical strain, dust, and noise. Aside from the blasting, with its obvious implications for human discomfort, the mines employ drills, scrapers, and underground locomotives, which in the confines of the shafts and stopes create an unbelievable din. Jackhammers, each operated by one or two Africans, weigh 22 kilograms and have a 6.4 centimeter bore. These hammers deliver between 1,720 and 2,200 blows per minute. The effect on the body and especially on the hearing, of operating this kind of equipment must be experienced to be appreciated.

The gold mines consist of series of deep shafts, with tunnels, called "stopes," running off the shafts. These angled stopes must be continually developed and supported to create the conditions under which the veins of gold can be accessed and removed. The gold ore has to be blasted to create tunnels (stopes). The tunnels must be cleared and hand trams installed so that the ore which is drilled free can be loaded and removed to shifts; from here rock skips (huge lifts) haul the ore to the surface. The miners ascend and descend like the ore: in giant cages each holding fifty to a hundred men.

Most of the work Africans do is dirty, irksome, and irritating to the senses as well as physically strenuous. The drilling creates acrid rock dust despite watering for cooling and keeping dust down. The stopes are dangerous even after development, affording extraordinary danger during the not infrequent rock-bursts and cave-ins.

The jobs done by Africans include the following phases of the mining operation: (1) rock breaking: shaft sinking, development of the face of tunnels, opening small tunnels (stoping), machine drilling and hammering of ore on the face of the stope; (2) shoveling and tramming: shoveling the broken ore into tramcars and pushing the trams up the incline of the stope to central shafts; (3) sweeping: literally sweeping up the finely broken ore into piles for tramming; (4) support of workings: opening and preparing the tunnels by placing of timber supports and by packing waste rock into proper places to help support the working surface and ceiling; (5) underground mining department: ambulance, first aid, piping, truck repairing, track laying and repair; (6) underground engineering: hoist and winch operation and repair, pumping operation (much underground water to be controlled), general mechanics' helpers, and drill sharpening.

Recently it has been suggested that Africans be allowed to participate in the blasting operations. This has been strongly resisted by the white unions. There are numerous surface jobs, but the underground African work force outnumbers the surface African work force by about three to one.

Work underground poses numerous health hazards, especially to a population that comes to the mine with various physical handicaps, notably malnutrition. The most common diseases acquired or exacerbated in mine work are: silicosis, heat stroke, miner's cramp (from salt loss), heat rashes and boils, lung infections (particularly pneumonia), hookworm, numerous epidermal parasitic infections, and of course tuberculosis. Mortality rates are hard to come by but Biccard-Jeppe (1946, p. 1, 784) reports (for 1943) 3.2 deaths per thousand employees in the mines due to diseases. Under current employment levels this would mean about 1,200 to 1,400 deaths per annum from diseases for all mines in South Africa, but the rates reflect the figures for Witwatersrand gold mines only. Therefore the estimate of incidence may be in error. Accidents also take their toll in life and limb. In the two-year period 1937–39, 135 miners were killed in Witwatersrand gold mine accidents (Biccard-Jeppe 1946, p. 1, 786). Francis Wilson (1972, p. 167) reports death rates at three gold mines for the years 1958–63 that vary between .9 and 1.6 per thousand persons employed per annum. Accident rates for the period 1952–63 at the same three mines vary between 50 and 70 per thousand per annum. About half of my respondents in Botswana could show me clear evidence of severe mine injuries acquired during one or more of their contracts. The most serious and most common causes of accidents are: rock bursts, where the pressure of the surface bearing down on supporting rock makes the rock fracture and explode, causing the ground to fall in on the miners; explosions (dynamite), and finally machine accidents, especially those connected with the operation of underground vehicles—drills, winches, and so forth.

The miners work forty-eight hours per week, six eight-hour shifts, which excludes time spent preparing for entering and leaving the mine. Miners typically do not eat during a shift but instead have a meal before and after the shift. Because of enormous water loss, the miners must drink continually while working. As an observer I would describe the setting of underground work as a maelstrom of noise, dust, and yelling,

amidst which can be discerned a coming and going of workers, equipment, and ore. Much work must be done crouched, bent, or in other
awkward positions as the stopes are seldom more than one and a half
meters high. (Stope comes from the Germanic "to stoop"—a word with
an African viewpoint!) Behavior underground is continuously timed
and under surveillance. The noise at the workings is so loud that little
conversation is possible. Interaction is confined almost entirely to what
is formally administered by the management.

The end of a day leaves any miner filthy dirty, his lungs and throat
coated with dust, his limbs and back aching from exertion, his body
completely fatigued.

Physical Characteristics of the Compound

The surface operations of the mine, the organization of factory industrial work, and the life of an industrial or mining compound all have
something in common that is not shared by underground mine labor:
the possibility for *secondary adjustments* to the primary requirements
of work. In all these places of work the individual has some freedom—
that is to say, some power—to maintain his autonomy apart from the
system of work organization. All of these in turn differ from the life of
a town or "location," for in these places one is aware that the chances
of escaping the manacles of work organization are infinitely greater.

I quoted Goffman's apt formulation of a total institution as a system
for generating assumptions about its inmates' identity—their human
nature. The relegation of Africans to a rather undifferentiated proletariat in the mine reflects an assumption: that Africans—especially "raw"
Africans—are mainly suited to heavy, simple work. The compounds of
factories and mines reflect other assumptions made by the management concerning the species nature of Africans.

Compounds vary enormously in size, from 50 to 100 men working
for a small factory to the giant compounds of the largest mines which
house up to 15,000 men. In the mine compounds one finds far greater
ethnic heterogeneity than in smaller factory compounds. Typically six
or eight ethnic-linguistic groupings will be found in any one mine compound. Many of these compounds house their workers in ethnically
segregated quarters. In the older compounds twenty Africans would be
housed in a barracks six-by-seven meters. In the newer compounds,
the trend is to make the barracks smaller, but decrease more than
proportionately the number of occupants. In the newer mines, for
example, in the Orange Free State, the barracks are simple cement

structures—clean, airy, heated, and electrified. Each barracks has a "prefect" or elected spokesman who carries complaints or requests to the *induna*—the compound boss for the ethnic group in question. Each ethnic group has one or more *indunas* to supervise compound life. For every 100 or so miners there will be one "police boy"—a watchman who assists the *indunas* in surveillance of the men. In the newer compounds, miners have a choice of buying their own food and preparing it themselves or getting it from a communal kitchen. Different schemes operate from mine to mine for paying for rations. Some provide food "free" as part of the contract; others give the food allowance to the miner and allow him to purchase his food or meals.

In my research in one large Orange Free State compound the food was very good, diverse and nutritious to an extent far exceeding what is typical in Botswana. Miners are well fed. They may eat all they want. A common sight is the miner who has just finished a shift loading up a huge basin with one or two kilograms of food: meat, maize, sorghum porridge, greens, beans, bread, potatoes, fruit, and a two liter bucket of beer. This will be wolfed down in a few minutes and the individual will return for seconds.

The compound often has a loudspeaker system that blares news and music to the miners. The noise of the underground makes the compound appear quiet, but the bustle is quite considerable even so. Messengers and other "enforcers" maintain a discreet presence all the time. The crowding in the compound is apparent only at the beginning and end of shifts when thousands of miners are entering or leaving the cages (the lifts). Lines hundreds of meters long are formed when men check out or check in their gear: carbide-lamp hats, boots, and jackets. The surface life in both mines and factories appears very casual and unregimented compared to that in the underground work site.

Let us turn from this overview of the physical plant to a closer look at the organization of compound life itself. In the process I shall refer to the organization of other industrial work sites, as many of the adaptations made to compound life are to be found in factories as well as in mine compounds. Moreover, my own personal observations were made in factories and factory compounds in Johannesburg as well as in the compound of one large mine. Hence I shall combine my descriptions of compounds into a general characterization of common elements and include the observations I made in factories and in the surface operations of one large mine. In the compounds much of the social organization that generates assumptions about the nature of

African species being is to be found. We will begin with a look at the
beliefs of the Europeans as embodied in the "science" of personnel
management.

The Underlife of Work for Africans[2]

Personnel Folk Psychology
The majority of South Africans, including many South African personnel psychologists, hold that any individual African is more or less a
microcosm of his "African" culture. Africans, unlike Europeans, are
believed to be pretty much homogeneous replications of one another.
The questions Europeans ask about Africans often indicate this stereotype. An eminent South African psychologist asks: "Do Africans
possess the basic potentialities to enable them to respond adequately to
the vast changes occurring in their environment and upbringing . . . ?
Are their intellectual capacities, manipulative dexterities, and temperament makeup suitable for the demands which would eventually be
made on them?" (Biesheuvel 1952, p. 49). Not only are Africans often
regarded as psychologically homogeneous; they are also made to be
near prisoners of the culture that gives rise to this invariant personality
type.

> Drive and capacity for sustained effort are virtues typical of Western
> civilization. Does the African possess them to a sufficient degree?
> When allowance is made for these [cultural deprivation and social-
> legal disabilities] there remains nevertheless some doubt about the
> African's ability to maintain a high level of endeavor in his work.
> This doubt is based mainly on the apparent failure on the part of the
> African elite to make forceful use of the opportunities that have
> come their way, and of the indifferent progress of their communities
> where they have played a dominant part." [Biesheuvel n.d., pp. 3-4]

Many white South Africans, including industrialists and their psychological minions, ignore the nature of the social disadvantages borne by
Africans when making judgments about African ability. To assume that

2. The following section is extracted from an earlier publication: Hoyt Alverson,
"Africans in South African Industry: The Human Dimension," in S. J. Morse and
C. Orpen, eds., *Contemporary South Africa: Social Psychological Perspectives*
(Cape Town: Juta [© S. J. Morse and C. Orpen] 1975). Reprinted with permission
of the editors.

one can measure or determine the direction and height of a man's ambitions in a context where all but the most lowly of these ambitions are illegal is curious indeed. Moreover, it cannot be assumed that a black man's performance in his place of work is a measure of his capabilities. At work he is surrounded by insult, ridicule, and mistrust, and he must contend with incredible insecurity in return for sub-subsistence monetary rewards—surely a most unusual setting in which to measure achievement motivation.

While European intellectual mythology constitutes an aspect of the industrial milieu, it is the activity at the work site and in the compound that comprises the actual conditions of work for Africans. In nearly all of the administrative divisions of South African factories and mines there are two aspects: the European "side" and the Bantu "side." The personnel departments are examples of this. The Europeans who hold down the "Bantu side" possess credentials as overlords of the Bantu proletariat. The compound managers or personnel managers (always Europeans) typically speak one or more African languages or pidgin dialects. They are self-made men who have worked and lived with Africans all of their lives (or so they readily claim) and "really know the 'Bantu.'" These men often lack professional training or education. Their knowledge of the "Bantu" is amazingly uniform from one personnel or compound manager to another, across firms. And it is predictably consonant with the domineering, austere, paternalistic role played by the manager vis-à-vis the African worker. The requirements of the office of personnel manager, the rather inferior status it has, and the low pay it consequently provides, select for conservative and traditionalistic white South Africans. These men have developed from their own experience an ethnology of the African that is a charter for their role as captains of the fate of African industrial workers.

Below are comments made to me by five personnel and compound officers in five firms. While these clichés mean little in isolation, they are a representative sampling from a rather small group of stereotyped myths that "rationalize" the role of the white non-European personnel manager.

1. "The Bantu come from a simple background; their needs are simple; they want someone to tell them what to do, how to do it, and make sure they do it right." "The Bantu are bewildered [*verbysterd*] by the White Man's world. They need someone who will show them what they need to know and protect them; keep them from going wrong." "The Bantu are tied to the soil—all these men you see here

would be much happier if they could be back at their kraal, donned in their skins, tending cattle."

2. "The Bantu have never had a chance to learn responsibility. That's why we don't give them none. They need someone like me, who will make sure that no harm comes their way, and that they'll do what's right."

3. "The Bantu are always getting 'hung up' [verwikkel in] in witch-craft and superstition. I spend a lot of my time just sorting out these men's problems with the witch doctor [toordokter]. They're always trying to get someone killed, or someone's trying to kill them. They know they can come to me for protection."

4. "My job is to keep down tension, and make the Bantu feel at home here." "They got nowhere to turn if they can't turn to me. Yeah, my workers really like me—mind you, they aren't cheeky; they really respect me. . . . it's like a kid and his old man."

5. "No one pushes my Bantu around. I really look out for my Natives. They know they got someone here'll get in their licks for 'em."

These few statements suggest the paternalism of the compound manager. He protects the Africans from the "evils" in the modern world, and he helps insure that they will remain subdued, simple, subject people, protected from all the forces of change, especially those dangerous ones—enlightenment and political consciousness.

The breadth of activity permitted the non-European personnel department or personnel manager varies among firms—factories or mine compounds. In some organizations personnel work is little more than house- and record-keeping on the "Bantu side." In others the per-sonnel functions are quite elaborate. Here personnel activities range from the usual record-keeping to employee evaluation and testing, job placement, coordination of the training programs, and adminis-tration of recreation and welfare programs. Yet in all the firms studied it was clear that an overriding aim of non-European personnel policy is to assure the satisfaction and contentment of Europeans. "We have good labor relations" means: "We engage in no programs of African uplift that might arouse the ire of European labor unions." An African doing "unauthorized" skilled work, an African unavailable to bring tea, an African being "cheeky" to a European or even dealing with the European as an equal are all events that can cause labor unrest. Hence a major task of the non-European personnel department is to reconcile the contradiction between the demand for a "rational" use of African labor, on the one hand, and demand of large segments of the European labor force that Africans remain helots, on the other.

Another important activity of the personnel departments and their officers, black and white, is "settling" disputes between black workers or between two parties one of whom is black. In practice where disputes arise among Africans they are settled informally outside the purview of any formal structure. Where the disputes involve members of both racial groups, the non-European personnel department strives to settle the matter in such a way that all the Europeans involved will be content with the outcome. In other words, in practice the personnel department strives to assure all Europeans that the Africans will act "appropriately." In reality, the personnel department mediates in only a small percentage of disputes. The mechanisms of redress and settlement are largely informal.

An Outline of Role Conflict

The networks of social relationships that link African workers to one another and to the European-dominated organizational structure are a key to understanding much of the work behavior and work "attitudes" of individual African employees.

To the African boss-boys, clerks, and *indunas* falls the task of making the organization, its policy and directives, intelligible to the Africans. These African supervisors play particularly important roles in transmitting interdepartmental directives, formal and informal. Whether it is a requisition for paper clips, which must be made informally to be effective at all, or a major statement about changes in the conditions of work, African emissaries mediate the information. As a result of this, a relatively *small number* of literate, educated Africans dominate the communication channels that connect low, middle, and top management with the mass of African production workers. Communication across racial lines is fraught with misunderstanding, mistrust, deception, and purposive withholding of information. Moreover the structural position of the clerks and many of the *indunas* in factory and compound social systems is extremely marginal vis-à-vis both black and white social classes. Although the African production workers have some limited working arrangements with the black clerks and boss-boys, the social distance between the two groups, with its accompanying suspicion, distrust, and rejection, is quite profound. Thus just as blacks are rigidly separated from whites and communication between them almost nil, so the flow of information between black line workers on the one hand and black clerks and boss-boys on the other often becomes equally reduced and constricted. This situation not only precludes "feedback" from African workers about the effects of one's directives, it also makes nearly impossible the flow of information down the line from white supervisors to black production workers. Europeans are generally abrupt and often unclear in giving directions to their African boss-boys. The boss-boys usually know from experience what the European is trying to imply. Yet in giving orders to the black production workers, the boss-boys typically use the curt and abrupt manner and ambiguous phraseology of their European superordinates, exacerbated by the lexical impoverishment of *Fanakalo* in the case of the mines. Explanation is seldom offered and complaints are never listened to. The boss-boy prefaces and closes his directive with: "The white man says."

Informal delegation of work by Europeans to Africans is commonplace, especially in factories, but frequently in the mines as well. In the ninety-six departments studied (in five firms) much of the coordination and supervision of production formally assigned to European personnel had been, in turn, *informally* delegated to Africans. In twelve of the departments, the European foremen and superintendents had delegated to Africans almost all the work assigned to them in their formal job descriptions and spent their days literally sipping tea. In shops where European artisans performed skilled operations, such as welding, toolmaking, and other manual craft work, they were assisted by one or more African helpers. I observed that during the course of the day many African helpers would frequently perform every operation the European performed. In some cases this performance of the same task by Africans and Europeans occupied up to 50 percent of the total work cycle. In brief, the nominal apprentice relationship was often more a communal work setup where African and European did the same work side by side. In one shop I observed the European operator leave the floor on several occasions, allowing the African to carry on the entire operation alone.

A common sentiment expressed to me by Africans to whom much work was informally delegated was resentment at doing the white man's work. They believed themselves competent to do it, yet they resented receiving no reward: no extra pay, no recognition, not even a thank-you. In the mines it is not at all unusual to find Africans performing one or more of the chores connected with the role of blasting. Theoretically blasting is a job "reserved" for Europeans. In practice it is often done by Africans.

A particularly resented form of conflict arises when several Europeans simultaneously delegate work to a single African. This usually entails work that no one in the firm may legitimately ask any subordinate to do. An African has, in effect, as many supervisors or superiors as there are Europeans close by. It is customary in South Africa that any African does any European's bidding. Every day one sees numerous examples of Africans at all organizational levels being approached by two or more Europeans who will demand services of him, none of which is legitimate in terms of company policy and none of which the African is willing to do. Yet obey he must. In one extreme case I observed, an African *induna* was approached by four Europeans in the space of ten minutes and asked: to fetch European A a spanner; to fetch European B tea; to take a message from European C to a foreman in another shop; and to arrange for an African woman to meet European D outside the gate at noon. A check showed that none of the Europeans (save one) had any direct formal authority over the African.

Another less flagrant conflict occurs when an African is required to perform "legitimate" services for two Europeans simultaneously. The Europeans often interpret an African's failure to perform for them expeditiously as laziness, whereas in reality it is often simple "role overload" resulting from conflicting simultaneous demands. This propensity of Europeans to blame Africans uncritically for their failings has a corollary in the general unfounded scapegoating of Africans by Europeans. Africans as an aggregate are regularly blamed for all manner of organizational malfunctioning. Machine breakdowns, failure to meet production quotas, and lapses in quality control are often blamed on Africans, although no evidence may exist that any African worker has in any way performed his role improperly.

A rather diffuse conflict stems from the fact that many Europeans expect Africans to behave at work as mature, critical, intelligent human beings yet simultaneously expect them to remain at all times docile and submissive. Africans are continually remonstrated with for not taking initiative or showing imagination and intelligence. Yet in practice an African engaging in "unsolicited" behavior is usually soundly condemned. One African informant told me that when he saw his boss about to make a serious mistake, he yelled at him to stop. He was then belted across the face by the European. The African now knows he must wait until the error has been committed; he then approaches the European concerned and informs him that "we," the European and the African, have made an error.

Some Common "Secondary Adjustments"
among African Workers

> Informal organization . . . is composed of the animosities and friend-
> ships among the people who work together . . . [their] primary
> groups, cliques, and congeniality groups that develop in shop or
> office. It consists of the folkways, mores, norms and values which
> guide the behavior of workers, sometimes in fulfillment and some-
> times in blockage of the goals of the formal organization. [Miller
> and Form 1964, p. 119]

Given the primary adjustments to the pattern of work with its system
of privileges and mortifications, we would expect to find that Africans
make a number of "secondary adjustments" to their abject status, that
is, that they change the meaning of what they experience through subjective subterfuge or fantasy. This is the case to a limited degree in the
mines, but very prevalent in the factories. The secondary adjustments
most commonly found in Western total institutions are to be found
among African factory and mine workers: (1) situational withdrawal
(e.g., getting drunk, leisure activities, absenting oneself in day dreaming); (2) intransigence (rebelling in order to maintain one's pride or
integrity in the face of an egregious assault on one's identity); (3) the
colonization of mind (coming to identify with the mine as a part of
oneself; internalizing the mine world as a part of the stock of beliefs
one holds about oneself); and (4) playing it cool (taking the system for
a ride, exploiting its organization and resources for one's own ends).
A critical corollary to the discussion is the question whether African
workers employ these strategies individually or collectively, that is to
say, as a class. It is primarily in compound life that one finds these
secondary adjustments manifest. Underground work is far too exact-
ing and well supervised for expression of anything but proper role
behavior.

One of the African's secrets of survival in South Africa is to keep
the white man as ignorant of him as possible. The white man's ignorance enhances the black man's chances of realizing at least a small
number of his aspirations. There is a constant guard against divulging
anything perceived as information the white man could use against
him. This, of course, makes social research very difficult. Through
development of close association with key mine and factory personnel
my research associates and I unearthed some spotty but nonetheless
valuable data on the informal organization of African workers—data

which would never have come to light through routine interviewing procedures. I will discuss briefly the least equivocal aspect of this data—that relating to informal patterns of "leadership" or interpersonal influence.

It is impossible to discuss "leaders" independently of the total context in which this leadership is exercised. Leadership is, after all, but one way of talking about followership, and vice versa. For our purposes here and for lack of data I will simply assume that where certain individuals have an influence on the system-relevant behavior of others but where the influence does not work through the established structure of the organization, we have an instance of informal leadership.

I have documented three kinds of informal leaders: (1) the "cultural brokers" or "old hands"; (2) the leaders of work groups; (3) the racketeers.

Anyone who has information about the work site or compound which clearly exceeds "common knowledge" is to some extent an expert. Through time many individuals who remain with a firm acquire a fund of specialized knowledge exceeding that of the newer arrivals. Some of these experts on the factory or mine compound organization, formal and informal, are mere repositories of data; others use this data for purposes of personal or collective aggrandizement.

The majority of African workers have very little usable knowledge— primarily because they are given none—about the intricacies of the formal and informal hierarchies of authority and the division of labor in the total organization. This ignorance is manifest in the inability of most Africans to make distinctions among the relationships of Europeans to one another. Most Africans interviewed could only distinguish between immediate boss(es), the "big" boss, and other whites. (Several informants in the mine said the big boss was named Jan Smuts.) To do one's job this is about all one needs to know, if one is an unskilled African laborer. There arise occasions, however, when more detailed information about given authority figures is required. This is often obtainable from one of the "old hands." I will give two cases to illustrate the roles of the old hands.

Case 1: In a welding shop in one factory an African was fired by the superintendent for a series of breaches of interracial etiquette— not an uncommon occurrence in this shop. This African liked the work he was doing and wanted to get his job back. Supplicating the superintendent to recommend he be rehired was to no avail. He was approached by one of the shop's old hands who advised him to go to the home of the superintendent and without any formalities simply begin doing work in the man's garden: weeding, turning soil, cutting grass, and so forth. Also he might nightly wash the superintendent's car. After one week he should return and ask the superintendent for his job back. The African did as he was advised and was reinstated in his job.

Not all or even many Europeans would have responded to this kind of ingratiation. One African in the shop knew this particular superintendent well and could advise an African in trouble how he might redeem himself in his eyes.

Case 2: In all of the firms studied it was customary that a new recruit for a position be sent with an African clerk or boss-boy supervising the job to the work site, where he would be introduced to this work and the immediate surroundings. This introduction entails far more than explanation of the task requirements. The new recruit will be clearly told how to get along on the job. This means above all how to please the Europeans who will be working in the same area. The new employee will be informed of the peculiar or idiosyncratic prejudices of the Europeans working there; how to please them; what extra work-demands they will make; and how to fulfill these demands. The patterns of surveillance will be described, along with the techniques which can be used to make oneself unavailable when the straw boss comes around. The amenities will be pointed out. These include not only the bathroom and cafeteria, but also the local shebeen (illegal brewery or bar), the local *dagga* (marijuana) pusher, and undoubtedly the plant *fah-fee* agent (bookie). If it is relevant he will also be informed within a few days either by the boss-boy or more likely by one of the old hands on the line how to steal materials from the factory.

This last case introduces the topic of extralegal but factory- or compound-based activities, which are important in many aspects of the informal organization of an African workingman's life on the job. Directing or facilitating many of these extralegal activities are the "racketeers." The pastime of Africans at work that is most striking to a careful participant observer is the astonishing amount of drinking that occurs on the job, unbeknownst to most of the Europeans. To be sure any European will be aware that certain Africans have been drunk on the job. But this is simply a superficial indicator of a rather complex network of leisure-time social activities bolstered by drinking. On given days as many as 30 percent of the workmen we interviewed were too inebriated to respond to our questions—although in this state they often volunteered interesting, unsolicited information. (During a typical day, four of us would interview twenty individuals, and as many as six or seven would be intoxicated.) This fact led us to look into the drinking more closely, particularly in one factory where this pattern was well developed.

In this particular plant where we investigated drinking patterns there was a liquor distributor operating within the factory. He worked in cooperation with several women who distilled the liquor outside and brought it to him on a daily basis. He then sold the liquor to African factory personnel. We could never ascertain how the profits were distributed among the various functionaries in the bootlegging operation. Regularly, at lunch and teatime, Africans in considerable numbers would discreetly appear at the "bar" and have their tea cannisters filled with beer or some home-brewed hard liquor, usually a whiskey made from fermented brown bread. The patrons would consume part of the liquor there or, more often, return to the work site where they would drink with their African friends what appeared to be tea. There is apparently an elaborate communications system which is used to inform workers when the liquor is available and when it is safe to come for a drink. We were unable to document the communications system, although its operation was indubitable.

There are a variety of lotteries among Africans in the mines and industries in South Africa. Formal organizations are very conducive to the support of lotteries. The participants are bound to one another in a variety of ways, making welching or nonpayment of debts difficult. The bookie or other agent has easy access to an almost captive group of potential participants; and the element of craze or fad, with attendant social pressures to conform, operates to insure maximum participation.

There are, of course, a number of *inyanga* (*dingaka* in Setswana) or specialists in the practice of magical or supernatural arts and crafts. "Witchcraft" in many of its forms seems to have useful industrial and mining applications. Many Africans seek supernatural assistance through a diviner, sorcerer, or herbalist for obtaining promotions, finding redress for wrongs committed by fellow workers, settling disputes, and even placating angry Europeans. We could collect only spotty data on the extent of the participation of *inyanga* in the informal structure of the factory and mine compound. But there would appear to be ample reason to assume that magic and supernatural belief together with the requisite practitioners form an important aspect of the informal organization.

The final category of informal influence I will mention comprises informal work groups and their leaders, particularly as they affect the realization of organizational goals. The phenomenon of restriction of output by informal work groups has long been known and is well documented in North American industries. My data suggest that Africans, too, have developed production folkways that are expressed in informal associations of workers. The importance of this phenomenon is many-faceted. It is apparent that the role into which the worker is socialized is not simply what is officially defined but includes a complex of norms and expectations which are by-products of the formal organization and of a variety of interpersonal relations which exist because of or in spite of the industrial process.

I have recorded forty-three instances of workers whose work is done in isolation from others (e.g., sweepers, cleaners, batchers, "tea-boys") who indicated that at some time during their initial trial period they were instructed by individuals who do similar work or work in the same area how much work should be done and at what pace. "Rate-busters" are soon brought into line, much as they are in our own industries. Usually rate-busting is unintentional, stemming from the uncritical acceptance by a naive worker of the guidelines set down by the European supervisor or African boss-boy.

On the assembly line and in other systems of interdependent work, pacing is usually accomplished through the group following the lead set by an informal group leader. This leader is usually the individual whose position in the work-flow logically permits him to determine the speed of work for the group. For example, three assembly line operations were observed where the individual who loaded the conveyer determined the pace. All of the workmen interviewed in these three situations agreed that one man paced the others. By this means they were able to avoid any suggestion that there might be one or two goldbrickers. The belts were always full and everyone appeared busy, although the pace of work seemed leisurely indeed. In two documented cases, a group slowdown accompanied a rather peremptory introduction of an incentive scheme. The workers perceived the scheme as a device to determine how fast the men could work. Once this measurement was made, the workmen thought the scheme would be withdrawn and new higher minimum standards of acceptable performance set. Although this was an incorrect interpretation on their part, their action was rational in light of it. The fact that three of four men together deceive the organization indicates close informal cooperation.

This extraorganizational activity forms as important a part of industrial work as does the machine, the assembly line, and the egregious European bureaucratic authority structure.

Many of these "adjustments" do not take place in the underground operation of the mine, though they are found in the compounds. A crucial question raised by the presence of these colorful secondary adjustments is whether they are simply individual or group acts of social banditry or whether they could indicate a nascent consciousness of oneself as a worker—as a member of a political class. As political class is a province of meaning as well as a thing-in-itself, we will take up this point when we discuss the *meaning* of work experience.

These observations suggest that the ecology of work for Africans includes far more than the role pressures and role behavior deemed relevant and appropriate by Europeans. Thus the explicitly stated job requirements are but a small portion of the adaptive problems with which Africans must deal in the industrial setting. This setting includes minimally these additional elements: (1) the goals Africans seek in and by means of industrial employment; (2) the peculiar hurdles and disabilities industry itself has placed on black men; and (3) the varied but limited solutions Africans can develop to cope with these industry-created problems of adaptation. Much of the normative order in South African factories and compounds has been introduced by African laborers and exists together with what has been imposed on them by European entrepreneurs and their industrial technology.

5 THEMES OF SELF-IDENTITY

Introduction

In the preceding chapters I have outlined the patterns of linkage and dependency between various groupings of Tswana and the surrounding political economy. The material and institutional conditions of that dependency have been the focus of concern. We turn now to the study of *conscious self-identity*, with a view ultimately to describing the correspondences that exist between these material, institutional conditions and the manner in which individuals experience their world.

My outline of the ecology and economy of Tswana communities has drawn heavily on the kind of commonsense observations that are made in the "natural attitude." But while the Tswana live materially embedded in the conditions I have described, it would be wholly unwarranted to claim that this constitutes an account of *Tswana experience.* To deal with Tswana experience, and in particular "self-experience," we must turn to the Tswana speaking—using their language to communicate their beliefs. Their language-in-use is our principal mode of access to the private, interior experiences that comprise *self-identity.*

Any inquiry into self-identity runs the risk that the researcher will create a reality by his very choice of initial questions. Questions in human language usually rest on numerous presuppositions of fact and belief. Respondents often give answers based on astute but ad hoc elaboration of the ideas embedded in seemingly simple and straightforward questions. When opening my interviews I tried to avoid this pitfall by reciting a number of well-known Tswana proverbs and aphorisms which I had interpreted as reflections of cultural principles basic to the individual's beliefs about his own social identity—and possibly his self-identity. All of these sayings contained as central themes the three questions: what is human nature (*botho-motho*), what is a proper, adult Tswana (*monna tota*), and what is the ideally good life (*botshelo jo bontle*). While I did not assume these were necessarily crucial for the Tswana in defining self-identity, I did assume they would open the inquiry with a minimum of direction from me.

Younger Tswana and almost all women were puzzled or confused by my commentary and discussion concerning "human nature." Younger people and most women claimed they did not think about such issues, and they suggested this topic was to be found only in "deep" or very old Setswana, of which they lacked knowledge. Older men differed markedly from the younger and from women in being very eager to express their views on the topic of "essential human and individual nature" and to hear "views from America." In contrast to the considerable variation I found among the Tswana on such topics as "things I want to do" (see below), questions about essential human or individual nature elicited remarkably uniform responses, including consistent citation of numerous homiletic proverbs and parables. This fact leads me to believe that there must be a concept of "essential self-identity" that comprises part of the philosophic stock of Setswana knowledge and is transmitted from generation to generation in the reflective conversations that older men reserve for themselves.

A Person's Humanity:
The Tswana View of Human Nature

Some knowledge of various aspects of the concept of self-identity as defined in chapter 1 is indeed contained in the wisdom of Setswana. One gains this knowledge through the accumulative processes that are part of growing old. Wisdom comes with age. Certain knowledge must be laid down before subsequent knowledge can make sense. I can best present this stock of belief as it was presented to me. The following transcriptions of six responses made in actual interviews have been minimally edited. Jointly they cover or embrace the beliefs espoused by twenty-three respondents (all older males) whom I asked to discuss the question of whether there exists in Setswana a body of belief concerning "essential human nature"—the putative basis for self-identity. The translation is into idiomatic English. I have not tried to preserve Setswana word order so as to make the texts appear exotic. They were given to me in idiomatic Setswana, and I have tried to preserve that stylistic register in the English translation.

Respondent A (elder from Kgaphamadi)

"An individual's nature is inborn. Even habits you cannot count on, because they are always influenced by a person's inner human nature [*botho-motho*]. You can never know what is inside another person. We say in Setswana, 'Unlike a field [which you can come to know every part of], you can never know a man.' The way people act is no reliable guide to what they are really intending [*go ikaelela*]. Training, even that of parents which molds [*go bopa*] the habits, cannot overcome the person's individuality. If a person is born to be a bully, if he has in himself decided to be a bully, there is nothing you can do to prevent him from acting that way. What a person essentially is [*boene ba gagwe*] is not changed by events [*ditirafalo*]. Take the Kgalagadi [the 'inferior' or junior tribal group attached to the Tswana]. Now these people are often treated like servants or like animals; but they do not become servants in their own mind. They retain their pride as human beings. The real inner self [*botho ba motho*] can never leave a person. A person may have been created [*tlhodilwe*] to be a servant all his life. This person may even accept this position and act accordingly in relation to others. But he never loses, because of this, his real inner self. Of course, some people have strength [*nonotsha*] to stand fast or act in the fact of adversity. Others do not. Still the inner self remains."

Respondent B (elder from Kalahari)

"Every person's thoughts are his own. Many thoughts may be 'the food of dreams'—they won't be fulfilled among fellow men, but they are the person's own. A person can act one way and be thinking something entirely undiscernible. For example, we say 'smiling teeth kill.' A person's actions can harbor any number of intentions. You can never know what a person is planning by looking at what he does. Every person has *thato* [capacity to act according to his liking, choosing, or planning]. People have *boitaolo* [freedom or power to do as they please in a negative sense; for example, to defy convention, as when a child defies his parent's wishes]. The only thing a person cannot change is his fate. We say, 'chieftainship cannot be bought [for oneself]; you must be born into it.' Many things in life are determined. Choice does not change them."

Respondent C (elder from Kgaphamadi)

"We don't have such a saying in Setswana [I had asked whether the respondent knew of a saying in Setswana with the same meaning as 'Stone walls do not a prison make, nor iron bars a cage.'] But it is true, indeed [*bommarure*]. No matter how the body is handled by others, the thoughts cannot be controlled. While one's circumstances may control one's actions, the suffering body will cause a man to make plans to decide to run away and look for better prospects elsewhere. No kind of ill-treatment can cause you to lose your inner self [*bo-wena*]. A person knows he has his humanity [*botho*] no matter how he is treated.

"In Setswana we say 'my thoughts are my guide.' I'm created by God just like the rich man. We both live and walk on the same earth. We both have the same ability to act according to our intentions [*boikaelelo*]. I can become determined to do anything I wish because of my intentions, even under heavy stress and suffering. But events cannot tell us what will happen in our lives, any more than our thoughts can. We say, 'ask me about whence I've come, for of whither I am going I do not know.' But, of course, one's persistence in seeking a goal can pay off. Effort is often rewarded. 'The seeker of a cow must persist like the digger of a well' [this means if you want something badly, you must seek diligently for it everywhere].

"A person's conduct can be shaped by good upbringing. But a person does not necessarily act the way he's been taught, because he is born with certain qualities that training does not change. 'I weeded for the tiny thorn, and after it grew, it pricked me.' Children can grow up to disappoint and hurt their parents who have tried to mold them properly. A person's conduct can be shaped by events which a person is powerless to change. 'The well dries up even as I am still looking at it.'

"Death, of course, is the ultimate unknown. We can never know when we will die. We can never know how our actions will end. It is always with us as a possibility. 'Death is in the seams of the blanket,' we say. That which overcomes a person is not his plans; rather, that which overcomes is death."

Respondent D (elder from Kgaphamadi)
"Someone can misuse your body by using coercion [*patikanyo*], but this cannot affect or change your thoughts. You are still able to grumble [*go ngongorega*], even if you are afraid to voice your protest. What we plan and what we do may be different things because of fear or lack of courage. What we think (believe) and how we usually behave [*botsalo*], nothing can change, except ill health. This is usually caused by relatives who do not wish you well because of their *hot spirits* (malevolent envy).

"Each and every person has thoughts which were given him by God, and by his ancestors, and all of these thoughts are unlike those of other people. No two people's thoughts are alike. We say, 'a person speaks with his heart.' A person's upbringing is designed to shape behavior properly. But any child growing up can refuse to listen. Refuse to obey. There is no way to force a person to become like what you want him to be. Ill fortune may befall those who do not listen to their parents' advice, but the child can still be stubborn and refuse to listen."

Respondent E (elder from Gaborone)
"A person's strength does not lie in the body; it lies in his ability to speak his thoughts. 'I am not strong in and of myself [*ke le nosi*]; I am strong in virtue of the word [*ka lentswe*].' Thinking and reasoning

make us different from animals. We live by rules and by law. That separates people from [wild] animals; every person is made [created] differently. Yet a person, we say, is a person by virtue of people. To be utterly alone is unthinkable. We are human because of the way we are brought up and live together with others. Our relations [*botsalano*] with others shape our behavior. But our thoughts are our own. They can never be known by looking at actions or by knowing the people of [one's] home."

Respondent F (elder from Gaborone)

"In Setswana we say, 'you can never build a kraal for a person.' This means that there is no purpose in building a kraal for a person, since a person cannot be confined. Humanity [*botho*] cannot be taken from you nor controlled as a kraal controls the cattle. Each and every person's thoughts and ideas are unlike those of any other. Just as people's physical appearance is never the same, so their thoughts are never the same. Reasoning ability is not removed by suffering. People can, of course, lose propriety. One can become ill mannered. But that is still within the bounds of a person's reasoning and his choice-for-himself [*boitlhopelo*]. Herding cattle at the cattle posts, you may be ill treated by the older boys there. You will resent this, but you continue because of necessity. You, also, may or may not become a bully. That cannot be known. Even people born of the same parents do not exhibit the same thoughts or feelings. In any circumstance people experience the same thing differently. We say, 'When I am bitter, everything will be bitterness to me; when I am kindly, everything will be kindness to me.'"

These six responses encompass all of the major points made by the seventeen other elders from Gaborone, Kgaphamadi, and the Kalahari whom I questioned about the nature of self-identity. There was a kind of consensus on questions of self-identity among the group of older people whose responses were most confident and fully articulated. Interestingly, this did not carry over to the other topics I raised, where differences showed themselves even among the elders. This was particularly true in their discussion of European institutions (see chapter 8).

Having elicited replies to my questions about the essential nature of the *self*, I asked those who had not responded to comment on the statements made by the elders. In this task of recognition there was wide agreement among respondents that what a person is capable of thinking and feeling is not necessarily manifested in what he does. Circumstances such as child rearing do not determine an individual's thoughts and feelings. The qualities of the *self* are largely innate, given by God or the ancestors or otherwise inborn. Furthermore, thoughts—especially plans, feelings, and intentions—are not something that can be known or inferred from behavior. As one respondent put it: "If a person wants to, he can in his mind turn the whole world into a tiny ball." The Tswana were unanimous in saying that the goal of child rearing is to shape behavior, but that the success of this enterprise is highly variable because of the freedom of the mind to accept or reject the "law" [*molao*].

There was no unanimous opinion among the elders as to whether this "essential, inner self" was mutable. Yet most agreed that there always exists an "ability to change one's mind." In fact, the Tswana enshrine in numerous proverbs and stories this ability, often exercised with caprice and abandon, to change one's thoughts or attitudes. In my estimation the consciously held Tswana view of the self, and hence of self-identity, comes close to that espoused by William James in *The Principles of Psychology*. That is to say, the *self* is comprised of the thoughts and beliefs actually held, especially those whose topic is the *self* as such.

While it would be irrelevant to discuss their concept of the self from a critical (philosophical) point of view, we must appreciate that this bit of Tswana philosophy represents an aspect of the self-identity of many individuals. It forms the horizon of the experience of self—explicitly for older, male Tswana and implicitly for the others. Self-identity must include, then, experience gained in the process of acquiring objective cultural knowledge during one's lifetime, especially one's adulthood. In the Tswana view, identity formation is not concluded in the early years of life, but is affected in important ways by knowledge acquired in advanced age. This knowledge affects, as I shall show, the entire "reflective gaze" the individual can direct toward his own past in evaluating his self-identity.

The Tswana stock of belief concerning the self appears to corroborate —at least it does not contradict—the claims I made in chapter 1 about the central role of the power to believe in constituting self-identity. The Tswana seem to hold that the individual is not determined by his circumstances. The individual is free—to some degree—to make meaning in the world. Specifically the individual cannot be fully known, precisely because he is not simply a function of the facts of the empirical world. Whether this belief is right or wrong in terms of some metacultural system of thought is irrelevant. What is important is that the Tswana beliefs, whether true or false, can be *true* in their objective consequences for the Tswana who believe.

Having assured myself that at least one element of self-identity ("human nature") exists for the Tswana and having obtained some idea of its content, I sought in subsequent interviewing to employ other proverbs, sayings, and aphorisms that appeared to extend the concept of self-identity in important ways. In response to my further queries the Tswana with whom I worked almost invariably articulated one central and three subsidiary themes, which emerged reliably, independently, and with little structured suggestion on my part: 1. wanting-to-do, 2. expectation (hope and fear), 3. evil, and 4. the hero. This implies that these themes comprise a shared cultural *schema* of self-identity.

In this and the following two chapters the four themes will be presented as "idealizations" within the stock of beliefs belonging to the culture of the Tswana. Unless otherwise stated, these will be *Tswana* idealizations of their own beliefs. However the actual beliefs held by individuals or by such groups of individuals as those found in the three ecologic niches or in the two age cohorts will be more or less unlike the beliefs in their most general, abstracted form. Thus the articulation of Tswana age cohorts and communities with the social stock of belief varies with the theme in question. There exists what is called in modern parlance an "interaction" between the particular theme of self-identity, age group, and community membership.

In all of the descriptions of self-identity themes I emphasize the responses given to me by members of the cohort called here "old" who live in Gaborone or in Kgaphamadi. While the older Tswana living in town have very different daily experiences from those who live in Kgaphamadi, there exists, nevertheless, a striking concordance in the way the two groups elaborate their beliefs, for example, those I describe under the theme, "wanting-to-do" (see below). The older men in town were all employed full time in wage labor—in "menial" work, either in local industry, government, or domestic service. Some lived close enough to their rural homes to take an active part in running their farms. Others were unable, because of distance from home or other reasons, to be actively engaged in agriculture. Nevertheless all held land that others farmed with them or on their behalf. In some cases the immediate families lived at home, and the older men, the respondents, lived most of the time in Gaborone, sending some portion of their wages home to help with expenses.

The older men in Kgaphamadi can be divided into two groups, depending on whether or not they undertook wage employment at the government research farm, three to six kilometers away. About half worked for wages, commuting daily on their bikes and returning home at night. The other half had no wage employment. The work the men did on the government farm was in all cases identical to what they did routinely on their own farms.

The urban were motivated for a variety of reasons (to be discussed below) to come to town in search of wage labor. In every case I recorded, this implied a loss of their labor to farming but the acquisition of a cash income. From my interviews and personal observation, I concluded that the urban-dwelling old were no more and no less "successful" in their farming than those living in Kgaphamadi. Yet the urban dwellers believed, for various reasons, that working in town and being at best a weekend farmer was preferable to remaining in a rural area as a full-time farmer.

Despite the differences in biography that distinguished the urban from the rural elders, their intellectual and emotional responses to these themes of value we will discuss were very similar. Every older urban man described his being in town and working for wages as an onerous chore necessitated by circumstances that prevented continuation of full-time farming. Each urban elder strongly wished he could leave town and return to the rural areas. None saw town life or wage labor as intrinsically enjoyable, despite their commitment to it.

Wanting-To-Do: Theme and Variations

Several basic presuppositions of Western knowledge may thwart an appreciative understanding of the Tswana concepts of "wanting" and "doing." In the West we intuitively make a close semantic connection between "wanting" and "desiring." Further, we designate objects or conditions that can satisfy a want or desire as "goals." Counterposed to goals are those resources, techniques, and actions we call "means," which are deemed to have value more or less in relation to how effectively or efficiently they lead to the attainment of goals. In our view, wants or desires are potentially unlimited. We believe every individual is capable of genuinely wanting an infinite variety of things and conditions *for himself.* But the means for attaining goals are, we are told, limited. We live in a cultural world predicated upon a belief in necessary scarcity, with finite means for pursuit of an infinity of goals.

In the industrial West we do not rigorously circumscribe the class of wants or desires by notions of personal need or societal necessity. Wants for us are in large measure the food of dreams. Madison Avenue and its coterie of fantasy merchants work feverishly to fuel, and keep pace with, the burgeoning of fancied wants. They help assure that our wants will run furiously ahead of any means or powers we as individuals or our society as a whole has to attain them.

This culturally decreed disjunction between means and ends, the instrumental and the consummatory, has an analog in our opposition between *doing* and *having*. *Possession*—whether of things, right of access to things, conditions, control of people, or whatever—is an essential characteristic of what we call goals in our society. Contrariwise, *working* or *doing* is usually considered a means, often onerous, to that consummate position of *having*. Most westerners, when asked what they *most want*, will in answering use the expressions "to have" or "to get." When asked how these goals may be obtained, they will use the predicate "to work for them."

We cannot understand the full meaning of the word "want" in Setswana unless we understand the conditions of belief that surround and inform the use of this and related terms in all acts of speech. In Setswana the word meaning very roughly "to want" [*go batla*] also suggests in most readings or uses the sense of "to seek after," "to quest for." "To want" in Setswana semantically implies the supposition that action is intended which itself comprises or will lead to what one wants. In other words, for the Tswana "to want" is "to want to do." Now the Tswana, like all peoples, have hopes that they admit may not be achieved. They have a world of fantasy and imagination. However most of what the Tswana articulate as wants in life are at once intentions of doing something—of seeking those wants.

This belief is critical to understanding the distinction between *doing* (i.e., doing which is desired) and other activities. In Setswana *doing* is not simply a general-purpose verb of action; rather, it denotes activity characterized by significant value—that is to say, desire or want. For example, agriculture and animal husbandry require many activities, almost all of which the Tswana describe as actions they want to do. To be doing them is a want. Yet there are other activities—for example, selling one's labor in the mines—in which one is not deemed by most Tswana to be "doing" anything at all. Indeed, to be at wage work is referred to by the foreign terms *go bereka* or *shebetsa*.

For older Tswana especially, wants are well circumscribed by the limitation: "what I can do." Desire beyond doing is not want but rather "acquisitiveness." Wanting-to-do leads to those works that affirm proper existence. To desire more than this is to "desire things." To desire things leads to stealing, to invidious comparison, and finally to "consumption violence" (*go iphetlha*), wherein the members of the community compete to gain commodities in excess of what is to be had—in excess of what there exists power to produce. Older Tswana agree that modern life, insofar as it increases the ability to do "great works," is a good thing, but insofar as it leads to *acquisitiveness* and *self-centeredness* is a destroyer of the Tswana's ability to affirm existence by doing. "It destroys values and leaves us unprotected in the world."

In Setswana there is no semantic antinomy between *doing* (working in the Tswana sense), on the one hand, and *play* or *leisure* on the other. On an informal word-association test, the two modally frequent words given in response to the stimulus word "doing" [*go dira*] were happiness [*boitumelo*] and sloth [*botshwaga*]. For westerners, the modally frequent responses to the word "work" would probably be play, leisure, or money.

In sum, we must bear in mind two important aspects of *wanting* and *doing* in Setswana which contrast with our own thinking: first, most Tswana do not partition the domain of wants into two distinct and different classes, *means* versus *ends*; second, the class of actions called *wants* or *desires* is defined in reference to intended action. For the Tswana, wants are not a limitless class of fancied things which one "wishes to have"; rather, the class of wants is substantially limited to intended action. By implication (and by testimony), because means and ends are coterminous, one cannot be scarce in relation to the other; and because *wanting* is *wanting-to-do*, there can be no opposition or dichotomy between thought and action.

What does a Tswana *want to do*? The term *what* in this designation calls for both a list of particulars and a set of features or conditions necessary and sufficient to define those particulars in terms of their essential common qualities. The Tswana enumerate a set of activities— "great works"—which, substantially, are what each Tswana "wants to do." They can also provide a description of the essential features of these enterprises—what makes them members of the category "great (cultural) works." These necessary and sufficient conditions are commonly described in terms of two kinds of considerations: (a) belief in the culturally beautiful, good, or proper; and (b) (valuation of) success, progress, achievement, and weal (wealth). These are aspects of all great cultural works. A brief discussion of the common meanings of the culturally "beautiful," "good," and "proper" will be given as we discuss the great works themselves. The notions of "achievement," "progress," "success," and "weal" (wealth) I shall describe briefly before we go on, as their significations in Setswana rest on ideas not common in the West.

Achievement (*go atlega/go kgona*). In contemporary Western usage this term means bringing to a successful conclusion; attainment of a purpose or end; a result brought about by purpose, resolve, persistence. It is a movement from one evaluatively described position to another by means of one's efforts. Very often we define achievement relative to the individual's position in society or to his own "definition of the situation."

In Setswana, *to achieve something in life* (*go atlega mo botshelong*) has two connotations usually lacking in our use of that phrase. First, achievement is a culturally standardized "absolute" condition; it is not relative to an individual's definition of the situation or to his biography of deeds. Second, the term in Setswana implies that *achieving* is the *achievement*. To achieve or accomplish a deed entails certain methods or routes which in Setswana are definitionally part of the achievement itself. All achievement or accomplishment is *process* for the Tswana.

Success. A similar inextricable union of what we partition into means and ends can be found in the Setswana notion of success (*senatla*), which signifies both: (1) advancement to a superior position in a project, and (2) that that is done by means of one's own resolve, tenacity, planning, and hard work. Indeed, success for the Tswana implies *qualities of coping* as much as it implies *fruition*.

This necessary union of means and ends, of process and fruition, in the concepts of *achievement* and *success* can further be seen in the way the concept of "failure" in Setswana differs from our own. The Tswana describe the negation of achievement and success in terms of the notions of "disappointment" and "being overwhelmed or overcome (from without) [*go palelwa*]." Since success and achievement both lie in process, there can be no "failure." Once a project is undertaken, failure as we define the term is by definition impossible, because striving is by definition a part of success. Further, since achievement is a culturally specified condition, one either will or will not attain it. But one does not suffer disapprobation—hence, the imputation of failure—since not-to-achieve is a result of being overwhelmed by circumstances. This leads to disappointment, but not to "failure." One simply does not achieve. The idea of personal responsibility, and the resulting blame, that can inhere in our notion of failure is almost never present in the Tswana concept, where "to fail" is to be overwhelmed or overcome in an undertaking. Success is moving in a project; it is not the end achieved. If success had any contrary in Setswana, it would be to cease moving in a project—to stop one's "progress." The Tswana who undertook to explicate the concept of success for me likened it to the notion of going on through life (*tswelelopele*), going forth in the direction one is facing in life. Furthermore, they tied success and progress to the notion of rebirth or rejuvenation—literally, a blossoming after dormancy (*tlhabologo*). Progress, and therefore success, is not projection into an indeterminate future but rather movement in a course of action.

Weal. "Wealth" in Setswana means roughly what was formerly implied by the Old English word "weal." All welfare, good, or virtue in communal life was "wealth." Today the word *weal* (wealth) is generally used to suggest economic utility or exchange value, and hence riches. Wealth today is power in economic production and exchange, and in social relations it is generally represented as mediated through commodities. The Tswana, first of all, do not divide their world into the economic and noneconomic. Communal and personal life depend on fulfillment of a variety of "needs," without differentiation. Wealth is thus the attainment of the personally and socially necessary conditions for a meaningful cultural existence. Therefore wealth does not—indeed, cannot—lend itself to a one-dimensional calibration. It is the condensation of value in social existence as such. Wealth is value, but only a small part of this is exchange value. Value is intimately tied to the "how of doing" and the "what of doing"; in short, it is the cultural prescription of wanting-to-do. Wanting-to-do, not exchange, is the touchstone of wealth. Thus children, cattle, fields, family, cultural knowledge, and so forth, are all described as "wealth," but this is not because some set of exchanges is possible among them. These varieties of wealth are all, to be sure, "capital," in the sense that they are crucially important to production of the means of cultural existence. But they have no "revenue product," because they have no cost derived from a capital market. *Wealth* in Setswana is, by definition, at once resource, asset, means, end, factor of production, and final product.

Because wealth (weal) both creates and derives from communal cultural existence, *scarcity* is not, as it is for us, simply a function of exchange in an arena where supply and demand are significant social forces. Scarcity in Setswana means scarcity in relation to culturally prescribed wanting-to-do, not in relation to a proliferation of idiosyncratic fantasies tied to an all-purpose money. The moral, the proper, the fair, and the good are all the same in Setswana; and wanting, achieving, succeeding, and weal should be represented in all one's doing.

Wanting to Do "Great Works"

Doing "great works" is correlative to the individual's wanting-to-do. To be doing great works is to have achieved. To be achieving by dint of carefully laid plans carried out by industrious hard work is success. The result of achieving by success is weal or wealth. The "great works" (achievings) cited by the Tswana, both in town and in rural areas, are—

1. to be free of want (poverty);
2. to be doing agriculture and animal husbandry (for oneself);
3. to be building a family and home (for oneself);
4. to be keeping community and the law;
5. to be building one's "name" (this topic is treated in chapter 7 in the context of discussing the hero and "praising oneself").

Each of these is at once the means and the end of wanting-to-do. Each is both resource and asset. All are weal or wealth. To be doing these is to be a content and fulfilled individual.

Wanting to Be Free of Want

The most salient want for all Tswana is gaining *freedom from want*. Current deficiencies in the material basis of their subsistence strongly influenced their expression of "what I want to do." To be free of material want, said every Tswana, is his fondest desire. For a westerner this statement raises the question of what endowment of material resources and assets a Tswana would identify as constituting "freedom from want."

Almost all the older Tswana interviewed evaluated material resources in terms of the yield of farming (i.e., agriculture and animal husbandry). They hoped to be able to farm such that the product would (1) reliably feed the household; (2) leave sufficient surplus to raise cash for a readily delimited set of material objects; and (3) provide sufficient "surplus" food to feed the poor of the community in return for any labor they might render. In short, every older Tswana saw freedom from want as a condition wherein he himself, his family, and the community were sustained with food. The "surplus" of farm production desired (described by the Tswana as that harvest which "equals" certain requirements other than eating) was no greater than what was needed to pay for wage labor. Each Tswana town dweller wanted to raise sufficient surplus to buy the same goods and services (exclusive of food) now being bought with his current cash income. All Tswana agreed emphatically that reliable subsistence for the family plus a surplus equal in exchange value to the cash revenue they now spent on nonfood items would constitute *freedom from want.*

The reaction of rural peoples employed on a government farm was the same—to be able to raise enough to feed the family and to sell such surplus as would produce the cash they currently spend on nonfood items. Rural elders not working for wages listed a set of commodities that have to be purchased with cash. Each said the costs of these items must be met out of agricultural surplus. Were he able reliably to raise this surplus (equal in cash value to about eight Rand per month), he would be "free from want" or "outside the bondage of poverty."

I put to all respondents a proposition derived from their own testimony—that to have reliable subsistence farming plus a "surplus" equivalent to about eight to ten Rand per month per family above eating requirements would represent complete freedom from want. To this all the elder Tswana agreed, and most added that such a situation would be a most desirable life—living by farming.

The older Tswana stated that lack of rain prevents farming from being a reliable form of subsistence. This high variation in the reliability of agriculture was seen as the principal cause of poverty among the Tswana, the source of most misery and fear, and the reason that many undertake wage labor to buffer themselves against the devastating effects of famine (*leuba*). In typical years, rain is sufficient only to raise enough to eat. No surplus for sale or other exchange is derived. During the best years a small surplus may be obtained by the farmers with the biggest fields. In bad years famine visits everyone.

For older Tswana especially, *freedom from want* is a necessary but not sufficient condition for the ideally good life and the making of a content, proper, and fulfilled person. The good life as a whole requires the other great cultural works.

Agriculture and Animal Husbandry

Age is a necessary condition for achieving. This is particularly apparent in arable and animal agriculture, where the amassing of resources is a long and slow process. While some fortunate young people may receive an inheritance of cattle and lands, periodic drought can reduce them to nothing. These erstwhile fortunate ones then begin over at the same starting point as the pauper: clearing and preparation of fields, accumulation of seeds, acquiring children (a most important source of labor), the reliance on natural increase in one's stock of animals (both for food and for draft power), the saving of money to purchase tools. All these require much time and much hard work in a setting where a drought can destroy in a single season almost all that one has painstakingly produced and accumulated. In societies like that of the Tswana, where cultural insulation or environmental control is much less than in industrial societies, holding on to the fruits of success is very risky. But recall that the Tswana believe that achieving and success lie in *striving*, not in the predictable attainment and accumulation of material results.

Cultivating fields and husbanding cattle are works of such value that the oral literature of the Tswana is filled with their apotheosis. Many of the oral accounts of husbandry and agriculture are purely aesthetic expressions making no reference to economic or utilitarian importance. Indeed, the elder Tswana's conception of "Botswana" itself is not the nation state with its government, but rather the habitat as defined by the material conditions for a successful cultural life. This means principally rain—rain sufficient to make fields and herds possible. This richness or fecundity of the habitat is called the "beauty of Botswana." The "beauty of Botswana" means fields with crops and stocks of healthy animals. Most of the elder Tswana say of agriculture, "Wealth is plowing." Cattle are referred to as the "Bank of the Tswana" or the "Tswana's 'Standard Bank.'"

I have heard Tswana sit and talk about nuances in the physical appearance, behavior, or history of a single cow for an hour. They can recite eulogies to cattle and to fields under cultivation, revelling in these verbal descriptions.

The elder urban men, for most of whom engagement in rural agriculture was tenuous, referred with obvious reluctance to plowing as their premier want-to-do. In simply expressing a want whose undertaking is a remote possibility, they showed unmistakable signs of dejection. For these older Tswana, most of whom were materially rather well off in town, there was always bitterness and disappointment expressed when they described plowing and husbandry in the conditional or subjunctive mood. A want for them is an *intention to do*, and to speak of a want-to-do hypothetically is a cause of anguish.

Most of the older Tswana have had many experiences "being overcome" in their pursuit of fields and cattle. All had lost most or all of their cattle in the drought that occurred throughout southern Africa between 1965–69. Yet each of the elders described his project of raising cattle as an achievement, a success, which though finally a "flop" (in our terms) lived on as achievement and success in the consciousness of the individual and in his reputation.

To experience something of the meaning of fields and especially of cattle, we must turn to their formulaic verbal representations. There are two kinds of "predications" on cattle which we should attend to. First, there is the class of praises to cattle which predicate upon them their meaning to people. Second, there are the predications upon people or institutions which are based upon metaphors derived from the significance of cattle. Through this literature we can appreciate something of the way in which the Tswana deepen the objects, cattle and fields, into rich experience and see why the Tswana call agriculture and animal husbandry "the treasures of Setswana culture."

I. Stout-one of arms (weapons)
   Preparer of liquid food.
   God with the long, straight nose,
   When it lows, saying "moo,"
   Women say, "it says, 'moo.'"
   Men say, "it's saying '[to] arms again!'"
   Ah! Animal of my father—red female.
   God with the moist nose.
   A short sip of something hot.
   [This] god has eaten my father,
   And as for me, he'll eat me too.
   Animal with the moist nose.
   . . . .
   To corral the cattle is done only by a man with many sons.

II. Beast with such palatable gravy
   Animal with the moist nose
   Sniffer with both nose and tongue
   I lacked one, I lacked sleep,
   I had one, I lacked sleep,
   I didn't sleep, I didn't want to,
   I sought [it], I sought also my child
   My child has fallen into the river—the pool of the hippo.
   He has been driven astray because of cattle
   Cattle of Moselekatsi [Mzilikazi].

III. Heavy wooden bowl of my father
   When I have eaten from it, my heart is glad
   For it is the bowl of my parents
   Wooden bowl for sweet gravy of the cow

Lovely cattle of our home
One, alone, is sweetness
Missing one, alone, is sorrow
Dark, blue-grey cow—one who robs of sleep
Cow with the many spots
One with the melodious tongue
Stout-one of weapons
Preparer of liquid food
God, with the moist nose.[1]

Consider the following phrases, each of which is a metaphoric reference to a Tswana chief:[2]

Eulogy to Chief Senwelo of the Kgatla
    son of the cow-like person,
    compared to a cow—he surpasses it.
    He surpassed the cow . . .
    [The] one who resembles a cow.

Eulogy to Chief Bathoen I, Ngwaketse
    light-colored cow . . .
    the ox at Kanye . . . satisfies us fully.

Eulogy to Chief Tshekedi Khama of the Ngwato
    A chestnut cow calved in the field . . .
    a yellow cow of Khama and Sekgoma.

A closer look at these brief excerpts will elucidate further the points I have been making. Note that this poetry is formulaic, in the sense that many of the individual lines are standard formulas whose use is determined by the narrative intent of the reciter or poet. Between them he may use lines of his own composing. Further, he is free to vary the order of formulas and the total length of the poem. Many of the formulas are found throughout southern Africa—for example, "preparer of liquid food," "god with the moist nose," "stout-one of arms [weapons]," "a short [small] sip of something hot," and so forth. These formulas reflect the cultural sentiments that accrue to animal husbandry from its place

1. These selections were translated by me from original versions appearing in a collection made by D. F. van der Merwe, "Hurutse Poems," in *Bantu Studies* 15 (1941): 307–37.
2. From the collection made by Isaac Schapera, *Praise Poems of Tswana Chiefs* (Oxford: Clarendon Press, 1965), pp. 50, 162, and 236.

in the structure of Tswana society. To be sure, not all Tswana nowadays embrace these sentiments. The older Tswana, both of Gaborone and Kgaphamadi, knew most of the formulas—I could begin almost any of these lines and the respondent could finish it or add to it in a mood of obvious contentment.

Without going into the underlying structure of these poems, let us look at some aspects of the narrative content.

In poem I the cow (first line) is referred to as "stout-one"—strong, powerfully built—and "of weapons." This latter phrase indicates that the cow in former times was a cultural treasure and often had to be defended in war. One fought to protect cattle, one fought to recover cattle stolen in raids, one fought to take cattle as retaliation for previous cattle raids by others.

The cow is a preparer of liquid food (i.e., its milk). The cow is food which itself produces food. The reference to god is laudatory and implies all it would in our own culture if we referred metaphorically to someone or something as a god. When the cow "moos," women simply acknowledge such; men are reminded that the lowing is something that is sometimes purchased at the price of war. Cattle are a part of social relations—in particular, the lineage which is the source of one's inheritance. Thus, the significance of the phrase "animal of my father." Parentage is acknowledged and celebrated as is the patrimony, the cow. "A short sip of something hot" is a synecdochic reference to the sound that milk makes striking the side of a milking pail—like the rushing noise made when one sips something hot quickly. Cattle are often responsible for death, in this case the death of the reciter's father, who was probably lost in a cattle raid. Heroically, the reciter anticipates his own death in defense of this cultural treasure—"and as for me, he'll eat me too." The last line suggests the intimate connection between animal husbandry and the home as a conjugal economy. A person needs much labor to husband many cattle. If cattle are to increase, one's own progeny must increase too.

Note the many references in each of the three poems to the aesthetic aspects of the cow's physical appearance: "stout-one," "god with the long straight nose," "god with the moist nose," "red female," "sniffer with both nose and tongue," "dark, blue-grey cow," "cow . . . with the melodious tongue." The cow is not here a salable commodity, an item of exchange. It is the object of ecstasy.

Consider the individual's emotional investment in cattle, indicated by these lines from poem II:

I lacked one (i.e., one of the cattle was gone, missing)
I lacked sleep (this was enough to cause me to lie awake in worry)
I had one (i.e., the cow is recovered; I still don't sleep because now
  there is the burden of protecting it from raids, from wandering off,
  from predators)
I didn't sleep, I didn't want to (better to lie awake and plan than sleep;
  being concerned about the cow is more important than sleep)

Consider the "costs" of cattle implied in poem II:

I sought [it] (my cow which was taken in a raid)
I sought also my child (who was tending or seeking also to recover the
  cow)
My child has fallen into the river, the pool of the hippo (because of
  cattle my child has died in a certain river where perhaps he attempted
  to steal in retaliation for the loss of the first cow).

Note that the expression "falling into a pool of hippos" is an allusion to
being wasted in war. These lines from poem III reveal the same emotional
investment in cattle:

Lovely cattle of our home
One, alone, is sweetness (a single cow is enough to bring joy)
Missing one, alone, is sorrow (no matter how many cattle one has, to
  miss one is sorrow).

The elder Tswana still cleave to these values, albeit as an ideal. Times
of famine force the selling of cattle for cash to buy grain from South
Africa. Cattle are eaten willingly only on festive occasions or when an
animal dies of disease or starvation. They are sold to the abattoir by
these elder Tswana as a desperate measure dictated by "need." Many
older Tswana told me that they still consider the selling of a cow a sign
of "failure"--that is to say, a sign that one has been overwhelmed by
circumstances. No fault or guilt inheres in such a step; it simply indicates
that circumstances in the life struggle have gotten the upper hand.

Most of the older men in my sample had some kind of herd. Between
1965 and 1969 most of the national herd of Botswana was killed in the
extended drought. In market terms, this represented for many individuals
an "economic" loss of about 90 to 95 percent of their worth. Still, this
kind of calculation is meaningless to the Tswana, who view the loss of
cattle much as we would the loss of a great objet d'art—that is to say, as
incalculable.

To be a subject of eulogistic poetry is a suffcient but not necessary condition for an institution, custom, or belief to represent a central value in the life of an individual or community. Thus agriculture as well as husbandry is a "want-to-do" among the Tswana, yet the former does not appear as a topic in their oral poetry. Agriculture itself is called "plowing," cattle being the source of draft power. As grain comprises over 90 percent of the diet, the connection between cattle and arable agriculture is close and direct. Plowing extensively, cultivating large fields, and reaping beautiful harvests are the highest joys. "Plowing is the life of a Tswana."

Town dwellers were in some cases reluctant to state that extensive farming was something they personally would pursue because they felt the chances of living off their land were remote. But they did say categorically that, were they able to, they would return to the life of farming and leave town.

In the work of farming, unlike that of cattle husbandry, women have a central role. Many of the oral formulations of the cultural meaning of "doing" in agriculture are found in what may be called women's and girls' work songs. While these songs may be sung at work, typically they are women's dances, accompanied by singing, which are performed in moments of communal festivity. The celebration of the *work* of agriculture, from plowing to harvesting, grinding, food preparation, and eating, will be the focal point of such activities.

Building Family and Home

In Setswana family and home imply independence and autonomy. Before turning to a discussion of these values, some semantic background must be given. "Family" in Setswana (*bantlo*) is literally translated "they of the house." The possessive "my family" is "they of my house."

Kinsfolk are denoted by different terms, depending upon the class of culturally significant kin-types they fall within. The "people of the stomach [*bampa*]" are siblings and other descendants of a common mother. The "people of the vein [*balosika*]" are patrilineally related descendants. Consanguineous relatives in general are called "those from the same blood [*ditsala tsa madi*]." The values of kinship and the family are the kernel of each Tswana's social personality. Older Tswana especially see a sharp contrast in meaning and significance between ties of family and lineage and those of "mere friendship" (*ditsala fela*) or co-residence (*baagelane*).

Tswana consider family to be their paramount achievement—a great work that brings both pride and satisfaction. Family is the result of hard work and careful planning. Building a family is a result of wealth and also a producer of wealth—it is a factor of production which is necessary to those other works, cattle and fields. Family is the only social grouping that each adult Tswana sees as a direct extension of himself. Within the family, moral and social support is unequivocal. It is that social product which survives and whose presence and value remain even in the hardest of times. It remains even after one has died. Family is the one Tswana grouping within which invidious envy and jealousy are, ideally, kept to a minimum by trust based upon regular exchanges and reciprocal obligations. Family is the primary unit of coping against a hard life, the group within which hardships and troubles can be openly discussed. The larger community in Tswana society is one in which the individual feels obliged to present a good face and a strong exterior, to hide his weaknesses and failures. The family is the group within which he can admit his problems and work out solutions.

Family is the one source of children who are "of the vein"—over whom a person has the rights of parenthood. Children are paramount—the extension of oneself into the future. Children are also one's principal source of labor—labor based on fealty as well as on material interdependence born of specialization and exchange. The husband must work very hard to accumulate wealth to convey to his wife's family if he is to gain rights of paternity over her children. He literally has to earn his entitlement to the role of father as he builds his family.

The Tswana carefully distinguish the status of progenitor from that of parent. To sire children (out of marriage or before completion of the bride wealth payment) is easily done, but it does not entail the status of legal parenthood.

All of my respondents described family as the greatest of the works in their life—more important even than fields and cattle. The family is the center of satisfaction and pride. Younger Tswana who are either not married or who have not completed payment of bride wealth say, "We want families but have not yet achieved them." Most of these younger Tswana, nevertheless, had children.

To see how family is a "great work" and the necessary condition for a person to be known as a "proper man," we must understand the instition of bride wealth (*bogadi*). All older Tswana see *bogadi* as necessary to constituting a proper family and becoming a proper man. Why is this so?

"The woman is a cow who is going to produce a nation at her husband's place. This is going to increase the ward of the husband, yet be of no benefit to her parents who brought her into the world and raised her. Thus the receipt of cattle from the husband's people seems like a reasonable compensation to the wife's people for their loss of her. Without *bogadi*, women (daughters) would become foreigners. All one has done to bring them up—feeding clothing, schooling— would be lost as they would run off to live elsewhere as soon as they were impregnated. Also the pains of the woman in delivering the children are the pains of her people. Cattle are compensation for the bringing of children into the world." [Gaborone elder]

The cattle given by the young man and his father assure that the wife's father must continue to care for her throughout the marriage. If the husband and wife should come upon hard times or the wife cannot work, it is the obligation of the wife's father to slaughter *bogadi* cattle to help out the young family. *Bogadi* also assures parents of the loyalty of their children. It assures that they will not run away and neglect their parents. The young man gets help in accumulating *bogadi* cattle. He gets this in return for his help to the parents in running the house. If there were no *bogadi*, children might not stay to help their parents but would run away and neglect them. With the cattle they inherit, they can pay proper *bogadi* to their wife's parents." [Gaborone elder]

"Giving *bogadi* assures that the husband is the root of the house. He receives the wife and children as his to protect. [Question: Some people in Europe think that *bogadi* represents a kind of commercial transaction where cattle are 'paid' to the wife's parents in return for their sale of their daughter.] [Answer:] This is rubbish. When you buy something you get all the rights to it; there is no question of the wishes of the seller being considered after the transaction. A wife lives with her husband, after receipt of *bogadi*, under a condition of law— mutually agreed to, by both sets of parents. The daughter is not lost or neglected in *bogadi*-marriage. In fact the obligations of her parents continue *because of bogadi*. Thus, when there is friction between the husband and wife, the wife's parents must help settle the dispute. *Bogadi* helps assure a smooth marriage by assuring the mutual interest of both the wife's and the husband's parents. They can put pressure on both children to live amicably. If the marriage is not smooth, then everyone stands to lose because of *bogadi*. *Bogadi* means the husband can complain to the wife's parents and the wife can complain to the husband's parents concerning marital problems." [Kgaphamadi elder]

"Bogadi means the husband-to-be and his kin have achieved. It means the man is ready to marry. Even if a family is destitute, when their daughters marry, the first daughter's *bogadi* [when received] must go to be the *bogadi* [still owed by] her father. Thus, even if bogadi is not paid at the time of a man's marriage, when the man has daughters who marry, he will not receive her bogadi cattle; rather his wife's father, to whom he is still obligated for bogadi, receives them." [Kalahari elder]

Bogadi *represents* an investment of wealth in kinship and family. It is simultaneously an *entitlement* to rights over women and children, a *warranty* for the performance of both husband and wife, and an *indemnity* against possible misfeasances of husband or wife. Further, it is a way in which the son's fealty to the two fathers is assured, and the alliance of husband's and wife's lineage cemented. Bride wealth is almost always a substantial portion of the total wealth an individual can accumulate. However, the debilitating financial obligation to convey cattle, on one's own or one's son's behalf, is offset by the prospect that one will receive cattle in return for the marriage of daughters. Any conduct that might upset this flow of wealth could well have devastating consequences for the individual's capacity to remain within the system of social reciprocities. The system requires diligent, assiduous performance. An individual not only produces *for* himself but actually produces his entitlement to be a social person. A Tswana must literally make his social personality, in part by the processes of accumulation and conveyance that are involved in the exchange of people and cattle in *bogadi.*

Another reason family is considered a great achievement is that it provides social security for the individual in his old age. Tswana see family as an investment. The man must work to provide for his family. In return, he expects fealty and loyalty both now and when he can no longer provide for himself.

The family is the most important source of all labor in the domestic economy. Children "owe" their parents labor. In return the children can expect assistance, not only bride wealth paid at marriage but also a patrimony paid at the time of the father's death.

Many older Tswana claim that their children are the main reason for accumulating livestock. They say they have few or no animals themselves since the herd is going to be inherited by their sons. Most older Tswana see this husbanding of animals for their sons as an activity superior to raising animals for sale or slaughter. The Tswana are fully aware that this continuing accumulation of what ultimately will be a bequest assures that the sons will stay around and work hard and loyally for their parents. There are tensions in this patron-client aspect of the relationship between father and son. Thus when the son is under pressure to be tending his own fields, he may be obligated to work for his father. The wife may well resent the husband dividing his scarce labor between his own father and herself and family.

Family is also a great achievement because the parents can acquire new knowledge for themselves through the education of their children. Education affects the life chances of the children and the family as a whole. The literate child can provide many kinds of counsel and aid to parents unfamiliar with the "world of paper and numbers." Children's education is their parents' adaptation to a changing world. Parents therefore realize and expect that the culture of Setswana will play a diminishing role and the knowledge of the Europeans an increasingly important role in their children's pursuit of farming. Even those elder men who find the nation state, government, town life, and European ways incomprehensible, nevertheless strongly believe that a European-style education will allow their children to understand and cope with modern life and in turn enable them to continue to support their parents.

Interestingly, it is women rather more often than men who state that they want to have their children educated for the sake of knowledge itself. Men tend generally to see the education of children as an "economically" necessary step in assuring that the family will continue to thrive in a changing world. Women, on the other hand, speak of their children needing "the light" to "understand" the changed times.

Success and Doing-for-Oneself

The values of farming and building a family both imply the value of "doing-for-oneself [*go itirela*]." Undertaking farming and cattle husbandry or building a family is best done on one's own—by dint of one's own hard work and careful planning. In practice, any person is dependent upon many others in Tswana society for most of life's undertakings. But the ideal is to do as much as possible autonomously. In my observation, this value is at once an aspect of success and achievement, as we have seen, and an attempt to reduce the risks that arise from the intimacy, propinquity, and interdependence found in virtually all human communities.

Most Tswana are quite emphatic in saying that the community generally—friends and co-residents who are not kin—cannot be relied upon or trusted with one's "secrets." Friendship in Setswana is a fair-weather and casual matter. Many Tswana I interviewed dismissed the importance of friendship as an asset or resource, some claiming they had no friends at all. Underlying this mistrust of relationships based largely on affection and common interests is fear of envy and jealousy and their debilitating effects. As one Tswana put it: "Friendship is like a river (in the desert); it can be there one day, and the next day it is gone, leaving no trace." Tswana fear the evil effects of others' envy as well as the jealousy they feel in themselves when desiring to hoard their own accumulated wealth.

There are two basic Tswana strategies to combat the fact or the imputation of envy and jealousy: first, to gain through one's own hard work, and not by asking or receiving aid from others; second, to be generous to others, thereby creating a prima facie situation where one cannot be accused of being envious of others or jealous of one's own property. Gain not associated with hard work is believed generally to be a result of "dirty tricks"—deceit. If one does gain, then generosity in sharing eases the hot envy of others; it soothes the pain felt because of invidious comparison, and it creates obligation on the part of others to help with the donor's tasks. Avoidance of dependency on others, whose help and counsel may be fickle and unreliable, and removal of oneself from situations in which one can be envied or in which one will jealously hoard can both be achieved through doing-for-oneself. It is primarily in agriculture and the building of family that this functional autonomy is sought. When I asked one respondent which aspect of Setswana culture aroused the greatest pride and satisfaction, he answered: "Our greatest satisfaction as Tswana comes in having complete control over our lives and our possessions. We can do what we want. Whatever we have or don't have, we have decided how to live and work. This is our great cultural treasure." This value of doing-for-oneself in the domain of agriculture and family has many implications for understanding how the Tswana react to the economic and psychic alienation they experience working in European institutions. I will take up this point in chapter 8.

Doing-for-oneself is considered an aspect of success and achievement. "Success means working hard with your hands." "Success means planning and thinking wisely [go ruluganya ka botlhale] about the future." "Success means starting with very little and through doing-for-yourself improving and progressing in life." "Hands and intelligence are the secrets of success."

Doing-for-oneself does not guarantee progress, however, because individuals differ in their allotment of good fortune (lethlogonolo). Life can be so hard that a person is overcome by circumstances no matter how hard he tries. But in general the successful are considered to have done-for-themselves.

There are additional canons that define doing-for-oneself. It cannot be an egotistic struggle against others in the community. Doing-for-oneself does not imply license for personal isolation. It is industriousness carried out in the context of social engagement with others. Tswana freedom is not the alienated autonomy of each against all. Rather it is freedom from unwanted encumbrances. Thus dependency based on cooperation with others in an appropriate cultural manner is not inconsistent with doing-for-oneself. The success that results from doing-for-oneself must be evidenced by both generosity and sharing. It may mean hard work done immediately for another, but in the long run it is to one's own benefit. Successful people are people whose industry is redistributed in the form of help to others.

Because success is essentially doing-for-oneself, relative success cannot be a significant category. The significance of a person's doing is gauged by the individual in relation to how he believes he has worked and what struggles he has undertaken. It is not gauged by reference to some one-dimensional measure. Among the Tswana invidious social comparison is discouraged. Tswana make a great deal of effort not to conspicuously display or talk about their wealth, whether material or other. When I asked respondents to comment on the material well-being of others, they typically stated they "do not know the well-being of others, because success is felt by a person himself. It is something a person knows in relation to his own awareness of his efforts." Gross differences in material accumulation are noted, but these are not conceived as evidence of success or how one has done-for-oneself.

In this regard several older Tswana said "to compare oneself to another [in terms of some material norm] gives a person a bad impression both of himself and of what is really important." One said: "Comparison is bad; the only comparison that bears on success is the relationship between how one has striven and the meaning of what one has done. A person may have lots of properties, but he may be a prisoner of them. Hence he is not successful. The meaning of things cannot be known from their appearance."

Recipes for success among the Tswana include qualities of coping other than doing-for-oneself. The qualities cited by almost all respondents include: (1) commitment (*go ikgolega*), meaning literally to inspan oneself to a task; (2) planning and cunning (*go ruluganya ka botlhale*); (3) patience (*pelo ee telle*); and (4) well-grounded, purposive action (*boitlhomo jwa boikaelelo*), which means literally "the well-foundedness of one's purpose or goal." Most Tswana asserted that these attributes are necessary to success, and therefore define success itself. However, they are not singly or jointly sufficient to guarantee success. Every person is affected by the created order (*tlholego*) and by a good or bad fortune which no amount of struggling or coping with life's problems can transcend.

In traditional Setswana these recipes for doing or coping are given in knowledge at hand to be used when culturally prescribed. The tenacity of belief in the efficacy of these recipes was shown in the way Tswana responded to a counterfactual question I posed: "If you had your life to live over again, what would you do differently (if anything) to achieve more of your wants and avoid those disappointments we have been discussing?" In our culture we might expect such a question, asked under conditions of good rapport, to unleash effusive verbal fantasy. Two contrary reactions were obtained which amplify our understanding of doing-for-oneself. First, all but a few respondents questioned the meaningfulness of this question by stating that the issue in doing and success is commitment and hard work and not dreaming up variegated strategies. "One must face the realities of life and not be overcome by them." Few Tswana offered the view that the efficacy of coping could be enhanced by using varied approaches to life. Planning is not seen in terms of a variety of discrete approaches, each of which can be related to a single goal in terms of efficiency principles. Second, most respondents who did go on to provide an answer suggested that they would have done or not done some single act or would have done it differently. But no Tswana answered by positing major values or ways of doing that in any way differed from those that currently governed his life. The principal change in coping that most younger Tswana mentioned was to get an education. The principal change in coping mentioned by the older Tswana was not to have spent so much time abroad at work, but to have tried to live at home doing agriculture. More effort put into agriculture, they speculate, might have yielded greater progress in life.

From this I conclude that in imagining pure possibilities the Tswana are not at all alienated from the indigenous conditions of their work and their life as a whole, despite its material hardships and struggles. A difficult situation met with struggle that "succeeds" even to a limited degree has little chance of alienating people. *The sources of alienation from work or other action in life must lie in factors quite different from hardship and poverty alone.*

This acceptance of life as it is stands in contrast to the clear alienation caused by European industrial and mining organizations. In these settings the Tswana discover that remuneration and other job outcomes are totally unrelated to those qualities of *doing* they most value—industriousness, commitment, work with the hands, purposiveness, and so forth. Rather they see wages determined by such "irrelevancies" as skin color, language skills, clothing, and education. This is one reason why the Tswana seldom speak of wage labor as an instance of wanting-to-do. Wage labor violates the very definition of "doing."

Ideally Good Community Life

The interdependence between physical ecology and social relationships is so close for the Tswana that they seldom draw any distinction between them in discussing community life. Both material prosperity and propriety of conduct are believed to hinge on the same behavior. Habitat and social life are enriched and preserved by each person "doing the truth [*go dira bommarure*]."

Rain, the sine qua non of Tswana life, is "what makes everyone joyful." "Abundant rain well distributed means that everyone can live the ideally good life." "When there is rain, the land [*lefatshe*] provides all that a person requires. Then all of life is smooth indeed." This theme of sufficiency of habitat is reflected in two other aspects of Setswana life that most respondents articulated: (1) the Tswana's ability to have absolute control and say over what they do; this means effectively that *in times of sufficient rain what each Tswana wants most to do and what each Tswana is obliged to do coincide*; (2) in times of rain the Tswana can obtain almost all their material requirements from the local habitat: food, building materials, medicines, and so forth. The Tswana are quite consciously proud of their intimate and extensive knowledge of the "natural" world. This knowledge enhances their independence of the marketplace and their freedom from the need to seek help outside the community in pursuit of "great works." "We make everything we want from local materials, while Europeans have to spend money in stores. If only there is rain, each Tswana can do everything that must be done for himself."

In discussing the habitat, Tswana are very careful to stipulate that a rich environment is one in which there is not only abundance but also an even distribution of that abundance among all people. "Community means sharing; it means making a contribution [*neo*] to everyone's well-being." Traditionally, Tswana claim, one of the principal burdens of chieftainship was insuring that the resources of the tribe, including rainfall, were evenly distributed. Wealth has no meaning if it enriches a few.

On this point the Tswana contrast traditional tribal government (*puso ya bokgosi*) with modern national government. Almost every respondent asserted that modern government (*goromente*) ensures an opulent life to a small number of people in town and does nothing for the rural multitudes. Being rich in town "causes our leaders of today to lose touch with their people. They all have big stomachs; they've forgotten what hunger is like and what must be done to save hungry people. They don't feel hot sand on their feet. They travel on their buttocks (i.e., in cars). They can't listen to their hearts because they are removed from Setswana life" (Kgaphamadi elder).

Most older Tswana attribute what they perceive as an increasing harshness of the environment to the decline of traditional institutions and proper social conduct. Like most African peoples, the Tswana believe there is an intimate connection between conduct and natural events. The decline of traditional chieftainship and the extinction of traditional initiation schools are seen as contributing both to the general changes in personal relationships and to the decreasing fecundity of the habitat. This radical change in social life the Tswana describe as the "death of their origins" (see chapter 7).

Sentiments of Community: Hospitality, Peace and Law

Despite their awareness that many important institutions and beliefs of Setswana no longer exist or at least no longer work as they formerly did, most Tswana strive to maintain the traditional life-at-home (*botshelo jwa gaetsho*). While theory and practice seldom coincide in any culture, the Tswana claim that today there is a greater gap between cultural ideals and daily life than there was before Setswana lost its origins.

This gap between theory and practice is very conspicuous to the Tswana for they define sentiments in strongly performative terms. Recall that in Setswana want or desire, which we tend to think of as a mere idea, is an intention to seek after. The same intention to do or act is an aspect of other important sentiments of community. The Tswana presume the existence of certain sentiments on the basis of behavior seen in public life. This union of thought (or sentiment) and action holds not only for emotions such as generosity (*bopelonomi*), the desire to cooperate (*tuisanyo*), and the desire to reciprocate (*go amogana/go ruanya*) —all of which have an obvious performative reference—but also for emotions such as love, empathy, and the desire to be truthful—all of which we think of as purely internal.

In the industrial West our most revered and eloquent formulations of love, truth, and understanding seldom make reference to anybody *doing* anything. Indeed, "doing" is often conceived as a profanation of the ethereal profundities of thought and emotion. For the Tswana, love, "truth," and understanding obey performative principles; the very words in Setwana point to action. For example, the Setswana words *go rata* (to like) and *lorato* (affection) are often used to translate our concept of love. The meaning conveyed, however, is "to like very much [*go rata thata thata*]." For the Tswana, to be a person who *likes* someone is to be a person who *shows affection* for someone; to be one who *knows the truth*, one must *act or do the truth*; to *honor or respect* someone is literally to *present that person with material goods* which insinuate that respect; to *become friends* in Setswana is to *present gifts to one another*; to *understand* is to *hear* someone; to *do the truth* means to *be trustworthy and reliable* in terms of proper cultural performances.

In a small, face-to-face community, living precariously close to the margins of survival, unperformed sentiments have very little value. The unity of thought and action is a biological imperative for people who are directly and immediately dependent on one another. Failure or unreliability is not, nor can it be, absorbed by giant institutions which dissipate misfeasance and accountability in an imbroglio of bureaucratic machinations. Performance and failure, blame and credit, are out in the open—public and unambiguous. Anonymity and privacy are impossible. People live cheek by jowl in full consciousness of everyone's every move. In such circumstances a person's qualities of conduct cannot be modified or dressed up with a rich superstructure of motivations and intentions. A person *is* how he acts. And since almost all acts are public, a person is how he appears. That a person *can* believe himself to be other than he appears is possible in Tswana culture, but it is not important. It can become important when one goes to another world, into town, for example; but at home a person is judged to have "intended all the reasonable and probable consequences of his actions." In such a setting candor and sincerity must be subordinated to the higher values of proper performance.

Hospitality and Sociability: The ideally good life is filled with visiting, entertaining, giving and receiving food, conversation, and festive work, in an extended, unending network of reciprocities. Giving and receiving hospitality is both a "want-to-do" and an obligation. The importance of hospitality and sociability is not comprehended by our notion of "having fun." No Tswana describes hospitality as "fun," though fun is a frequent outcome. Hospitality and sociability mean, first of all, greeting (*maitiso*) and taking-the-news (*go tsaya dikgang*). Greeting and taking-the-news are in part functional equivalents of reading the daily paper. They are aspects of being informed about and participating in civil society. Often it is when greeting a person for the first time during the day that news is best communicated. At that time opinions can often be obtained or formulated, and guides to action set. To report plans, visits by strangers, and deaths or illnesses is crucial to the maintenance of communal life. If someone regularly fails to play a part in this face-to-face exchange, the Tswana presume he is ill, depressed, bewitched, or harboring malign feelings.

Greeting and taking-the-news are part of necessary "face work"—presentation of one's social personality in the larger world. Failure to engage socially in this world is not simply a violation of etiquette or decorum; rather it is an attack on the very basis of communal solidarity. It is in greeting and taking-the-news that the community publicly affirms its very existence. While it is through books or the mass media that we invest national life with meaning, the Tswana accomplish this in the conversations that comprise hospitality and sociability.

Hospitality and sociability are not felt as coercive or onerous. A Tswana seldom wants to turn away a caller. Generosity (willingness to extend the offer of exchanges seemingly advantageous only to the recipient) includes most prominently hospitality and sociability. While these exchanges of "dessert" have many very direct social consequences beneficial to all parties, they are not simply ceremonial covers for truck and barter. They are part of the ideally good life as such—they are pure *enjoyment*: what the Tswana call "eating well."

Hospitable sociability is the occasion for "great words"—for the verbal art in which most Tswana revel. But this conversational art form is dying —both the ability and the actual practice. To many Tswana, including younger Tswana, it has become, not priceless—as any art form of great worth should be—but a thing that can fetch no price. Accordingly, more and more Tswana are losing their skill in manipulating the language of ceremonial hospitality. Conversation is giving way, many say, to mere prattle.

This is not my lament alone, as an ethnographer; it is that of many Tswana who see their young losing not only the law (*molao*) but also the words (*dipuo*) of Setswana.

Hospitality implies offering food and drink. The word to be hospitable (*go thelesetsa*) means literally to assist someone by supplying food.

To be hospitable is to help. All the Tswana I came to know said that a result of success in agriculture is that one is able to be generous and hospitable. "Generous hospitality attracts many people to one's place." "Having people around to appreciate one's works means good company—where people come because they want to exchange good work for good food; this is good company."

Traditionally much of the "doing" that produced the necessary conditions for cultural existence took the form of hospitality. Pleasure and hard work were frequently combined into a single social transaction—for example, the communal work-party. More and more today, even in rural areas, the labor that produces the necessary conditions of communal existence is traded fee for service. Sociability loses many of the functions it formerly had. Still it exists, more or less freighted with its traditional significance.

Peace: In describing the ideally good communal life, almost every Tswana respondent cited *peace* as a fond hope, second only to food and family. Many, however, feared that war was possible. The Tswana as a whole, irrespective of age or habitat, describe peace as domestic tranquillity—harmonious relations among members of the community, among communities within the tribes, and among tribes within the land. All Tswana are aware of the wars that have plagued other parts of Africa. Some are aware of World War II, and all know firsthand about the state of military siege that South Africa exercises over its castes of black people. Violence, war, and "bullying [*boganka*]" are all, equally, contraries of peace (*kagiso*). *Boganka* (bullying) is a term that describes both valorous conduct in battle and the kind of destructive aggressiveness that can exist within a community. The Tswana distinguish between violence done in war and domestic violence, arguing simply that the former is necessary but the latter evil.

The Tswana claim explicitly that peace and tranquillity exist in Botswana, unlike in Rhodesia and South Africa. This peace is one of Botswana's treasures. Continued avoidance of conflict or fighting in Botswana is a strong desire expressed by every Tswana. Most Tswana express the hope that they as individuals will not even *inadvertently* give offense to others, or cause anger or harm, lest conflict be provoked.

Daily behavior and explicit belief testify to the Tswana's love of peace. Yet aggression and conflict have a "proper" place in Tswana life. War in olden times had its heroic elements. Valor and reputation were enhanced by conflict. War, especially in defense of right, was always better than a coward's peace. Many of the praise poems of olden chiefs eulogize acts of war and the fearsome, aggressive qualities of political and military leaders. Traditionally people could become "heroes" through their conduct in war.

In Tswana daily life, interpersonal relations among *unequals*, particularly between those of different age-grades, are typically filled with aggressiveness and bullying banter. Politeness, decorum, and deference are contingent upon the statuses of the people interacting. The older can expect deference from the younger and are entitled, conversely, to dominate and bully them. Only among age or rank equals must deferential face-work be mutual. Prescriptions for behavior in any culture have their criteria of relevance—the situations within which they are obligatory, those within which they must be suspended, and the zones of ambiguity in which individual choice and strategy may prevail.

In general, peace is as thoroughly grounded in the culture as physical or verbal aggression, which is sanctioned in very few contexts in current communal life. There are many heroes and other mythically defined archetypes of traditional life that commemorate the virtues of propriety, tranquillity, and a peaceful approach to interpersonal relations. The peacemaker, the wise man of words, and the conciliator are as likely candidates for herodom as the warrior. Generals do not have such an exclusive presence in the Tswana culture as they do in ours (to judge from the monuments of municipal greens).

While I was doing my field work, the South African police were strongly suspected of sending a bomb through the mails to a Tswana political refugee in Botswana, which exploded and killed him. The first reaction of the Tswana I interviewed in Gaborone was to say that this confirmed the "lack of humanity" of the Boers. One elder respondent offered this observation: "The homes of the fierce (warlike) are often in ashes; those who are meek still live in virtue of their meekness [*Marope a bagale melora, ba bonolo ba sa tshedile ka bonolo jwa bone*]." Among literate Tswana attending the university in Gaborone the reaction was much more Western—to express a desire for vengeance or "to see the South Africans trampled at the feet of some [hypothetical] liberating army." Few of the illiterate Tswana endorsed the idea of revenge, even when I posed this as a possibility.

Keeping the Law: The final and perhaps most fundamental of the three key aspects of community among the Tswana is the concept of law (*molao*). Most Tswana, especially the older, consider law to be the

foundation of a proper life, both private and communal. In popular
speech the Tswana use the term *law* to refer to: (1) substantive and
procedural law (law strictly defined); (2) obligations sanctioned informally through various social pressures, and (3) self-imposed obligations.
In a context that calls for precise, technical discourse, each of these is
distinguished from the others. However, law as commonly understood
is not coterminous with what concerns formal courts. In Tswana society
it is often the case that the formal body which serves as the arena for
litigation—and hence for the making and enforcing of decisions concerning obligations—is not a court but rather a family, an extended family,
the ward leaders cadre of "old men," and so forth. These can be either
the "courts of first instance" in litigation or the only arena of litigation
for certain offenses or conflicts of obligation. Hence, the term *law* in
Tswana, as they define it, covers a much broader domain of behavior
than it does in our society, where we define as law only what concerns
the courts.

In the ideal life, sentiment and law should be one. Many elder Tswana
told me, as I have suggested, that in former times "what one was obliged
to do, one wanted to do." The reason for this happy coincidence is, as
one Tswana put it, that "children are reared with the law, so when they
grow up, they will have the law, so they can live the law." Many Tswana
state that success and achievement in the ideal life, and in their own
lives, come from being one who "abides in the law [*motho yo o nnang
mo molaong*]."

Contrariwise, in our society, with its proliferation of civil law and
resultant "private" delicts, we tend to take an entrepreneurial approach
to life and hence to think of "the law" as a kind of "risk structure" to
be taken account of in *maximizing* opportunities. If something is not
proscribed, it is privileged behavior. Law is for us a "game plan"—a list
of dos and don'ts which, when fully specified, leave much leeway for
free choice and strategic action in pursuit of private interest.

This view is quite foreign to the Tswana, for whom the means-ends
dichotomy implied in such a conception of law does not exist. The
Tswana want to act by the law. Faced with uncertainty—for example,
in the situation that follows the incursion of Western industry—many
older Tswana look for "legal" guidelines to action, even to the point of
persisting in traditionally chartered conduct when outsiders clearly perceive this to be inefficient. Tswana seek moral and intellectual grounds
for action; this is part of their cultural stock of belief. In the face of
new circumstances—wage labor, for example—they seek similar grounds

for conduct. They attempt to turn action into a rational project. In the industrial sector this quest is often in vain, as their understanding of the relevant social forces is rudimentary. In changed circumstances the Tswana may be unable to find reasons for the behavior that is pre-scribed, and when nothing is clearly prescribed he may not know what to do, in which case he will often revert to the traditional approach in the face of uncertainty and seek guidelines from those with authority or a record of past success. The traditional Tswana would stop and think, seek advice, or look to copy a proven course of action. This behavior leads many naive observers to see the Tswana in Western settings as reticent and hypercautious, fearful of new situations, cowed by tradition, insecure, and filled with inferiority feelings. As we will see, this is a very mistaken account of why the Tswana choose not to act in the face of uncertainty.

In this connection many older Tswana describe recent social change as a breakdown of law, which they conceive of both as an institutional breakdown and as a loss of propriety in individual conduct. It is a commonly expressed sentiment that "children now make their own choices; they grow up and run around *without law.*" When a parent instructs a child on proper conduct and the reasons for it, he is said to be "giving his child the law." When institutional changes occur and the parent is no longer able to prevail on the child to accept his instructions, it is said that "the child lacks law"—that is, norms by which to act. Younger Tswana, especially those who are quite deeply involved in social changes stemming from labor migration or town life, often regard traditional parental control (law) as onerous. Many young Tswana today rebel against parental authority and other obligatory reciprocities of kinship. Several younger Tswana said to me, "I left home, because there I am 'held' by the law." In contrast to this, over one-half of all elder Tswana interviewed told me that "having kept Setswana law all one's life was a person's greatest pride." "No one can be a proper adult who does not seek to keep the law."

6 THINGS-I-WANT-TO-DO: COMMUNITY AND AGE-COHORT CONTRASTS

Introduction

A person's desires—to be free from want, to do agriculture, to build family, to do for himself, to keep community and the law—are not simply internalizations of values given in the system of culture. They are also provinces of meaning in the individual consciousness. It is necessary first to recognize *that* these themes of self-identity are cultural typifications which exist in consciousness and then to analyze them *as* they exist in consciousness.

An "intentional" analysis of "wanting-to-do" requires that we know something of the individual's life-project. Important material aspects of Tswana life and variations therein have been presented in chapters 2, 3, and 4, where I described the significant ecological contrasts presented by Gaborone, Kgaphamadi, and the Kalahari. In some measure these differences in the material substrata of communal life also distinguish the life-worlds of the people. But, as we have already noted, "age"— that is, the duration and sedimentation of experience—is also an important aspect of the life-world, and one that cuts across environmental variations. Ecology and age jointly permit us to construct a "grid" of the material substrata of the life-world which will represent important variations in the way Tswana express and explicate the cultural theme wanting-to-do. In other words, the way this theme exists in consciousness can be shown to correlate with objective features of the person's age cohort and his community's ecologic niche.

On the basis of the way they interpreted the value theme "things-I-want-to-do," Tswana respondents fell into three categories: (1) the old of Gaborone and Kgaphamadi; (2) the young of Gaborone and Kgaphamadi; and (3) both the young and the old of the Kalahari villages. Within each of these groupings the respondents were for the most part agreed on the meaning of things-I-want-to-do, but between groupings there were marked differences in belief. (The numbers of male respondents intensively interviewed were: twenty-one in the first category; twenty-one in the second category; and eleven in the third category.)

The fact that the Kalahari respondents, old and young, constituted a group by themselves shows that the degree of embeddedness in a Western political economy corresponds with variations in the content of theme values. The variation in the Tswana value wanting-to-do is not antecedent to the experience of Western institutions. Instead values with origins and foundations in traditional society have been differentially affected by the Western presence.

The typified account of the theme wanting-to-do presented in chapter 5 corresponds quite closely with the one expressed by older Tswana both in Kgaphamadi and in Gaborone. The task at hand, then, is to describe how the people of the Kalahari (both young and old) and the young people (both in Kgaphamadi and Gaborone) differ from the old upon whose views the account up to now has been based. In the following descriptions I report those aspects of wanting-to-do that contrast with the account given above. That an aspect of wanting-to-do is omitted indicates that it is similar to or identical with what was reported for the elders of Gaborone and Kgaphamadi.

The Tswana of the Kalahari

Three small villages made up the Kalahari sample: Ditshegwane, Takatokwane, and Dultwe. Absenteeism from these villages at any time can be extraordinarily high. During my study 60 to 70 percent of the adult population (males and females) were away elsewhere in Botswana or in South Africa. On the assumption that the people at home at any one time may well *not* be a random sample of all people who live in these villages during some portion of their lives, I carried out this study in two separate seasons—winter 1973 and summer 1974–75. The comparison of responses obtained in the two seasons, if quite different, would suggest serious problems of sampling error. This turns out not to have been the case.

There was one other important sampling problem. In each of these villages about half of the population there at the time of my study were

Kgalagadi and the other half were Kwena. The Kgalagadi have been throughout their history an attached grouping of Tswana who occupy a position of ethnic yeomanry vis-à-vis the Kwena. They speak a dialect of Setswana quite different from what the non-Kgalagadi call Setswana. They are a people colonized twice over –first by the Kwena and then by the Europeans.

In my preliminary surveys it became clear that there were significant differences among the Kwena and the Kgalagadi of the Kalahari and that I should confine my study to the relatively better off Kwena in these three villages. To be sure, the presence of such an "inferior" class as part of the social structure of their villages affects the life-world of the Kwena as much as the presence of a superordinate class affects the life-world of the Kgalagadi. These divisions do not exist in villages in the Eastern Kweneng. My assumption is, however, that the principal contrasts between the Kalahari and eastern Tswana villages are to be found in the marked differences in the degree of material autonomy of their economies and accordingly in the variations in amount of reliance upon labor migration to South Africa as a central feature of economic and social organization.

For the people of the Kalahari there is one overarching project in life—avoidance of hunger. Whatever alleviates hunger and restores the physical body to equilibrium is called success, achievement, weal—in short, the ideally good life. Specification of wanting-to-do beyond attainment of "freedom from hunger" is unnecessary; to do so is possible, but trivially unimportant. Food or its lack is a monomania. They claim this explicitly as their fundamental preoccupation, and their behavior as I observed it testifies to the sincerity and accuracy of the claim.

While respondents in the Kalahari could and did discuss all aspects of this theme (wanting-to-do), they did so as if describing a hypothetical reality. Indeed the values of Tswana culture as a whole have become, in one respondent's very poignant words, "killed at the root. We have been severed from our beginnings by the pangs of hunger and left unprotected in the world." Said another: "We can survive only by living in a world we don't understand [the European world]. The important thing is that money is there; more money now than ever before. We live there, for that is where we can eat."

When I inquired into the meaning of agriculture and stock farming, a formulaic response given again and again was: "Agriculture is finished; there is nothing [*Temo e fedile; ga go na sepe*]." Of course, it is not literally "finished." In some years there is almost no harvest, in which case almost all food must be bought from wages remitted. In some years agriculture is possible, and a harvest of some sort can be reaped. Livestock, especially goats, are kept and do provide an important food supplement as well as an item that can be sold to raise money. Yet the stark, simple fact that the Kalahari environment is materially more precarious, less fecund than that of eastern Botswana affects the way Tswana typify the whole of their social and cultural life.

The Tswana of the Kalahari describe the values of success, achievement, community, and weal by use of the words "I want *to have*," "I wish *to have*," "I hope *to have*," or "if only it were possible *to have* [*Ke batla go na le; Ke eletsa gore ke kabo ke na le*]," etc. This implies to me that the cash nexus between labor and commodity has broken the cultural link of wanting-to-do, which in the east still unites the world of desire, effort, and commodity into an existential whole. Progress in improving material circumstances is seen as success, achievement, and wealth. But no Kalahari respondent spoke of that value which almost all of the elder eastern Tswana described as the underlying meaning of all success: increase in one's capacity for self-determination and self-reliance—being one who can *do-for-himself*.

When I asked about doing-for-oneself (*go itirela*), the Kalahari would acknowledge their belief in this as an ideal but would aver that doing-for-oneself *really* means "having change in one's pocket." To have money—to have food, to have things—is *to be free of want*. Having commodities or the means to them—money—is sufficient to be free of want and hence to be a proper man (*monna tota*).

The value of doing-for-oneself as conceived by the eastern Tswana is that it betokens personal autonomy. Having possessions reflects successful doing-for-oneself. They express in condensed form the effort that has created them. Among the Kalahari, however, this contingent meaning of property does not appear. For the Kalahari, possession itself is sufficient—an unquestionably consummate and satisfying goal.

Another aspect of successful doing for the eastern Tswana is the capacity it creates for being generous. If their doing is successful, they will show it through generosity. The Kalahari reverse this recipe. When speaking of success, they often express the hope that other people will be generous toward them. The Kalahari, unlike the eastern Tswana, readily cast themselves in the role of supplicant, as demonstrated in the pleas I heard very often: "I wish someone would provide me *mafisa* cattle [cattle lent by an individual to another who enjoys their "usufruct," in return for herding them]," "I wish the community would care for me in my wretched condition." With many Kalahari I could not elicit evidence of any aspiration regarding wanting-to-do that went beyond a hope of receiving the means of subsistence through charity. In sum, among the Kalahari Tswana wanting-to-do-for-oneself seems to have been supplanted as a value by *wanting-to-make-do* by means of help from others.

The Kalahari do not dismiss the belief that hard work done for oneself is, or at least begets, success and progress. But they frequently describe bases for success that I rarely heard in the east: chance or good fortune. "Successful people are inspired by dreams." "It is often the gift of god, but I haven't seen a successful person yet." One Kalahari respondent stated: "Success is a thing of the past. It is no longer possible. Success means one must think in terms of the future, but we don't know what the future is, so how can we think in terms of it?"

The importance accorded planning and working for the future in the eastern Tswana's descriptions of success set these people apart from the Kalahari. The Kalahari spent much time in interviews wishing and fantasizing about improved circumstances and how to obtain them. Several Tswana said they wished the government of the country would give them *mafisa* cattle. (No one knew of such a thing ever happening or being proposed.) Several said that they could not think about the future or plan because they were starving. Several said quite candidly they hoped they could continue to work (either in the mines or in small cottage industry) in order to "avoid becoming a thief."

A similar fatalism or dependency appears in discussions of achievement, especially *family*. Kalahari, like eastern Tswana, say their most important achievement is family and children. "My success is in harvesting the fruit of the loins; the children and family are my one achievement." "I have achieved for I have children who are taking care of me." This frequently heard refrain suggests that the family is seen, even more than among the eastern Tswana, as a refuge from the vicissitudes of life. Friendship gives rise to misunderstandings in the community. The community cannot help. Only family inspires confidence: *"Bana ba motho ba kgaogana yantsi* [The children of one person share the head of a fly]," implying the ability of Tswana families to continue to share and exist despite near starvation.

The family in the Kalahari, as in the east, is the principal economic institution. Wages remitted from labor undertaken abroad are distributed within the family. Children are the most important capital a person can control. "I want my children to get an education so that when I am old and unable to work, they will be able to take care of me the way I have taken care of them." This sentiment was expressed even by young Tswana who had no children of their own. Children, whatever else they may be, are an annuity for old age. As one respondent put it: "My fondest hope for my children is that they go to Johannesburg and earn lots of money, so they can return here to take proper care of me."

These statements should not be construed to suggest that the Kalahari have lost the familial sentiments of love and affection. However, in discussions of the meaning of family, community, and habitat, the saliency of deficiency leads respondents to emphasize the role of the family in material subsistence.

Despite rather uniform poverty, the topic of *relative* success, achievement, and weal, which the eastern Tswana considered inappropriate for discussion, was of keen interest to Kalahari Tswana. Invidious comparison apparently does not seem so threatening to social solidarity when all are believed to be made equally miserable by life. In the Kalahari reliance on wage labor has had a considerable leveling effect on wealth, as has the lack of rain, which has a detrimental effect on all agriculture and decimates everyone's herds. At the mines a youngster can earn as much as a man of forty-five or fifty. As one young man put it: "When we are at the mines eating well, we know that back home everyone is starving. So we all suffer at the mines equally; we all send money at the same time. The people at home receive the money at the same time. We're all in the same position."

The kinds of people the Kalahari, young and old, frequently pointed to as successful were not the big farmers or cattle owners, as was the case in eastern Botswana. The local ideal of success was the shopkeeper, the man who has money. Their route to success, according to my respondents, was to accumulate earnings from the mines and buy goods which were then "hawked" through the small villages. Eventually they earned enough to buy a mule and cart or even to build a small shop and stock it with a wider range of goods. Evidence of success for the Kalahari lay not only in the ongoing business; equally important were the kind of material possessions such local businessmen could purchase from their earnings: cattle, plows, planters, furniture, iron roofs, radios, and so forth. Despite this interest in accumulation, the young without exception said the ideal life consists of a definite and delimited inventory of goods. In this regard the younger people of the Kalahari do not see the community and the ideally good life much differently than the adults. The younger Tswana expressed hopes that Botswana would have trains, mines, town entertainment, and—most important—jobs for the illiterate and not just for the educated. Few saw this in terms of action that the national government would take; the hopes were, in fact, disconnected from any conception of how they might be achieved. Furthermore the respondents had no conception that they personally could play any role in bringing them about. In fact, many of the Kalahari Tswana are dependent even in hoping, as shown in such frequently made statements as: "We hope that the whites will come and settle in Botswana so they can open mines and give us work. Also they can dig bore holes (wells)." Europeans are widely seen by Kalahari Tswana as somehow the proximate cause of jobs and money. In the east hardly anybody wanted white people coming to settle en masse in Botswana.

As in the east, the contrary of succeeding is "being overcome" by circumstances. But it was only in the Kalahari that I found people ready to describe their entire life—their biography of deeds—as a continuous "being overcome." The Kalahari seem to accord to circumstances a more important role in what will happen than do the eastern Tswana. One respondent put this aphoristically: "The Jackal said 'I am fast,' the field said, 'but I have (already) spread out.'" This alludes to the belief that no amount of skill or will (want-to-do) available to the individual can exceed the capacity of situations to overcome the person.

The Kalahari Tswana do not attribute being overwhelmed in their wanting-to-seek success in life exclusively or even largely to the harsh and capricious environment. The eastern Tswana claimed this to be the first, if not the only cause of being overwhelmed. Most of the Kalahari Tswana stated that a basic reason for their failure was that they had been *bewitched* (*loilwe*), either directly through the intentional efforts of others or indirectly under the generally debilitating influences of the envy found in their factious communities. Young and old claimed a life history of bewitchment and efforts to combat it.

Discussion of bewitchment often arose when I asked about the role of community in affecting a person's pursuit of agriculture or of a Setswana life generally. The following is a not atypical response: "The community neglects me, hates me. Despite my being medicinally protected from witchcraft [*go thaiwa*], I am bewitched. People gossip about me. I am trod upon in the community, as one who is insignificant. I lack words to explain my fears about my community. How can I explain it—look, I have no fields. Agriculture is finished. I have no job. I was born in this country, and I still don't know where to go. I am bewildered by my poverty. I'm afraid I'll steal. . . ." On the role of community in the pursuit of agriculture and Setswana life, another complained: "I fear community. Nobody is taking care of me. I am worried because I dream of countries and people I do not know. Even my uncle rejects me." Such frequent, strident statements about community envy, jealousy, sorcery, and witchcraft were not made to me in eastern Botswana. While the *distribution* of witchcraft accusations in the Kalahari is similar to that of the east, the number of cases that appeared in the context of accounting for "failure" of crops and loss of cattle was much greater in the Kalahari.

I interpret this as a sign of the general hopelessness and despair that is a not uncommon reaction to a widespread and seemingly unconquerable shortage of food. In our own culture despair or depression are often systematically expressed as lassitude, fatigue, fatalism, and unwillingness to act. Even at a time when there were abundant rains, many Tswana took a very pessimistic view of the probable outcome of *any* effort they might make to grow food. In the year after my initial visit to the Kalahari, there were unusually abundant and well-distributed rains. Yet when I arrived in the Kalahari for my second visit (December 1974 to January 1975), many Tswana who were there were not planting anything. Several people I spoke to about this looked somewhat embarrassed at what my questions must have implied—my belief that their lassitude was the cause of their claimed misery. When I asked bluntly, "Why aren't you planting?" two or three people said, "It's raining, and you embarrass me." Others would smile sheepishly and offer some statement to the effect that they were simply "throwing a few grains over the fence to see if they would sprout," and then they would add something like: "I'm just playing till I (or someone in the family) goes to the mines again." Others referred to the inevitable confounding effects of envy and sorcery on their efforts to plant. "What's the use; I'm doomed to fail in everything I do. I ran away from my people, and now I'm paying for it."

Preoccupation with the fact and the fear of hunger has another important consequence that the Tswana are consciously aware of and articulate readily. Mass famine, say the Tswana, produces bullyishness and meanness in people. Older Tswana decried the fact that rudeness and bullyishness (*boganka*), once confined to the boys at the cattle posts, are now to be found in the villages. This they saw as part of the general violence brought about when "that which one man eats must be taken out of another's mouth."

From my observations in one of the three villages, I conclude that there was much more aggressive verbal exchange, semipugilistic pushing and shoving, and rowdiness on public occasions than I observed in the east (except possibly in the case of the young people living in Gaborone). The decorous and formal air that pervades almost all face-to-face contact in the east has been supplanted in large measure by a much more aggressive, less polite form of conduct in the Kalahari villages. The fact that these villages contain numerous younger people, many recently returned from the mines, could mean that this behavior is related to age and the temporary influence of mine life and does not result from a normative change in the canons of public conduct in the culture of village life.

Older Kalahari Tswana claimed explicitly that the food shortage produces that "consumption violence" I referred to above. A chronic food shortage diminishes the size of the groupings within which civil, generous conduct can be relied upon to prevail. Within the family in the Kalahari, public behavior was much like what I found in the east, but between individuals of different families it was much less decorous.

Factionalism I found to be much more explicit in Kalahari villages than in Kgaphamadi or the surrounding villages. These differences in the degree of preoccupation with village politics are traceable to variations in the political structure of villages and the ways in which they are linked to tribal and national administration. But a mode of face-to-face interaction that is in general aggressive and belligerent exacerbates the overtly expressed political factionalism of Kalahari villages, whereas the distinct value placed on decorous public behavior in the east tends to ameliorate some of the emotional consequences of intravillage rivalries and feuds.

In this context I must note that the transmission of Setswana culture from generation to generation is profoundly affected by the interpersonal relationships maintained in village life. Children reared in Kalahari villages experience a quite different conception of Setswana law and tradition than do youngsters reared in the east. For example, in the Kalahari the concept of law [molao] seems to have acquired the connotation of statutes or rules that form part of the "game plan" one must know to live life well, in a strategic sense. Law is seen as part of an overall structure of opportunity and privilege rather than as a felt moral imperative. An effect of this coalescence of jealousy, factionalism, "politics," malevolent envy (witchcraft), and dire poverty is that almost all men and women try to arrange regular, lengthy absences from the small villages. "Home" in these villages is demographically a way station. With few exceptions, agriculture does not hold people to the sedentary existence that is more typical in the eastern Kweneng. Everything—hunger, fear of witchcraft, legal suits and countersuits, feuds, and so forth—converges to push people in and out of these villages at a high rate. It is not surprising in such a setting that discussion of community and law is seen by many, especially the young, as irrelevant if not unreal. Furthermore, the oral traditions—the singing of songs, the telling of tales, the fireside conversations concerning the meaning of life and the events comprising it—are less a part of life for youngsters in these villages than for those in the east. These activities represent important aspects of how life is experienced—how it is invested with meaning. This is shown by the fact that Kalahari Tswana, except for the very old, found it either impossible or unimportant to discuss philosophically many aspects of Setswana, including the notion of value (doing, wanting-to-do, name, community, etc.), about which conversation flowed so freely in the eastern part of the country. In sum, that the value of want-to-do in an environment of semi-selfsubsistence (Kgaphamadi) and the value of want-to-have in an environment of dire poverty (the Kalahari) spell very different consequences for the life-worlds of the Tswana.

The Young of Kgaphamadi and Gaborone

The "young" are not necessarily very young. As noted above, in my sample they range in age from nineteen to about thirty-eight. They are young in terms of the Tswana conception of the meaning of age as constituted by experience accumulated in living. All but five of the twenty-one young had either been actively engaged in labor migration or saw going to the mines as a possibility, but only as a backup in case of dire necessity. These young living in town gave the same reason for being there as the rural people did for going to the mines: to obtain cash for necessary purchases—for example, to buy food to complement what is grown but because of drought is insufficient for their needs. While the young in town were in most cases not as fully engaged in farming or in their villages as the Kgaphamadi young, they gave similar evaluations of their lives at home. Urban experiences described by the town dwellers and suppositions about town life held by the rural young were also concordant. This led me to surmise—correctly, it turns out—that "town" refers as much to an a priori life-project as to a nebulous concept that is slowly invested with meaning as the young person acquires experience in town. Town is from the beginning "intended as town," and this is as important for the total experience as the vague impressions and hopes that are fulfilled empirically and inductively as the person dwelling there copes on a day-to-day basis with its opportunities and burdens.

The young of Kgaphamadi and Gaborone who made up my sample of respondents were all born and raised at least to adolescence in rural eastern Botswana. Almost all had been to the mines. None of the rural young had ever lived in town however.

Material conditions such as climate can affect profoundly the project of life. The contrast between the Kalahari villages and those of eastern Botswana has illustrated this. But time lived and the experience of age is as important in understanding the meaning of experience as habitat and social structure. If the retrospective explication of events—the meaning invested in the past—changes as a function of age and the accumulation of new experience, this means that the cultural and individual meanings of any event are age- and experience-dependent. Values like wanting-to-do are not abstract, symbolically framed postulates that float around for people to take up. They are anchored in the material and existential conditions of living and are part of the life-project as such. Because the life-project is constituted in lived time—both past and imagined future—there must exist important correspondences between the content of a person's values and his age.

Young people, both in town and in Kgaphamadi, characterized success and achievement in much the same terms as their elders. The young people's response to the question, "What do you want most in life?" was, like that of the elders, "to do for myself [*ke batla go itirela*]," accompanied by emphatic gestures, placing both hands in clenched position in front of the body as though holding a plow. One young respondent from Kgaphamadi offered an interesting, though seemingly enigmatic, elaboration of doing-for-oneself: "The fat for a child is to be sent (on errands) [*mafura ya ngwana ke go rongwa*]." He explained that this means that the child, given his world of concerns and values, does not require tender meat as a reward for being sent on errands by his elders, because going on errands is itself happiness, desire, and want for the child. Applied to the question of doing-for-oneself, this implies that a person's pleasure or contentment lies in the doing itself; no extrinsic reward is required to offset perceived cost.

Contrary to this value, young people, whether they live in town or in rural areas, do not often lead a life typified by doing-for-oneself. Those getting started in life (*makolwane*) experience a general and persistent poverty, whether they cope by staying at the lands and migrating from time to time to the mines, or whether they come to town to seek work. While this kind of industrious coping may seem to us like doing-for-one-self, recall that the *doing* in Setswana presupposes culturally stipulated works. Labor migration and much town work are not examples of doing-for-oneself. Interestingly the Kalahari, young and old, would cite their treks to the mines and their earnings as accomplishments, and hence by definition as examples of doing. But the eastern Tswana, including the younger, denied that most town labor and any mine labor comprised doing-for-oneself, though they affirmed the necessity and propriety of these without hesitation.

For the younger, as for the older, the first and paramount want-to-do is to be free of want. But there is a difference. The young explicitly claim that whatever a person attains he will always want to do more. The young believe that a person's wants (want-to-do) will always exceed his actual capacity to do. The young, unlike either the old or the Kalahari, will describe things-I-want-to-do in terms of hopes and wishes which, reasonably, they assume will not come to pass. They do not dream wildly or have an aspiration level absurdly removed from what they can probably expect in life. But in my observation they spend a considerable amount of time projecting themselves into a future which they acknowledge is unlikely to be as they imagine.

The young have incorporated certain new works into the culturally defined concept of doing. Certain exchanges in the marketplace are acquiring the value of wanting-to-do, especially the sale of labor at a "good price." The young, whether in town or the better endowed rural areas, have experienced from their childhood a society which objectively and materially has opened its cultural horizon to include the principle of salability, including sale of labor. The market implies a universal means of exchange, a unidimensional standard by which all commodities become comparable. In this arena a person's essential *power-to-do*, to *become*, or to *have* is defined as the power to engage in exchange—to purchase and sell. When a single measure gains acceptance, it can open fantasy and desire to the possibility of expanding one's zone of operation in the world. Instead of cosmologic principles defining the separation of rich from poor, wise from stupid, royal from common, there is only one thing that separates any individual from his wants—scarcity of means. Since each wage-earning individual has some of that power, he can imagine himself with just a little more, then a little more, and so on.

The Kalahari, while involved in the world of cash, have *not* made the leap to "universal salability." Cash for most Kalahari is still "special-purpose money," a means to exchange labor, principally for the very same wants as were wanted of old—cattle and fields. The younger Tswana in the east also desire to make this kind of exchange, but they have gone on to want to do more than simply apply the power of cash to "traditional" purchases; they are as a cohort gradually expanding their culturally stipulated inventory of "great works" to include many activities and goods that are only available through the marketplace. The Kalahari are using purchase power to shore up, subsidize, and maintain a traditional rural life that would vanish were it not for that cash inflow. The common element of cash should not disguise this basic difference between the life-projects of the Kalahari and those of the young people in eastern Botswana. Furthermore, the old of Gaborone who are earning and spending money in town just like the young do not participate at all in this world view dominated by universal salability.

The rural-dwelling young who are committed to agriculture and farming are, like their age-mates in town, beginning to alter the traditional meaning of farming by entertaining in fantasy wants that can be realized in the foreseeable future only in the context of a monetized economy of universal exchange. The rural young of Kgaphamadi, living close to Gaborone (eighteen kilometers), have chosen to engage themselves in town and the economy that undergirds it, but the rural old have not. Now that there are opportunities for rural employment and possibilities for disposal of income in Gaborone, young people are beginning to want-to-do in terms of the urban market. While the rural old of Kgaphamadi make use of the urban market in much the same fashion as the young, the significance of the experience is quite different. In particular, the elder do not see themselves in fantasy participating in market exchanges except to compensate for deficiencies in their subsistence production.

The young share with the old of eastern Botswana the values of success or progress in life: moving from beginnings to fruition through "plans and hands." But the young allow into this recipe numerous definitions of the social-cultural positions involved and multiple "means" to these ends. The young define success in terms of prosperity, and prosperity *can* be defined in terms of the accumulation of things money buys. The content of success for young people depends on the individual in question. Success in town, they say, is necessarily different from success in the rural areas; but it is attainable in both. There is no necessary opposition between wage labor and farming. Indeed most saw their lives as ideally comprising both, provided they could determine the mix.

Interestingly the young people were almost unanimous in stating that they had achieved very little, if anything, in their lives. Those in the rural areas are fully aware that attainments in farming, in making a marriage and home, require a longer time. Those in town are aware that the pleasures of accumulation they had sought in town are generally precluded by the high costs of subsistence.

What has been said should not suggest that the young have simply substituted piecemeal the values of universal salability for the values of culturally prescribed exchanges. Nor have they been able to add the marketplace to their life-worlds, keeping all else constant. There is a dialectical conflict between the want-to-do made possible by the marketplace and the want-to-do of Setswana. In the pursuit of "great works"—escaping from want, farming, and making a family—this dialectic is subtly apparent. In the tasks of keeping community and the law and building one's name, the conflict is marked. Young people both in town and in Kgaphamadi claimed that "in the life of Setswana a person is bound or held by the law [Kwa gaetsho ke tswerwe ke molao]." While the elders feel that the Setswana of old has lost much of its pertinence in the "modern" world and left them unprotected, the young in the main feel that tradition "protects" them too much, for often the things they would like to do involve breaking traditional patterns of privilege and obligation.

All young people want to farm, raise stock, and bring up their families in "the life at our home [botshelo jwa gaetsho]." But the definition of successful, progressive farming for most of the young has come to include explicitly both methods associated with European farming and the raising of crops and cattle not only for household consumption but for cash sale. Ideally, the young say, "progressive farming" should give a person enough surplus to raise funds for home improvement and other investment by which to improve farming even further. The young differ from the elders in seeing cattle both as something beautiful and as capital investment, which to be used effectively must be sold when the animals fetch their best market price. Elders sell cattle in moments of desperation; to sell at all means that to some extent one has failed. When they do sell, they choose the oldest, scrawniest, and most diseased of their beasts, which usually nets them very little cash.

It is primarily the young who are receptive to the changes in agriculture that are being promoted by the central government. It is principally they who respond to the incentives to adopt "modern" methods and sell their surplus in rural cooperatives. Kgaphamadi proved a very appropriate setting in which to watch the impact of government-directed change in agricultural practice. The national center for training agricultural demonstrators is the Botswana Agricultural College, which operates Content Farm as its center of applied research. Kgaphamadi borders on part of this farm. Its "demonstration effect" on Kgaphamadi and other communities was maximal because it was visible to all on a daily basis.

This adoption of modern farming methods entails to some degree an extrication from the customary reciprocities of the traditionally organized community. Changing agricultural practice is never simply a matter of replacing one technique with another. It involves changes in a wide range of social relationships with many members of the community and in a variety of contexts. The young, while willing to risk this alienation, pay a high price for it in that they sever themselves from many traditional community benefits.

Let me illustrate. One of the changes in agricultural practice being promoted in Botswana is the fencing of cultivated land and the concomitant plowing under of cereal stalks after the harvest as fertilizer. Fencing protects crops from damage by cattle and keeps stalks from being eaten; the plowing under of stalks increases the humus content of the soil. On first glance it would appear that such an innovation would involve no "costs" other than the labor and materials required to fence. Such is not the case.

The young very often do not have their own oxen to use as draft power, or they farm in an area where only a limited number of oxen can graze locally during the planting season. Hence it is customary that certain kinspeople will lend out their cattle for use in plowing. This is also ecologically sound, for if each household had to keep a sufficient number of oxen at the farm lands, the grass cover would soon be depleted.

Now with the scarcity of grass cover at the agricultural lands, especially at harvest time after the cattle have been browsing all summer, a principal source of food is the stalks of the cereal crops which remain after the harvest. Cattle traditionally roam through everyone's fields looking for forage. Traditionally land becomes communal after a harvest for purposes of grazing. If a person insists on fencing and plowing under the stalks, he is in effect saying to any person who is in a position to lend him cattle for plowing: "Let me borrow your oxen, but your oxen cannot graze on my fields." The reaction of the owner of the cattle, very often an older person, is to tell the younger person to go to hell.

Another common example of severing reciprocities can be seen when a young person, either through wage labor or less likely through entrepreneurial farming, is able to hire for wages someone's cattle, someone's tractor, or someone's labor. He, by payment, ends in his mind any obligation to render return service either to the people hired or to the community in general. He, after all, has bought and paid for the goods and services with money he earned, so why should he be available to work for others who are not in a position now to do anything for him? Suppose he invests in a water-storage tank. He will often feel he should charge *money* to let others have drinking water from that supply. He could simply request other reciprocities in lieu of cash. But a person who is in a position to require cash for investment in modern farming usually does not need labor as much as he needs money. Charging cash for water is not considered wrong in Tswana communities, but it does place social relations on a new footing of fee-for-service where many people lack cash.

Should a young person decide that capitalization of his farm requires cash from outside, he may leave the community and seek work. Now money earned in this way he will look on as his own. He may feel obligated to support indigent parents, but the obligations to redistribute wage earnings are far less extensive than were the traditional obligations to distribute food, stock, and game animals. Moreover, because this person's absence prevents him from being of help to the community, he himself will have to buy and pay cash for many goods and services that he might have received on the basis of reciprocal exchange in kind had he remained an active member of the community. Thus young people often wind up having to spend their cash earned abroad on goods and services traditionally provided by communal reciprocities. In this case they are simply exchanging one form of economic expenditure for another with no net gain for use as investment.

Young people, both in Kgaphamadi and in Gaborone, say that they want to leave the rural areas because of dire necessity. But they also express a strong desire to extricate themselves from the many felt disadvantages and burdens of life at home. When a person leaves home for these reasons, the Tswana call it "escaping" the home (*go toba; go ngwepa*). Those who, for various reasons, continue to remain away are called "people who have become repulsed by the (home) breast [*makgwelwa*]."

Many of the young people in town reported that they rejected the village thinking they would escape onerous obligations, earn money in town, and return home in a more advantageous position. This project is usually thwarted because it is almost impossible to accumulate a grub stake in town, except perhaps over a very long period. The inability to amass money quickly, coupled with the continuing desire to avoid becoming enmeshed in village and family obligations, often forces the young Tswana into a pattern of circulatory migration, either between home and the mines or between home and town, even when the climate might permit a greater stabilization of residence on the farm.

The young *lekgwelwa* cannot completely sever his ties with the rural areas, however, as the farm provides some security against unemployment abroad and his inheritance of both stock and lands can be affected by his loyalty to his elders. However, despite the continuing importance of kinship ties in providing a structure for inheritance of wealth in the absence of a will, the increasing importance of cash as the connection among all people, together with a rise in the number of people absent from home, has served to undercut the significance and authority of many kinship-based relations. This is particularly marked in the changing role of lineage in building families. Since building families is one of the most important "great works" for every Tswana, we must examine how changes in this institution have affected the values of wanting-to-do.

The young have in the main sought to escape many of the obligations of traditional marriage, particularly as these involve the prerogatives of their lineages. Younger people wish to increase the autonomy of the nuclear family with respect to the obligation to share labor and decision-making with relatives on both sides of the family. This is particularly true as regards the burdens of marriage annulment and divorce—events of increasing frequency. While the young concede the importance of kinspeople in helping to make marriage payments (bride wealth) and in bequeathing land and stock, they wish to reduce many of the obligations entailed in these exchanges. In town the sentiments of love and compatibility are becoming conscious motives for marriage. While the legitimacy of marriage and rights over children are still felt by most to lie in the exchange of bride wealth, many of the young believe that the burden of making bride wealth payments is too great for what one gets out of it. The honor and dignity of the traditional conjugal union is readily acknowledged, but the "interference" of kinsmen in home matters which such a contract implies is becoming increasingly resented. Wage labor is now more than ever a means for a young man to accumulate the bride wealth that every father demands as a right in return for the loss of his daughter. This means that the young man's father has less control over the son in the marriage than was the case when he and his close blood kin provided almost all the cattle for making the bride wealth payments.

This ambivalence concerning the social controls created by bride wealth is reflected in young people's attitudes toward investment in their own children's lives. Elders all express the desire that their sons and daughters should be educated. While there are definite cultural stipulations of the kind of work men and women should aspire to, the older Tswana have similar hopes for the education and economic success of all their children, regardless of sex. The young, however, are very emphatic about not wanting to invest as much money in a daughter's education. They "fear their daughters will simply run away to live with their husbands and their people and hence no longer contribute to the support of the father's family." As one young Kgaphamadi respondent stated: "Daughters are foreigners. They will run to distant lands once they marry, and contribute nothing to their parents. So why invest in their education if it will only benefit their husband's people?" The elders, who revere the bride wealth institution and have all been married with bride wealth exchange, do not see investment in their daughters as onerous. What they resent are young men "trying to impregnate and steal their daughters without paying bride wealth." The young men, for their part, are quite ready to receive bride wealth payments, but they are keenly aware that there are plenty of men in the world who, like themselves, wish to be free from the responsibility of raising bride wealth. They want to invest a minimum amount in their daughter's productivity, at the same time hoping to receive a dignified, maximum possible bride wealth payment. I had no difficulty in pointing out this self-serving opportunism. While they concede this, they feel little guilt in holding such contrary views.

The obligations of a young man to his wife's kin and to his own lineage, which continue on into his marriage, are a central aspect of Setswana law. Young people's desire to reduce these obligations, the elders claim, is "throwing away the parents" or "throwing away the law." To do this the young person must often leave the home community and take up life elsewhere, increasingly in towns. Thus the whole family become "escapees." The tension and anxiety associated with rejecting one's parents in this fashion, while striving to "make it on one's own," are considerable. The world of independence is rough and insecure. Failure in many tasks is very likely. A result of this is that many young people expressed strong regrets at having thrown away their parents and rejected the community of kin. Associated with this conviction that escaping home was a mistake is the equally widespread belief that the kinspeople of the person are envious of the fact that he is seeking progress abroad. This envy leads them to attempt to thwart the young escapee in his project of work. Many setbacks and failures in town or in entrepreneurial farming among young people are accounted for by imputing malevolent envy to their own kin. On the other hand many would concede that failure to listen to parents and receive the law explains their current failings.

While the young are like the old in wanting to escape poverty, to farm, to build families, and with some modifications to keep community and the law, they place this wanting-to-do within new horizons. For the elder what a person must do and what he wants to do are nearly coterminous. Both the past and the imagined future are constituted in the light of a coincidence of want, necessity, and intended action. For the modern young, the province of wanting-to-do is becoming more vast than their felt powers to act. This divergence of want-to-do and power-to-do is associated with the younger Tswana's belief that he will probably never be satisfied in life. Prosperity for the young has come to include "things." The world of things, unlike the world of "doing," is potentially limitless. Many young have come to see their impoverishment in terms of the gap between the "properties" they actually possess and what it is theoretically possible to attain. They see in fantasy their zone of reach including much of the material world purveyed in the market. The elders, in contrast, continue to see this world of things as in large measure irrelevant to all their projects of action.

To some extent aging, which includes the process by which a person invests his lived past with new meanings, can account for the differences between young and old. But the material conditions of life in Botswana are themselves changing. The environment, the empirical ecology of values, is itself undergoing alterations. Hence we should expect that the age-related changes in the life-projects of the young, while indubitable, will probably not replicate the changes that occurred in the lives of their elders. Just how much the differences in value associated with wanting-to-do and its horizons depend on age cannot be asserted with confidence. However my impression, from the testimony of elders, is that the emphasis on materialism and accumulation and the schism between desire and performance cannot be traced entirely to changes in culture but are in part age-dependent aspects of a continuously changing project of life. In other words, the contrasts between young and old in eastern Botswana may be reflections of standpoints from which life is invested with meaning, standpoints which form a continuum from youth to old age. The regret and remorse expressed by many of the town-dwelling young at having escaped from home and rejected their parents' advice—merely trading town poverty for home poverty—suggests their deep, if ambivalent, identification with the essential values of wanting-to-do in Setswana culture.

Mother and child in the *lolwapa* (courtyard). "For women, wealth and pride are children."

Makonteraka (contractees) just home from the South African mines enjoying a *pafana* (gourd) of beer.

Inspanned oxen—a technique borrowed from Europe.

In town, ox and cart are replaced by horse and wagon.

View of Kanye, a large Tswana village (*motse*), capital of the Ngwaketse District.

View of housing in Soweto, Johannesburg, South Africa.

Dithapelo (prayers) are sung by women before the meal. The author participates, observes, and records.

Traditional doctor and herbalist in Kgaphamadi. He charges only if he succeeds in curing the patient.

Hauling water is young girls' work.

Children of the author's nearest neighbors in Kgaphamadi. The eldest girl attends school, as her dress uniform suggests.

Old men select a suitable animal for slaughter in preparation for a feast.

A feast means a slaughter and tasting meat. Here a goat is killed by piercing the throat and lower brain stem.

Rre Segatlhe "discerns" by throwing bones. He is foretelling events in the young boy's life.

The *saranguri* (derivation of the word unknown to author). The instrument is played both in solo performance and to accompany singing.

Cooking hut in a Tswana homestead.

7 THE HORIZONS OF DOING:
EXPECTATION, EVIL, AND THE HERO

Introduction

Like any behavior that forms part of a project of action, wanting-to-do exists within a horizon of symbolically represented meaning. This horizon includes the retrospective interpretation of the past in imagination—one's personal past and the past of the world—and the projection of present meanings and interpretations of the past into a future conceived in fantasy. I want to examine two important and interrelated aspects of the horizon of wanting-to-do: (1) expectation, in particular hope and fear, and (2) the most "primitive" beliefs concerning the nature of reality, especially time.

The Tswana, like all people, take account of "reality" in terms of emotionally held expectations or anticipations of significant events. Among the most important of the modes of expectation that constitute the future are hope and fear. The Tswana, like ourselves, believe that they live in a world where qualities of coping can make an important difference to what one reasonably hopes for or fears. But human action and will cannot *determine* existence, for existence is to some degree controlled by a transcendent reality (or, as the Tswana say, "created order [*tlholego*]"). No matter how *resolved to do and achieve* a person is, he is still to some unknowable degree *determined by creation.* While fantasy is free to depict a future of any form, the Tswana resist, as we have seen, the creation of an opposition between fantasy and intention to act. Intention to act, therefore, constrains the content of expectation, including hope and fear. As action is the principal mode of embeddedness in a material world, the Tswana regularly enlist even the "fabulous" in fantasy in the service of affirming a world to be lived.

The objects of hope and fear—events (including one's own actions) in the world—are constituted in relation to the Tswana cosmogony of the created order. In the Tswana view, the created order is essentially moral and purposive. Good and evil underlie all events in the universe. Expectation, then, is based on moral and purposive uncertainties, as well as on uncertainties associated with simple probabilities of the occurrence of events. In this chapter I will briefly examine the way the Tswana constitute the experience of uncertainty in terms of expectation (hope and fear), and how they relate themselves subjectively to the moral order in terms of lived time and in terms of moral assays of social action: evil and the heroic.

The Senses of Time

We cannot provide an interpretation of the hopes and fears expressed by the Tswana without first suggesting an outline of how the sense of time is constituted in Tswana consciousness. While the Tswana lack a systematic philosophy of time, their conscious hopes and fears (which, a priori, affect and reflect any projection into the future) cannot be understood without looking at the metaphysical, if tacit, concept of time they presuppose.

Time is fundamental; it is "one of the essential 'parameters' of personality" (Gurevich 1976, p. 229). "Representations of time are essential components of social consciousness, whose structure reflects the rhythms and cadences which mark the evolution of society and culture. The model of perception and apperception of time reveals many fundamental trends of society and of the classes, groups, and individuals comprising it" (Gurevich 1976, p. 229).

While I agree in general with Gurevich's position, I would argue that the phenomena designated by the word *time* are multifarious and that not all senses of time can be characterized in this summary way. For example, there is a sense in which time is a universal human dimension, an "inner necessity" for consciousness itself. There are particular conditions of knowledge, metaphysical and empirical, which define, measure, or signify time and which are themselves culturally and historically variable. The relationship of time to significance and meaning, existence and being, may have both universal and culturally particular aspects. In discussing the senses of "time" we must therefore be very clear what we are talking about.

As I have just implied, there is an intimate association between sub-

jectivity—as manifested, for example, in hope and fear—and time consciousness. The Tswana, like most preindustrial peoples, represent this
intimate association mythically. Merleau-Ponty says of these representations: "There is more truth in mythical personifications of time than
in the notion of time considered in the scientific manner, as a variable
of nature itself, or in the Kantian manner, as a form ideally separable
from its matter" (Merleau-Ponty 1962, p. 422).

To understand Tswana time consciousness, we can profitably reflect
on our own. But a crucial question must be borne in mind: what effects
do the conventional public measurements of time have on the subjective
experiencing of time, both the time of "inner duration" and transcendent world time? In trying to answer this question, I will be guided by
three suppositions which cannot be substantiated here: (1) overt cultural schemata for defining and calibrating time are functions of specific
provinces of meaning and are therefore heterogeneous; (2) the effects of
these schemata are limited to specific provinces of meaning in the life-
world and do not therefore globally affect time consciousness; (3) at
the most basic level of time consciousness, all peoples are alike. This
most fundamental time consciousness is one of the factors that constitutes our existence as a biologic species. An implication of these statements is that scientific theories of time in Western cosmology have no
more effect on the everyday time consciousness of Europeans than they
do on that of the Tswana. While the Newtonian conception of absolute
time has in limited spheres become part of our commonsense experience, it has not endowed Western time consciousness with any unique
attributes.

Kagame (1976) in a provocative essay on the "empirical apperception of time and conception of history in Bantu thought" has tried to
adduce the metaphysical foundations for "Bantu" time consciousness
through an examination of certain syntactic and lexical regularities in
the surface structure of various Bantu languages. While his findings are
plausible, they could, and probably do, apply to all peoples to one
degree or another. Any effable theory of time can find some empirical
support by analysis of the surface structure of language, for sedimented
in the faculty for human language as such is the capacity for representing any cognoscible conception of time. Given the freedom to pick
and choose one's linguistic domain, one could find structural evidence
or parallels for any body of cultural thought in any language. The only
way around this dilemma is to specify a priori the conditions under
which the analyst would *abandon* his claim that the particular concep-

tion of time adduced from the surface structure of the language comprises the phenomenally "real" conception of time found among the speakers of that language.

In my view evidence of the *variable* aspects of time consciousness is to be found in particular social formations—in the material aspects of life and the way they are experienced—not in surface linguistic structures. As life is not homogeneous, neither is time. The "time of the ancestors" makes use of a very different temporal sense from what is deployed in establishing "the best time in a foot race." The Tswana have and always—as far as I know—have had at hand both these and many other concepts of time, as we do. The difference between us lies in the degree to which we make use of these varying conceptions in daily life, in the conscious or unconscious knowledge associated with specific domains of action. No society has a unitary time consciousness.

If one undertook to understand Tswana "time" by examining locative constructions in Setswana, one might conclude the Tswana have discovered both that the coordinate system of space includes that of time and that duration cannot adequately be explained by reference to linear, quantified time. The tense system gives evidence of the existence of Newtonian absolute time, including the notion of time extending into an infinite future and into a finite past. But this is all quite trivial and arbitrary. Much more central to us and to the Tswana is the fact that most time is not empty—that it is filled with a plenitude of meaning and participates in that meaning inherently.

Thus the key to understanding specific hopes and fears among the Tswana is a knowledge of the cultural meanings which connect past and future in terms of the overall Tswana conception of time. It is also necessary to understand how the advent of European institutions has altered both cosmogonic ideas and the particular meanings that connect past and future. A pictorial representation will help me to present the "traditional" Tswana cosmogony as it was explained to me by various Tswana respondents (see figure 1).

What this pictorial metaphor highlights is the *two-dimensional* and hence spatial character of time. To understand lived time it must be realized that there is a coordination of progressive but atemporal cosmologic time with progressive world time. The Tswana believe that there was a creation—a beginning to the cosmos—but that beginning continues throughout cosmologic time and is hence always present. It is an eternal existent. World time is orthogonal to cosmologic

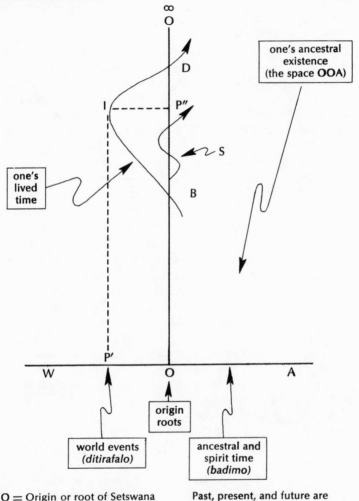

FIGURE 1
PICTORIAL METAPHOR OF TSWANA
TIME-CONSCIOUSNESS

one's ancestral
existence
(the space OOA)

one's
lived
time

world events
(ditirafalo)

origin
roots

ancestral and
spirit time
(badimo)

O = Origin or root of Setswana
B = Birth of an individual
D = Death of an individual
S = Spirits
I = Individual at given moment of existence = [P', P'']
O–O = Cosmologic time (atemporal, eternal present)
O–W = Axis of world time; space of world time: OOW
O–A = Axis of ancestral time; space of ancestral time: OOA
A–W = Existing time, union of world and ancestral time

Past, present, and future are
points in *two-dimensional* space.

time and is finite. Moreover, existing time has two aspects, both of which are given in the origins: world time and ancestral time. World time and ancestral time, while in complementary positions vis-à-vis the individual, parallel one another, each participating continuously in the origins of the cosmos. The basis for both the cyclical and the unique, progressive nature of world events, lived time, and ancestral time requires the conjoint role of cosmologic and existing time. The movement of the arrow along the axis of cosmologic time describes a path that takes one from the origin through life to death—that is to say, back to the origin. While the origin is atemporal and eternally present, existing time (world time and ancestral time) moves along the origin continually, sometimes close to it, sometimes far away.

These two senses of time (existing time and cosmologic time) are required to understand Tswana lived time: age and aging. Age for the Tswana cannot be the linear and homogeneous spatialized time of Newton applied to a biological definition of life. For that matter, most nonliterate Tswana do not "know their age" if it is conceived in this way. For the Tswana age has its most important basis in a set of social and ancestral relationships. Age is one's relation to a social order whose duration can only in part be conceived in terms of world time, for social order is only partly in the world of the living. Life in the world of the living is an aspect of life as a whole, not a period of time. The social order includes essentially the existence of the not living, who in virtue of being ancestors are closest to the origins of the society and the people. Positive world time for the Tswana individual comprises a movement forward to a stage that is like the beginning. The condition of the past—the ancestors, God, and their union—lie at the forwardmost extension of a person's anticipation of his being. The past of the world (*ditirafalo*) is unclear to the Tswana but will be clarified in the "time to come"—that is, when one is united with the ancestors who embody the final order established in the origins of Setswana.

In this context a person's age can be conceived of in terms of nearness to the ancestors—closeness to the cultural root (*modi*) which ancestral existence embodies. Age also represents the accumulation of experience. Accumulation of experience replicates to some degree knowledge of the past—that end to which the future is headed. To put this metaphorically, for the Tswana aging is a simultaneous movement in two directions away from a center: to a primordial past which is the goal of the future and to the end of one's future, which is defined in terms of experience accumulated while alive. The Tswana believe children are quite close to the ancestors, to the final order which is also the beginning. Growth cuts one off from this spiritual closeness to the ancestors. But with continued growth into the time when one will become "a man of long ago," closeness to the ancestors is again increased. Many Tswana claim that the very young and the very old understand one another well, in part because they share knowledge based on closeness to the origins of Setswana. While a young child's knowledge of deep Setswana is accounted for in terms of his recent propinquity to the ancestors—children "come from" the ancestors—the old man is wise both because he is growing closer to the ancestors and because he has world knowledge or experience. Moreover, the Tswana concepts of age and time are not uniform. The interpreted meanings of these concepts change with age, as the individual constantly redefines and reconstitutes his own biography.

Time, as I have said above, is not an abstract, conceptual continuum which exists in virtue of linear relationships between distance and velocity. For the Tswana time is composed of events. In virtue of this, living is an accumulation of time, not the passage of time, for living gives rise to wisdom and to the memory of experiences—the sine qua non of time. Because time is an aspect of events, the past is rich with experience and "deep in time." The future is shallow and, in imagination, rather impoverished. Its existence is composed largely of events normally extrapolated into the future. "Possibility" for the Tswana lies in the interpretation of the past, not in the imagining of an indeterminate future.

Time cannot be scarce, nor can it be lost. A Tswana does not suffer from shortage of time as he grows old. Time is not a resource and is never thought of as a scarce commodity. Time has no opportunity cost.

These qualities of time intersect with the qualities of age in determinate ways. Aging is experiencing. Aging is "seeing with one's own eyes [boitebatebelo]." Influence in the community depends on the degree to which one has accumulated experience. Experience, to be of value, must be remembered; it must become a part of the self. In Setswana the idea of "advice" or "counsel" is closely linked to the concept of recalling prior experience. Knowledge for the Tswana is "remembering things past." The Tswana equate forgetting with lack of knowledge or ignorance. They say: "To have forgotten is similar to being puzzled."

It is against the horizon of these beliefs concerning time and age that I shall try to explicate hope and fear. Both hope and fear have reference to emotionally freighted uncertainties and are predicated upon the temporal style of existing time and upon beliefs concerning cultural origins. In this discussion we shall see that the fundamental grounding of hope and fear lies in the individual's believed-in closeness to the atemporal continuum of cosmologic time: that is, the ordinate of cultural origins.

Expectations: Hopes and Fears

A fundamental fact of life for most modern Tswana is that the known world as well as possible imagined worlds no longer exist in terms of the traditional conception of creation—the cultural origins. The European invasion of the Tswana world has challenged their conception of the created order. Hope and fear for self, family, government, work, and habitat no longer orbit around culturally circumscribed moral uncertainties; *they participate in uncertainty about the basis for uncertainty itself.*

In traditional Setswana the world-time future is shallow or thin because it partakes more or less directly in the cultural origins. While cosmologic time is atemporal and infinite, making possible an open future, only specific deeds and events are unpredictable, because the "time to come" participates in the cultural origins as much as does the past. Tswana cultural cosmogony—like a grammar—does not specify what is to happen; it simply provides a scheme that allows a person to know that whatever happens, it can be understood and coped with in terms of the cultural knowledge at hand.

Now many Tswana frankly admit that certain events, especially the advent of the Europeans, have "falsified" this cultural competence. These events have shown that things can happen which they cannot interpret by means of the knowledge at hand. The trajectory of lived time and world events is leaving the cosmologic axis of ordinates. In the traditional cosmogony, meaning lay in placing events in the context of the created order. The history of events was a changing but undeniably meaningful manifestation of cultural postulates. Time for the individual was oriented not to a temporal past, present, or future, but to an atemporal and omnipresent origin with beginning but no end. Today for most Tswana the questioning of belief in cultural origins has created the spectre of *a future that is not only infinitely more open but also unintelligible.*

These observations are aptly summarized in the following words of an elder from Kgaphamadi, whose sentiments were echoed by most of the other fifty-three males and twenty-seven females interviewed:

"We do not understand this idea of modern government [*goromente*]. We do not know if it will ask us for our hopes, so how can we have any hopes in the government that it will do anything at all? *With the past gone, what can we know of the future* [emphasis mine]? To hope means to have knowledge; we lack knowledge of the future because we have been cut loose from our origins (roots). The future is just confusion. Rain is all we hope for. We know that makes everyone happy. Everyone should have enough to eat, to have cattle and plow extensively."

While the Tswana claim to have been severed from their origins, one aspect of the tradition that remains is that they continue to express their hopes and fears in terms of a collective orientation. All of the specific objects of hope—rain, jobs, minerals, cattle—should be available throughout the land (*lefatshe*) in order to avoid "consumption violence." A curious corollary of this collective orientation and keen awareness of fair distribution is the surprisingly widespread desire to have Europeans come to Botswana to lend a hand. Consider, for example, the following words of a young woman from Kgaphamadi:

"Europeans are not like Tswana; they are idea-sharing people. They are willing to come and teach us what they know. Tswana are idea-hoarders. We need a light for the future. We seek therefore close relationships with Europeans who come to Botswana to share their knowledge and abilities. Europeans have a constructive attitude toward the development [*tswelelopele*] of the Tswana people. They realize our problems, yet they are aware of their own limitations and their mistakes. Europeans do not moralize about their strengths and weaknesses. They do not try to hide their mistakes. The Europeans can bring a light to Botswana."

"The light for the future" harks back to my remarks about the way the future is grounded in the cultural origins. Almost all Tswana express similar hopes and fears for the future. But the horizon of those hopes and fears—their relation to intention to act—sharply distinguishes various groups of Tswana. All Tswana hope for rain, employment opportunity in Botswana, peace in the land, education for their children, productive agriculture and animal husbandry which will net a cash income as well as food subsistence. The only fear expressed by any Tswana which entails a negation of their hopes is shortage of rain. For almost no Tswana did significant fears center upon the *failure to realize hopes*. Thus few or no Tswana feared their children would lack education, feared lack of employment in Botswana, feared agriculture would not produce a surplus for sale. Fear is rather related to current problems projected into the future: fear that current deficiencies will continue.

This non-mutually exclusive, nonexhaustive distribution of hope and fear is consonant with the overriding predominance of the value of "want-to-do" in Tswana culture. The Tswana do not spend time in creating fantasy worlds, either optimistic or pessimistic, and then systematically comparing them with their actual lived world. They use their imagination primarily for coping with reality as it presents itself in their culture. In their thinking about the future, both hoping and fearing are clearly subordinate to the intention to carry on and struggle within the limits of current resources and liabilities.

In the West we tend to celebrate hopes and fears: psychiatrists diagnose them as projections of fundamental anxieties or other basic personality traits; businessmen tout them as the basic stuff of entrepreneurship; Christmas is a time when children's fantasies come true. The Tswana do not accord that kind of importance to the hypothetical future.

There are, nevertheless, marked variations among different groups of Tswana in regard to the role played by hope and fear in "extending" individual existence into the future. These variations, while circumscribed within the basic scheme of wanting-to-do, comprise a horizon for that wanting-to-do which imparts to it an added dimension of meaning. Most Tswana who have lived extensively in town and the younger Tswana of the self-subsistent rural areas relate themselves to the uncertainties of the future by identifying with some aspects of the colonial political economy. The elders of Kgaphamadi are resolved to struggle against the "confusion" of the future but have little concrete hope or fear that "modern" institutions will help them. The Kalahari Tswana exhibit a striking and quite un-Tswana dejection and negativism toward the future.

These observations are suggested by the following citations from Tswana respondents, one from Gaborone, one from Kgaphamadi, and one from the Kalahari:

> "We can no longer work toward our purposes [boikaelelo]; we work instead for money. With money we can hope to achieve our purposes. . . . Our hopes for the future are therefore hopes for what money can do for us. We want to work and make money in order to progress in life." [Young man from Gaborone]

> "The key to progress in this modern life is not hope about the

future or wishes about what one might have done but rather the determination to struggle with life as it is. To count on government to help is useless. Is the government going to ask me about my hopes? Of course not. Can the chiefs help? No, they lost their chiefly roles [*maano*] when they became government employees. The future is confusion so determination is the only hope." [Elder from Kgaphamadi]

"As for me, I hope we have white people come and settle here. We're Kaffirs (niggers), so if white people are around we can survive by working for them. Whites can drill boreholes for us. When there's no rain, they can help us with food. . . . I hope the government will make good laws to govern us well. I hope it makes jobs and will offer us rain, cattle, sheep, goats, and yellow meelies in drought times." [Elder from the Kalahari]

Urban Dwellers and the Rural Young

The urban dwellers and the young of the rural areas hold out great hope that the government will somehow be able to help provide a means to successful farming. It is among this cluster that the clearest and most articulate concepts of the nation Botswana and its government [*goromente*] exist. These concepts are somewhat distant, but they are associated with specific hopes and fears. Indeed, the fears of this group primarily have to do with physical habitat (lack of rain), while the government is a focus of hope—the hope that it will provide the resources necessary for the continuance of traditional life. Most of these Tswana express the hope that Botswana will never become a land of police and passes like South Africa, with which all of them have had extensive experience. Equally they hope that there will be no wars or "terrorists" in Botswana such as they hear of in the parts of Africa to the north. While all see civil society in Botswana as the antithesis of that in South Africa, they use South Africa as a model of the kind of productive economy they hope the government will allow Botswana to have: jobs, minerals, and extensive plowing.

In regard to agriculture, all these Tswana hope for cash cropping and animal husbandry which entails some combination of the value of wanting-to-do and purchase of the good life by the means available in an industrial economy.

The hopes these Tswana express for their children exhibit the kind of protean fantasy typical of Western society. Both in its stereotypes and in its formless optimism, this hoping departs remarkably from the restraint that characterizes the traditional Tswana formulation of plans and purposes. The Tswana hope that their children will have prominent positions in the government, hold high-paying jobs in firms, or work as wage-earners in agriculture. The old, but not the young, express a strong desire that their children will have prosperity, though they stipulate that they should not become so wealthy that they despise others. The elder envisage their daughters and granddaughters, as well as their male descendants, getting an education and working in the wage sector. The old, with one exception, said that their hopes for their daughters were the same as for their sons. Furthermore, in my observation they had in fact invested equally in their daughters' education. The young, on the other hand, stated explicitly that daughters are less worthy of educational investment than sons. "Daughters are foreigners. After one has paid for their education and upbringing, they leave to live elsewhere, no longer contributing to the wealth of their home" (young man from Kgaphamadi).

The old have hopes that in the future appropriate bride wealth will be paid; hence the worth of a daughter is *enhanced* by education. The younger fear that others will do exactly what they themselves would try to do—avoid or minimize bride wealth payments.

Fears for almost all Tswana are current anxieties or worries protended into the future. Life is a struggle, as we have seen, and all these Tswana have experienced setbacks that they fear will continue indefinitely into the future. Among town dwellers and the rural young, there is little fear that the future may be worrisome because different from the present. Indeed many of their hopes are predicated on the world's being very different—in terms of opportunity for wage labor, for example.

The urban old are the only group in this cluster that fear government turpitude and exploitation at all. They are afraid that the work of distributing wealth will be subverted by a government bent on hoarding and creating wealth for the few at the expense of the many. They see the possibility that the government is a self-serving coterie of "big-stomachs" whose large salaries have undermined their ability both to reason constructively and to identify with the problems of the poor.

This fear, however, is clearly subordinate to their fear that they will not be able to continue to support their families. Loss of work, famine, and inflation are all pressing. Yet their attitude toward these fears is one of determination to struggle against them. Several older Tswana said that "fear is something within one's consciousness (thoughts) [*dipoifo di mo kgopolong*]" and not something of the world. One town-dwelling elder made the following sage observation: "In Setswana of olden times, when fear existed, it was called ghosts or witches or wizards. I do not believe in ghosts; therefore, I am not afraid.

Most young people, but only a few among the elders, feared that their wants would continue to increase at such a rate that they would never be able to satisfy them. Said one: "Our abilities fall short of our wants, no matter how much progress is made in life." Several replies of younger respondents echoed this sentiment—for example: "We live in a world of money; the more we earn, the more we want. Acquisitiveness seems never to be quenched in humans. My shortages grow as I get more. I fear I will never be fully satisfied."

A corollary of this fear of growing wants and the "need" to attain them is the fear expressed by the rural young concerning envy and witchcraft. While only *one* town-dwelling respondent mentioned envy (*dikgaba*) and witchcraft (*boloi*) as objects of fear, *all* of the rural-dwelling young people mentioned them. This differential saliency of witchcraft and malevolent envy cannot be traced to "cultural" differences separating town and rural dwellers. All are equally acquainted with these fears, and all admit formally to a belief in witches and the potency of malevolent envy. Witchcraft and malevolent envy, both as objects of fear and as explanations of why one is being overcome in one's works, are usually imputed when it is perceived that someone is conspicuously progressing in life by other than completely accepted cultural formulas. One rural respondent put it this way: "Wealth in the modern world means trickery [*boferefere*]." While town dwellers concede that "success" in town does not represent traditionally defined progress, the association between tricks and wealth gained in town is deemed to be nearly inevitable.

Rural young people live in the context of ongoing communities where many concepts of labor and economy derived from institutions in town are being integrated into the practice of traditional agriculture. This is being done almost exclusively by younger farmers, often in explicit violation of elders' wishes and expectations and in contravention of many usages of traditional Setswana. Whether the young "entrepreneurial" farmer succeeds or fails, his "deviance" is obvious to all. Many younger farmers recognize that this individualism in the pursuit of progress in life is behavior that flaunts traditional culture—in the first place because they place themselves outside the community norms that restrict individual effort, enterprise, and accumulation. One very hard working younger farmer said to me: "I fear my own progress in life." When I asked why, he responded: "I fear *dikgaba*—the (malevolent) envy of others in this community, which can cause me to be overcome in my work."

In fact, none of the younger farmers was any more "successful" in farming than the majority of older rural people, who lacked almost completely such concerns about witchcraft and envy. The young people are simply thinking in terms of cash cropping and capitalization of farming outside traditional conventions. Their life *as intended* is quite different from that of the elders, though their *objective* behavior in terms of accumulation is no different. That this new life is being pursued within the context of a traditional rural community is creating far more "culture conflict" than is caused by the contrast of town life with rural life. The perception of deviance—flaunting of tradition—seemed to me to be far more acute in the case of young "entrepreneurial" farmers than with town dwellers, young or old, for they look on town as a province largely cut off from the cultural origins.

The fact that young rural Tswana sought wage labor on the nearby government farm—which deviates from traditional Setswana practices—did not arouse fears of conspicuous progress, for that work was undertaken merely to provide a subsidy for customary life. For the young, some of whom were engaged in no wage labor at all at the time, their intentions for a life of cash cropping created more felt conflict with the community (hence fear of envy and witchcraft) than the supposedly deviant act of finding wage labor away from home.

For most of the rural young and the town dwellers, "progress" in the future is seen to lie in the adoption of foreign practices, which they believe to be efficacious even if they do not fully understand them. They feel ambivalent about government and monetized exchange but do not find them totally mysterious. Both rural young and town dwellers are actively striving to cope with these new Western-style practices, in the belief that the new world is one in which one still wants-to-do. Most of the people I interviewed in town did not decry town life as corrupting but simply looked on it as an unfortunate necessity. These observations are mirrored in their answers to my questions concerning how they would dispose of a windfall of wealth. For example, I asked: "If some rich and generous person were to give to you five hundred Rand simply as a *gift*, what would you do with that money?" All of the respondents expressed wonder and puzzlement at such a highly improbable event. But after expressing this, they went on to state quite matter-of-factly, and in considerable detail, that they would invest this money in herds and capital equipment for farming.

All of the Tswana in this cluster responded after this fashion: "One must think carefully how to use such money. But I would buy a tractor, improved seeds, build myself a nice home at the lands, buy cattle, buy a plow, and escape the money expenses of town life." About half the rural respondents, but none of the urban respondents, stated they would invest the money in some piece of capital equipment which had little to do with farming and go into business (*thekiso*): to open a small shop and to buy a lorry and go into the transport business were two often-mentioned possibilities. All of the respondents except one mentioned banking part of the money as a hedge against the risks of investing entirely in stock and agriculture.

All of the respondents were awed at the size of this sum of money, and none seemed to realize how little of what they wished for such a sum would in fact buy. Most important, however, is the unanimity of the wish to find the wherewithal to live at home while engaging in a life project that entails a vastly increased dependency on the market economy and, hopefully, an increase in material prosperity. It is interesting that many rural young people proposed to spend the money on a commercial venture while all the urban dwellers wanted to return to fulltime farming.

The Rural Old

The rural old contrast markedly with town dwellers of all ages and with the rural young. These rural elders hold strong beliefs about the importance and efficacy of industriousness. This colors almost all their expressions of hope and fear. "Life is doing. The only purpose [*boikaelelo*] in life is succeeding by doing." For these people—even more than for the previous group—hopes and fears are the simple projection of current conditions into the future. While the town dwellers and the rural young speak of the future being uncertain because of the changes worked by modern institutions, the old say that the future is opaque because the new ways "have caused us to lose touch with our origins; these new ways have caused the past to die."

This opacity of the future is manifest in the universal lament of the rural elders that while a central purpose of life is to "form children into proper adults, in the modern world this is no longer possible. Children now make their own choices. So we cannot even hope that our children will grow to be proper people." The Tswana are just as aware as anthropologists that child rearing—the forming of proper adults—is the sine qua non of maintaining the culture.

Two hopes expressed by almost all of the rural elders were: (1) that the application of new (European) farming techniques would help overcome current shortfalls in agricultural production, and (2) that God would hear the prayers of his people and bring a better future—that is to say, one with current deficiencies remedied. Many who said this were not Christians, nor did they pray to God. They said that they did not pray because they were not sure that God heard prayers or, if he did, that he responded. *None* of the elders save one was making any effort to adopt modern farming techniques. In fact they were a core of resistance to their adoption.

The rural elders' hopes were invariably directed toward a traditional value currently lacking, especially cattle and productive farming. Several respondents said as an initial response to my inquiries: "We all hope for rain—a life removed from the troubles that now plague us." The reference to "rain" in this context implies that the good life requires no more than the *means* necessary to live in the traditional manner. Hope does not run ahead of what the culture prescribes. While rain for the town dwellers and the young is a crucial factor of production, for the rural elders it is a symbol of the ideal life as such.

The great fear for rural elders arises from their belief in the decline or death of the past. While many elders concede that modern administration, first the British and now the government, has checked the former tyrannies of the chiefs, they nonetheless claim that the power of chiefs to make rain has been squashed in the process.

The lack of rain makes periodic wage labor necessary. Most of the elders hoped for wage employment close at hand so as to be able to "work during the day and be home by night." But few of the elders expressed hopes to gain jobs, though in fact half of them were currently employed in wage labor at the nearby government farm. Clearly wage labor is much more peripheral in their fantasies about the future than is the case among those who have had town experience or who, like the young, see money and wages as a central part of their project of life. The rural elders again and again stated that their wage work got in the way of their doing anything. When I asked, "What are your most important daily activities?" several people employed at the farm responded: "I am currently doing nothing important, as I have to work at Content Farm."

The older women expressed views similar to those of the men, but they added one hope that not a single elder male mentioned: the desire that education be readily available to all in the future. The men would mention the hope that their children receive any education that was available when I asked specifically for their hopes concerning their children. But none mentioned education off the top of his head; whereas all the women did.

Older women would very often elaborate on this hope by stating that their husbands were "shrouded in darkness"—that they could not understand the modern world. In this connection the women often prove to be more adaptable than the men in seizing on ways to earn an income—cottage industry, petty trade, and so forth—and this income often exceeds in cash value what men can get by their preferred mode of earning money—the slaughter of livestock. The elder males have lost their dominance in the conjugal economy, and this together with their perceived powerlessness to understand the modern world produces a low self-esteem in comparison with that of town-dwelling people and the rural young. Part of the reason the young people's efforts to adopt new farming practices are perceived as threatening probably lies in the elders' declining self-esteem.

When I directed the attention of these elder respondents toward hopes for their children, the most frequent response was: "My children should prosper, that I may be helped in my life." Children are seen as part of the traditional system of kinship reciprocities, and their futures as a continuation of obligations to their parents. At the same time these elders realize that children more and more tend to "throw away their parents [*bana ba gompieno ba re alatlha*]."

Unlike the younger Tswana, the elders hope that their daughters and sons will receive equal educations. Indeed, most of the elders who had school-age children were sending their daughters to school at the same age as their sons, and just as regularly.

The prominence of traditional beliefs in the world of these elders is reflected in their response to my question concerning how they would dispose of a windfall of five hundred Rand. Most of the elders were bemused or perplexed by the simple content of this clearly counterfactual question. One said, "If such a person ever lived, he's now dead for sure." Another said, "I don't know what such a gift could possibly mean." After some prodding to ignore the meaning of the event and simply concentrate on how they would dispose of the cash, all but one of the elders said they would "first thank this person for his generosity in some way"—slaughter two oxen for him, name a child after him, and so forth. Thereafter each elder said he would buy cattle and farming equipment, and make improvements to the homestead. There was no discussion of investment strategies as such, simply a statement that they would purchase two or three items of capital importance to farming. Not one male elder mentioned educating his children with this money. Contrariwise each of the rural women mentioned sending her children to school. Women, I am quite convinced, are very influential in seeing that a share of the "surplus" of the household budget goes to educating some of the children.

The Kalahari

The single most distinguishing feature of the Kalahari in comparison with eastern Botswana is its very harsh environment, with the resultant poverty and dependence for continued existence on money sent home from abroad. The Kwena of the Kalahari have the same culture and traditions as the Kwena of eastern Botswana. But the material conditions of poverty profoundly affect the way they think of the future.

In gathering material in the Kalahari, the questions I asked were the same ones I posed to the other Tswana. The responses showed that the Kalahari Tswana desire and hope for a life-style quite like that of the materially better off Tswana to the east: rain, fields, cattle, a fine homestead. An ethnographer might conclude from the content of their hopes (and, perhaps, fears) that the expectations of the Kalahari Tswana are like those of eastern Tswana. This would be, however, a mistaken conclusion.

For example, I asked the Kalahari the question: "When you see the future in the best possible light, what do you hope this future will hold for you and your country?" Two answers were given frequently—one familiar, the other not encountered in the east. On the one hand, most respondents mentioned rain—"the rain of olden times." But most said as well: "To have white people here." Almost all of the Kalahari respondents expressed the view that white people could be a positive resource, especially in hard times. They also expressed hopes for the government which contained the same suppositions of dependency. For example: "I hope the government makes good laws to govern us well. The government can make a good life for us. I hope the government makes jobs for us and also will *offer us* [*go re neela*] rain, cattle, sheep, and goats." Said another: "I hope in the future the government will give me *mafisa* cattle."

These and dozens of similar responses conveyed to me the impression of a general hopelessness. The future in these answers is seen from the standpoint of idle fantasy. I probed insistently about how plausible it was that the government would *give* stock or rain. I also questioned whether it was desirable to have white people living all around. While conceding my objections, they insisted that this was better than the starvation they faced under current conditions.

There was indeed extensive hunger and malnutrition in these Kalahari villages during the time I worked there (1973-74, 1975-76). This led to a conspicuous look of fatigue and helplessness. For example, when I asked one man about his hopes for the future, he said flat out: "I have no hopes—we're all starving." Several respondents offered the answer: "I hope I do not have to become a thief" (the implication being that this might be necessary to survive).

When I turned the discussion to children, the kinds of hopes expressed for them reflected quite directly this dependency and helplessness. The most common immediate answer was: "I hope to see my children working (in jobs)." Respondents used the Afrikaans word *go bereka* or the *Fanakalo* word *go šhebetsa,* both of which imply selling labor in the European world. All elders hoped that their children would not have to go to the South African mines, but rather that there would be jobs in Botswana—mining jobs, to be sure. The youngsters in the Kalahari almost all said they were *most eager* to go (or go back) to the mines, as there was lots of money to be made there. They hoped to use that money to make purchases of material goods and livestock for themselves. The young, being very much preoccupied with migration, hoped that wages would continue to rise in the mines as they had in the past two years (1973-75).

Most elders presumed that their daughters would not work in the wage sector and most did not mention education as a feasible hope for them. Typically elder males said: "Women cannot work for themselves, so they should get married by *bogadi* (cattle payment to the bride's father), so they can pay back my feeding of them." For sons the elders' hopes were education to avoid mine labor and seeing them in "high positions" as salaried employees. These hopes were very diffuse and seldom included a specification of the kind of work they would like to see their children or grandchildren doing.

When I turned the attention of respondents to their fears and worries concerning the future, I received answers quite unlike those I encountered in other parts of Botswana. The following are typical of those made by older Kalahari.

"I fear illness, 'short blankets' (poverty), low wages, no jobs. Towns are leading to robbing. God must help; I go about 'speaking by heart' [speaking but not being able to trace the words to reasonable thoughts]. I fear witches and ghosts at night. I long for the time of Lentswe [Kgatla chief]. Then we had rains. Drought has ruined our culture."

"In the olden times the children wore *makgabe* [short open shirts] for good health. Now we must wear dresses. Botswana has lost its living by traditions. There is no initiation [of children into adulthood]. They just go to the mines and are destroyed. Seretse [Botswana's president] promised us a better life under self-rule. But he's creating more problems instead. There's no money, no jobs. We can't have confidence in our country. I . . . fear planes and bombs. . . ." [A female respondent]

This is sufficient to illustrate the extreme anxiety, depression, and melancholy I found in the Kalahari. Only once or twice did any Tswana in the east mention fearing witches, scorpions, or mambas. In my view these fears can only be understood as a kind of natural symbolism. Witches, ghosts, mambas, dreams of people one does not know, and speaking without perceived reason are cultural representations (which I cannot explicate here) of fear and depression that have exceeded the capacity of an individual to cope in terms of *intention to struggle*.

The narratives given by Kalahari respondents, especially the elderly, were disjointed. Their remarks often wandered rather aimlessly along. They did not focus on fear as such—referring to it most often in terms of *go tlhobaelo*—literally, that which causes one not to be able to sleep, but keeps one awake tossing and turning with troubles and worries.

The young adult Kalahari Tswana displayed much less dejection concerning their surroundings and their future. They were visibly buoyed, in fact, by the present horizon of their life—going to the mines. The idea of taking care of older people who were dependent on their remittances gave these younger Tswana a source of pride and satisfaction, at least temporarily. They spoke positively of the future providing jobs for everyone, "work for illiterates like me." Few of the young men mentioned education as a hope for themselves or their children (unless I directed their attention to the question of hopes for their children). The women, however, both young and old, waxed eloquent on the topic of education whenever I inquired of their hopes for the future. One woman aged about twenty-five said: "For women fulfillment is children and education; for men it is cattle and fields. With education I could work on behalf of my parents, for it is they who have made me a big woman (i.e., a first-born daughter who is married and has children). A woman without a husband has no dignity."

Many of the fears expressed by the young Kalahari Tswana coincided with those of the elders, but there was more bravura in their answers. Thus the young mentioned *dikgaba* as a fear, but a supposition in most of their responses, unlike those of the elders, was that these debilitating social diseases had yet to strike them. The young spoke, in a very focused manner and without evidence of depression, about their fear of mine accidents and loss of life, tattered clothes (poverty), lack of money to pay the witch doctor, and unemployment. Some of the young mentioned mass bewitchment of the population as a fear, but this appeared to be more a parroting of the fears expressed by older people than a reflection of overwhelming anxiety.

The people of the Kalahari responded to my hypothetical question concerning how they would dispose of five hundred Rand in a different way than the other Tswana. There was no long period of initial puzzlement or belabored discussion of how to thank the person or what such a windfall would mean. Rather both young and old immediately listed a set of purchases they would make to improve their herds, farms, or homesteads. As one said: "I would build a house with an iron roof so that all can see I'm no longer in poverty." There was none of the discussion, so typical in the eastern Tswana, about investment or the careful thought that would have to precede any intelligent disposition of such a large sum. The Kalahari seemed to lack the idea of planning in their thinking about how to spend money.

Conclusions

Those affectively laden forms of expectation we call hope and fear help to constitute the horizon of wanting-to-do. What one can reasonably expect to do in life is not exclusively a function of the industriousness born of desire. Luck, fortune, fate, and circumstance remain independent of man's ability to manipulate the environment. Yet the quality of expectation is influenced by how effective a person believes he can be in creating and carrying out projects in life. The Tswana are aware that theirs is a habitat that can overwhelm the individual. All have suffered incredible pain at its hands: decimation of herds, years with no harvest, death of kin and neighbors, coercive labor migration. Yet only in the case of the older Kalahari Tswana did I sense that the habitat had been able to stifle the primacy of "wanting-to-do" as a value in thought and action. The additive effects of the harsh Kalahari environment and the rigorous control of mine labor together constitute an egregious assault on the Kalahari Tswana, who would appear

situationally at least to be "determined from without." Certainly the
responses of the elders reflected something of the burden of this external domination. But even they asserted that work was something one
should want to do, as we saw in chapter 6. By no means did the Kalahari
elders act as if they lacked freedom of choice and an understanding of
their world. At the same time the crushing experience of "objectifica-
tion" manifests itself in their expression of hope and, especially, of
fear, a remaining aspect of which—evil—I will now turn to.

Evil

Many anthropologists hold that a nonliterate people's fundamental beliefs about knowledge and being are to be found embedded
in the structure of myth, ritual, legend, folklore, and so forth. The
kind of inquiry into topics like evil that we call "philosophical" is
generally not to be found in preliterate societies—or so it is claimed.
Indeed, the initial responses of my Tswana respondents to the question
"What is evil [boshupo] or bad [maswe] or wickedness [boikepo]?"
consisted of simple lists of the actions or dispositions in people that are
classified as evil. Very little was offered that could relate these diverse
evils to underlying philosophic precepts. Most respondents would
simply look puzzled if I asked, "Why does evil exist?" However, some
respondents were more reflective than others, and a few individuals
offered insights which I could then pose in propositional form to the
more reticent or puzzled. Invariably these elaborated theses about evil
were accepted as accurate by most of my respondents, who would then
be able to add articulate commentary of their own.

While I do not deny that much of Tswana cosmology does not exist
in propositional form, I would argue that we as anthropologists may
often be too ready to conclude that a people lack conscious knowledge
of a given topic if our particular questions do not elicit fluent or
effusive answers. Cultural knowledge and the capacity and desire to
expound it in an articulate manner are not uniformly distributed. A
cultural inquiry, therefore, must not confound knowledge-in-the-culture
with readiness to explicate that knowledge for curious strangers.

Ten categories of evil were named in almost every interview I held on
the topic, quite independently and quite unprompted: (1) The
sekebekwa, the chronic bad actor; (2) the criminal (e.g., the thief, the
batterer, the rapist); (3) the seganana, one who behaves indecorously,

who insults or is rude to others; (4) one who gossips maliciously, especially one who falsifies or misrepresents the words of another; (5) the lazy, indolent, helpless, shiftless person (*setshwakga*); (6) the person who is self-centered, egotistic, inconsiderate or inhospitable; one who is indifferent to the suffering of others; (7) the delinquent or neglectful parent who allows his child to grow up without the law; (8) the person who is envious of others and jealous of his own possessions and position; (9) poverty which is so severe as to destroy the understanding; and (10) political repression and injustice. Note that while some respondents mentioned witches and witchcraft as being evil, most did not; instead they suggested that witches were "responsible" for evil.

All respondents agreed that for a person to be any one of these is loathsome and despicable. Yet they all acknowledged that such people are commonly found. Their initial explanations for why such people exist fall into four non-mutually exclusive categories. Each "cause" is sufficient in itself to bring about all the ten evils cited.

First, some people have a propensity toward evil conduct built into their natures—an inborn or innate trait called *mokgwa*. Second, some people simply intend to be evil for reasons known only to themselves. People are free to be evil if they so choose. Third, evil can be the result of nonhuman agencies which are themselves intrinsically evil: spirits, wizards, witches, and so on, each of which can afflict a person with or without his cooperation. Fourth, people can learn to be evil, that is, acquire evil ways through lack of proper training and upbringing.

What is apparent as a common theme in each of these categories of evil is also acknowledged by the Tswana—namely, that "evil disrupts and pollutes social relationships [*bo senya botsalano jwa merafe*]." These evils are direct attacks against the social order as much as they are offenses against given persons. Evil is "the destroyer of social living"; it undermines a person because it ruptures his moral embeddedness in the existence of other people. Personality or self-identity is conceived by the Tswana to be essentially social. That which destroys the person does so by destroying the social bonds that *are* a person's identity. As the Tswana say, "I am a person (human being) in virtue of other people," and similarly, "For one to be requires (at least) two; one (by himself) is nothingness (death)."

Several ideas that are consciously held by most Tswana inform these categories of evil and make them meaningful by showing that they are not a disparate group but manifestations of underlying precepts in Tswana cosmology.

Flowing logically from the notion that evil is a disturbance or disruption of social relationships is the notion that evil, like wanting-to-do, is essentially performative. No Tswana in my sample of respondents saw evil as a diffused force or spirit which hovers over humankind occasioning wicked acts. Evil is rather to be found in the patterned action of social life itself. While the ultimate reasons for evil and its basic meaning are problematic for all Tswana, its existence is indubitable. In conformity with this way of looking at evil is the complete absence, as far as I could discern, of any complex, mythical account of sin. There are no symbols of sin or even of general "species defilement," and consequently there is no conscious formulation of species guilt or innocence. Human being has a moral dimension, but this does not have its foundation in transgression (guilt in the juridical sense) nor in inheritance of culpability and pollution (guilt in the sense of sin). The idea of obligatory atonement by humankind for its very being is absent from Tswana cosmogony. To be sure, there are precise conceptions of purity and danger (Douglas 1966). Purity is conceived of as correctness and probity in acting; danger as taint or pollution vis-à-vis the common weal or particular social relationships. But there is no a priori guilt which humankind must atone for. There are only behavioral shortcomings which must be remedied by penitence, recompense, or sacrifice on a case-by-case basis. Even the continuous or regular defilement manifest in disease or feuding is conceived not as part of the human condition, but rather as a foreign invasion or an affliction visited upon those whose performance is deficient.

Conceptions of evil are intimately tied to ideas of volition, choice, and responsibility. Conscience (*segakolodi*) for the Tswana means in the first instance awareness and active recall of those acts that are proscribed and the horrors that come from transgression. For us the primary sanction of this recalling or conscience is "guilt"—that pervasive self-wounding that takes place even in the absence of public discovery and overt punishment. The guilty conscience is cultivated in Western society as an internal control that operates where shame or fear of reprisal leaves off. For the Tswana, as far as I can tell, the notion of guilty conscience is anomalous. For them, only a person can be "guilty" and only for publicly acknowledged misfeasance. When a person is found guilty, the general disapprobation and ridicule that follows will (say the Tswana) produce shame—literally "cause the person to hide his eyes like the badger for fear he will be caught [*go tlabisa ditlhong*]." What a person must or must not do in the Tswana view is always a social act involving at least one other person. What I must do is what another can legitimately expect of me. Failure to do what others have a right to expect brings shame. But the Tswana do not, as far as I can tell, have any conception of unilateral moral obligation, where a person sets a standard for himself and insists he must abide by it, but simultaneously denies the right of anyone else to demand that he do so. The Tswana notion of moral obligation is like our notion of legal obligation; that is, it is bilateral. Our notion of the moral act that may violate legal rules because is it sanctioned by a conscience following privately held imperatives is anomalous for the Tswana. For them the moral and the legal are both bilateral, involving at least two parties in a relationship. Their very word for conscience, which means to recall or be reminded of acts, suggests this strongly social and empirical base for feelings of shame. Conversely, it discounts the notion of principles existing in thought alone, never manifest in actual social transactions.

A powerful sanction operating in most small-scale societies is public disapproval for misfeasances that become known. Since most misfeasances become known, this sanction is highly reliable. But many private thoughts or secrets may well not become known; hence, they cannot be misfeasances and cannot be negatively sanctioned. Following from this is my observation that the Tswana, while obsessively concerned with shame, are not disturbed at all by thoughts or even acts that they are sure will not be found out. Self-inflicted feelings of guilt seem remarkably absent. Where there is minimal chance of discovery and retaliation (e.g., when one is abroad), what one recalls—conscience—remains "clean." This "shame orientation" has important implications for understanding the behavior of Tswana outside their home communities, especially in large, anonymous urban areas where the mechanisms of social control typical of small, face-to-face communities no longer operate. This will be explored in the next chapter.

An aspect of Tswana cosmology which is manifested in the way they think of evil is their curious notion of the relationship of existence to reality and the concept of (moral) causation. Two or three respondents made the statement to me that "that which is evil is not part of the created order [tlholego]." This, to my ears, was a semantic paradox. How can something which exists not be a part of creation—i.e., of the universe. The key to resolving this seeming paradox lies in the Tswana distinction between creation (the properly, morally constituted universe) and existence. The former is a subset of the latter. Not all that exists is natural or part of creation; this applies in particular to evil.

The universe is at base a moral universe. Underlying all notions of creation are moral principles. There need be no contradiction between statements using the predicate "is" and statements using the predicate
"ought to be" in referring to the universe. For the Tswana the universe
is fundamentally endowed with morality and purpose. Thus evil, which
is the negation of morality, is spoken of as unnatural or not part of the
creation.

This view of the universe makes plausible the Tswana claim that certain acts (e.g., incest and the European suppression of black people) are
"unnatural"; they are literally bizarre and aberrant. Such acts are truly
evil—outside the boundaries of creation. The thesis that the universe is
moral also makes plausible the Tswana claim that poverty is evil. It is
unnatural—as incest is unnatural—that people should be starving. The
fact that people are starving suggests that some fundamental force is
working to upset the moral order. This force is evil, and it may include
everything from ancestral malevolence for earthly transgression to a
woman's violation of menstrual taboos and the spoiling of the world
by war.

These statements suggest what several respondents claimed explicitly
—that the moral basis of the universe is also causal. How things happen
in a moral universe is necessarily different from how things happen in a
universe based on machines and mechanism. "What one thinks," said
one Tswana, "can affect not only what one does, it can affect directly
what others may think and do, including the dead and the not yet
born." Each person's existence participates in a network of moral connections that links all people. "Even one's intentions can affect another person's life." This is exemplified in the domain of evil by the
polluting and debilitating effects of malevolent envy (*dikgaba*) and
jealousy (*lefufa*). Thus in principle there is no such thing as a *necessarily
private* thought or act. "Any thought (e.g., envying another's success)
can lead to circumstances where that person who is envied may be
overcome in his life struggle." "Envy is truly an evil because it can
destroy lives." So it is with jealousy. "To want to hoard one's possessions, to resent requests for help, can destroy lives or create ill-feeling
which can pollute the entire community, causing storms, crop failure,
winds, or locusts." Said several respondents: "The hot blood of envy
can force families to break up and make people leave home and flee to
a life elsewhere."

Embeddedness in a moral universe might suggest to westerners that
responsibility for misfeasances, for improprieties, for natural disasters

and troubles like plague or disease, might be extensive but hard to pin down. Indeed the Tswana do not have the wide-ranging category of causation we call "acts of God"—chance occurrences with devastating consequences. The morality of the universe implies that responsibility for everything that happens necessarily inheres in morally responsible agencies, including responsibility for those most heinous evils—unnatural acts like incest, poverty, envy, witchcraft, and so on.

Responsibility (called "answerability [*go arabela*]" in Setswana) is always moral. Even that subset of responsibilities which can result in liability to legal action are tied intimately to moral responsibility. Responsibility—whether established by adjudication or in some other way—requires personal remedy, penitence, compensation, propitiation, or other acts which restore the moral balance of the universe. To be found responsible for misfeasance or delict is to "have the fault [*go na le molato*]." Fault is the result of discovering responsibility for a disturbance of creation. Fault can inhere in witches, ancestors, or living people, and it can be widely ramified, implicating on some occasions a whole community.

Fault is not guilt or sin. Fault means the liability to make restoration, after which the moral balance is restored and the fault vanishes. The Tswana hold a very straightforward view of both responsibility and fault. From the standpoint of prevention and cure, their view of evil tends also to be matter-of-fact. The cure for evil is finding or establishing responsibility, verifying fault and remedying it. Once this is done, the moral order is restored.

Some Tswana expressed to me worries that circumstances in their life might become so desperate that they might be at fault for evil acts. None of these felt guilty, as far as I could see, for expressing these worries. Several respondents—usually Kalahari—made statements in the course of very matter-of-fact discussions such as: "I hope I don't become a thief" or "I fear I'll become a thief."

The problem of evil in Tswana culture is basically tactical: evil is to be avoided because the costs are high. To be accused of evil is to stand to lose much. But once retaliation or compensation is achieved, life must go on. No group could survive if it allowed its way of thinking about evil to seriously interrupt social relationships.

For the Tswana, then, evil is not a philosophical problem; it is constituted by a set of concrete types of unnatural behavior which disrupt communal life. A curious illustration of this is a statement made to me by a young farmer from Kgaphamadi (an illiterate and not a

Christian) which all other Tswana present said was *nonsense* but which we, I dare say, would endorse. I asked this man, "What is evil in the view of the Tswana people?" He replied, "Evil is not something that people do. Evil is an attitude to things. What is evil depends solely on what you believe in. For example, Jesus was called evil by the Romans. Yet we call him a hero. Evil is made by men just like religion is. When we do not understand life's problems, we create beliefs to hide behind, like religion." Six or seven other Tswana who were present when this statement was made disagreed strongly. They all argued against the "relativist" position taken by this young man. However, the assertion that "Jesus was called evil by the Romans, but we call him a hero" aptly prefigures the next horizon of doing—the heroic act.

The Heroic as Predicate

Introduction

To the Tswana the heroic is in a sense the negation of evil. The performative orientation of the Tswana view of the self suggests that the hero, by definition a person of action, presents a key metaphor of wanting-to-do. True heroes are seldom to be found, and heroic action is infrequently observed. Yet the heroic is not necessarily unusual behavior undertaken in unusual circumstances; it is instead a *certain mode of engagement with the everyday.*

The Tswana use the epithet "man of heroism" or "heroic [*monna wa bonatla*]" in everyday speech to refer to the prowess, courage, and especially industriousness which bring honor to the person and the common weal. This characterization implies a certain inertia in the world and an efficacious and valorous mode of coping on the actor's part.

To appreciate the full meaning and significance of the heroic, we must first understand the power of naming and self-naming to create what one is. For an individual to name or call an act "heroic" is a way of symbolically creating experience. Among the Tswana a traditional part of growing to manhood entailed learning to compose skillful and artistic praises for the heroic in poetic form, especially praises *of one's own putative heroism.* In my view this culturally sanctioned practice of predicating upon oneself the epithets of the heroic is central to understanding Tswana self-identity.

If symbols were merely representations of the empirical world—of history and social life, common sense and science—symbol use would clearly play a role quite subordinate to direct experience of the material world in shaping beliefs about the self. Logical positivists, vulgar materialists, and others argue just that: the symbol is nothing but a physical signal with certain properties of association or iconicity that allow it to become a surrogate stimulus for another object or event. In this view the symbol and the object for which it has come to stand in the learned responses of the organism are related to behavior, thought, and feeling in a similar manner.

A contrary view, and the one advanced here, claims that no adequate account of the meaning of symboling, including literature and poetry, can be attained if its field of reference is confined to the putative facts of material existence. The very unity of any object of experience is necessarily symbolic—a result of meaning, which can come only from a system of symbols. It follows that since symbols *express*—project a meaning that is part of subjective experience outside the person—the referent of a symbol must necessarily be *in consciousness* and not in the world. It is through symbols that the contents of consciousness can become objective facts of shared experience. Through symbols we can have "objective" views of another's subjective experience. This is the particular genius of poetry and literature.

We can now return to the hero. The literary expression of the heroic largely creates the world of the hero and his community. The creation of the hero cannot take place within "factual" material existence alone, for heroism is constituted for the most part of meanings which have no ostensive reference whatsoever.

Now the question we must ask of the Tswana and of their oral literature (especially poetry and fable) is this: can we reasonably assume that the meanings constituted in the literature represent such a significant definition of the good, the true, and the efficacious that they comprise an essential aspect of the Tswana self-ideal? Does this oral literature not only *re-present* belief, but also *constitute moral and affective meaning structures* for thinking about the self? If this is the case (and I shall so argue), the study of the content of oral literature and how people make use of it should yield strong and subtle indications of self-identity. In the case of the Tswana the connection between self-identity and literature is quite direct as they, traditionally at least, use many formulaic oral narratives as metaphors for "self-praising" and self-naming. This cultural practice of composing poetic narratives in which a person asserts his own heroism provides a means whereby the individual can situate himself in a world that transcends the givenness of the everyday and the closure of common sense. The poet makes for himself a phenomenal world whose fundamental reality is in imagination, and hence "fabulous." Insofar as experience affects self-identity, the symbolic world—especially that made for oneself—constitutes a force in building self-identity. For the Tswana the force of self-praising is to be found in the explicit practice of "naming" or "praising" one's identity.

Name

Fundamentally name (*leina*) stands for a person's reputation; it is the public assertion and recollection of what a person has done and the significance of those actions. Name, while symboled by a simple word or phrase, stands in a synecdochic relation to the whole discourse that has been carried on throughout a person's life about who and what he is. In this sense name is the most direct public allusion to a person's self-identity.

The word "name (*leina*)" in ordinary usage refers not to a proper designation of a person but to a genre of oral poetry which every Tswana (traditionally, at least) was expected to master—as a composer—in the process of growing up. In former times young adolescents were sent to "initiation schools" where they underwent a complex and lengthy rite-of-passage into adulthood. This rite was an extended period of instruction in the knowledge and skills associated with leading an adult life as a responsible member of Tswana society. As part of this schooling youngsters were taught how to compose poetic formulations which would capture the essential meaning of the various deeds the child would accomplish in the school and later on in adult life. Each child was taught literally how to compose poetic praises of himself. Public, poetic self-praising was explicitly taught as a prerequisite to acquiring a proper adult social personality. These praise poems composed *to* oneself and *for* everyone are called *leina* or (literally) "praise names."

These praises, while based nominally on the recalling and celebrating of events, are more importantly an overt symbolic creation of experience and particularly experience of oneself. Throughout life each Tswana would, more or less artistically, continue to add to his repertoire of self-praises. Some very gifted poets would be called upon by chiefs or other patrons to compose praises which would be sung or chanted on important public occasions. Reciters of praises—really poets who composed, formulaically, impromptu poems—were in much demand as part of festive public ceremonies. The Tswana learned from very early in life the value of these poetic expressions of belief about the self.

Tswana of all ages and in all communities referred to their name (in the full sense outlined above) as a "treasure" and a "resource." Name, according to many respondents, is something "a person thinks a lot about because it is constantly being affected by what a person does and says and what a person has done to him or said about him." Name is constantly in the making; it affects kinfolk, especially descendants, who will carry it. Names can kill and heal, impoverish and enrich, make great works and destroy them.

Generally praise names or poems are eloquent and compelling compositions in which a person ascribes favorable personality and behavior characteristics to himself, or has a poet do so. The most important feature of these attributes is that they are almost always *metaphoric*—allegoric, synecdochic, metonymic, ironic, sarcastic, etc. In other words, the inchoate *I*, the ego whose identity is being created and expressed in these poems, is given concrete embodiment and phenomenal reality in a universe composed of ideas or ideals that can *only* exist in a metaphoric world—a world of meaning expressed and referred to in poetic language. The Tswana do not grow up in a world where they simply identify with literary figures and adventures or project themselves into a literary realm by imagination; they are a people who literally make themselves the characters of their epics. A person's praises are about himself and are a part of the objective world of spoken words that makes up the individual's environment. In other words, in and through a (praise) name a person *creates* experience which transcends the givenness of everyday experience. By praising himself, the poet can alter the signification of institutionally typified meanings. He can, I suggest, transcend the determinism inherent in a life governed by cultural codes, rules, and preinterpreted meanings.

In present-day Tswana society the practice of traditional initiation is moribund; the art of formulaic self-praising is no longer explicitly taught. However, belief in the value of public assertion of one's deeds in formal, polite, and often poetic style is still very much alive. The imago—the self-ideal—of the hero constituted in eloquent literary presentations is very much a part of Tswana experience. All Tswana informants with whom I worked were conscious of many parallels between their own lives, communities, and values and the content of eulogistic poetry and animal fables. There were, however, many parallels which I alone discerned and communicated to the Tswana, and these often evoked or provoked reactions of embarrassment, laughter, anger, or denial.

My intervention in the interpretative process raises a thorny issue: are people conscious of or otherwise affected by unstated, implicit, or "deep" textual structures? In my view current structural analysis, with Lévi-Strauss as its major prophet, lacks a theory of meaning—that is, a theory to account for how structures known only by the analyst come to have phenomenal meaning for the naive "indigenous" hearers of the text. To be sure, structuralists point to "parallels" between text and social structure, or among texts in different societies, as evidence that something "deep" has been found. The "parallels" found are, however, invariably tautologous with the principles of structuralist description itself. When they are not tautologies, they are ex post facto inferences— declared to be parallels by the analyst after his analysis. In my view we need compelling evidence to justify impugning the meanings (given to a text by an indigenous hearer) as "false consciousness." Unless we can adduce from a naive hearer a specific kind of response which we have worked out beforehand and can theoretically account for as indications of a given deep structure, we have no reason to be looking for deep structures at all. In view of this criticism, my principal warrant for asserting that praise names and animal fables constitute expressions of the heroic in the life world of many Tswana is that most of my respondents made this very claim to me. I am passing along to you, the reader, for your evaluation, a claim made by the Tswana about themselves.

Poetics of the Hero in Setswana
Superficially the eulogistic poetry of the Tswana and related peoples of southern Africa is an evaluative recording of the deeds of chiefs, warriors, hunters, and plain folks who have engaged themselves heroically with the everyday. Some of these poems are praises sung to animals and even inanimate objects. Schapera (1965, p. 15) summarizes what he considers to be the significance of praises composed by or for Tswana chiefs: "In general, we may say, the poems deal mainly with events in which the chief was personally involved, or . . . with what was expected of him; there is occasional reference to other members of his family, and to past history. . . . The contents always include eulogies to the chief himself . . . , but the eulogy is generally related to some specific event, so that the poem is, in effect, a flattering account of

what the chief had done to distinguish himself." As to how the Tswana themselves think of such poems, Schapera says that he did not inquire into the matter fully but that he had the impression that in assessing a poem people looked mainly at its content and language. A poem is appreciated (according to one of Schapera's informants) "because it is full of history." Schapera adds (1965, p. 15): "Praises in general do seem to be appreciated more for what they say about a chief than for how they say it; i.e., than for what we would call 'poetic beauty.' They are regarded primarily as sources of historical information."

My own findings do not contradict Schapera's inferences; however, my respondents hinted at and even stated explicitly meanings of this poetry that clearly go beyond historiography and flattery. Their suggestions lead me to believe that the anthropologist or literary critic faces an interpretive problem more complicated and richer than Schapera's claims imply.

Let me give a simple illustration for my suggestion. During my field work in Botswana I had occasion to travel by car to Johannesburg with Rre Segatlhe, my host in Botswana. When we arrived at the South African side of the international border separating Botswana and South Africa, it was necessary to show our papers, and Segatlhe went into the line for "Bantu" and I into the line for whites only. The black border official attending to Segatlhe began to puzzle over why he was with me and where he was going. While being treated quite deferentially by another (white) official, I said, somewhat short-temperedly, in Setswana to the black border official that "the old man was with me; we are both going to the University of the Witwatersrand to see his niece who works there, and besides this old man is my father; he's with me." Both Segatlhe and the black official were delightedly taken aback with the improbability of the whole situation. I then told the white official that the old man was with me; this official then turned to his black subordinate and began brusquely to tell him to fill out Segatlhe's forms and not delay the old man or me any further. Clearly this little incident impressed the old man as a "victory" at a border post where one can usually expect indifference at best and surliness at worst. But he said nothing to me at the time.

When we returned to Botswana a week or so later, I noticed that the old man was stopping everybody who passed by his kraal and engaging them in lengthy conversations. Etiquette prevented me from doing more than discreetly overhearing these unusual caucuses (*ditaba*). But I was able to discover that he was, in addition to delivering the news about his trip to Johannesburg, describing in actual formulaic stanzas his "victory [*phenyo*] at the border post"—attributing it all to his repute and power as a witch doctor with whom no one, not even the whites, had dared to trifle. He was singing the praises of the "medicine" he had prepared before leaving, which would ward off any indecorous behavior or harassment from whites. He was broadcasting his heroism.

Now the *events* that his self-praises refer to could be interpreted as arising from his medicine or from his being in the company of a white person in a racist, white-dominated society. But his poem *named* the event, its significance, so that as far as the little community was concerned the meaning of the event lay in the poetics of its creation.

The reality of that event in Segatlhe's language and in the minds of all the Tswana around can best be discerned by an examination of the verbal formulas that named and created the meaning of the happening. Unfortunately I only have a few snatches of his self-praise, but they illustrate my point:

It is I Segatlhe, who
Swatted pesky bugs that flew around my eyes.
Swatted bugs at Kopfontein Hek.
. . . .
Medicine smoothed the road, filled the holes,
And brushed aside thorny branches.
The medicine of Segatlhe.

While only a fragment, these lines are sufficient to illustrate the unique competence of metaphor to create meaning. This is not the place for a full discussion of metaphor—a subject of lively controversy in modern linguistics—but a cursory outline can be provided.

Note there is not one literal reference in this fragment of Segatlhe's self-praise. This is, as far as I know, always the case in Tswana praise poetry. Why would it be so important always to express praises metaphorically? What does metaphor do that literal language cannot? What is the nature of the world of experience that metaphor alone can create?

The signification or reference of any novel metaphor—as opposed to a dead metaphor that has become part of everyday speech—contains a "tension" or "twist" traceable to a three-fold set of semantic markings which become conflated in reading or hearing (Pelc 1971, pp. 142–94). The three interpretations or readings given by a hearer to any metaphor occur simultaneously. These are, first, the "ordinary" semantic reading or interpretation of the utterance form. This is normally a paradox or contradiction, for the ordinary semantic features of the individual lexical items cannot be projected on to one another without creating logical contradictions. Thus the phrase "medicine smoothed the road" is contradictory because in Setswana medicine cannot affect the topography of the land surface. Medicine is not semantically "marked" with the competence of agent or tool capable of smoothing dirt roads. The second reading of a metaphor is the actual or "metaphoric" reading of the utterance form, which means most simply the suppression of all semantic features of the individual lexical items which are ordinarily in contradiction. This would imply in the phrase "medicine smoothed the road" suppression of all the semantic markings of "road" that refer directly to geophysical and spatial phenomena, while retaining those that refer to route, means of progress, and so forth. Likewise all the semantic markings contained in the verb "to smooth" that refer to the abrasion of rough physical surfaces would be suppressed, leaving only those that refer to the amelioration of social and psychological conditions. The third simultaneous reading of the metaphor consists of a tacit recognition of the ordinary linguistic form which is semantically equivalent to the actual metaphoric reading. Normally, if uttered, this would involve an extensive, sometimes tortuous, paraphrase. This threefold structure is shown in figure 2.

These three readings take place simultaneously, and it is the tacit awareness of all together that in part explains the aesthetic "twist" of apt metaphors. But there is another equally important aspect to metaphor that cannot be accounted for in terms of this three-fold structure. Metaphor is, I believe, unique among linguistic forms in containing as an explicit part of its semantic structure an assertion of the *intentional standpoint* from which the reference of the metaphor is to be viewed. In other words, metaphor appeals to us because it is an invitation to adopt an affective or other standpoint in regard to the reference of the metaphor. The power of this appeal lies in the fact that it is embedded in the semantic structure of the metaphor and is not uttered as a separate proposition. If we assume that all objects of experience are apprehended from some standpoint—that consciousness is consciousness of something for me as well as consciousness of the thing itself—then metaphor has the unique ability to represent the intentionality of consciousness in its very structure. A single apt metaphor can convey the kind of psychological complexity that in literal language might require a whole volume. Metaphor is thus the literal language of

FIGURE 2
THE STRUCTURE OF METAPHOR
(AFTER PELC)

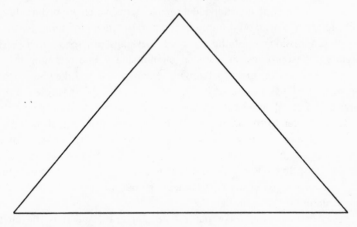

"Ordinary reading" of linguistic form
(implies semantic paradox)

"Metaphoric reading" of linguistic form (implies suppression of all contradictory semantic features projected on to one another by syntactic structure of the linguistic form)

Ordinary statement of metaphoric reading (implies a "literal" paraphrase) consciousness. This is only a seeming irony. If the subject of poetic or other linguistic representation is human experience, the only literal language for representing it is metaphor. Apt metaphor—as opposed to dead metaphor or linguistic mistakes—must be interpretable as intended by the speaker to be metaphor to the hearer, even if it is not always intended metaphorically by the speaker.

Let me illustrate this by reference to Segatlhe's self-praise and to praise poetry in general. The lines, "Swatted pesky bugs that flew around my eyes / Swatted bugs at Kopfontein Hek" probably seem enigmatic. "Pesky bugs" is a metaphoric reference to European officials at the border gate. It happens that etymologically the word for "Europeans" in Setswana is a homophone of a word for "buzzing insects [lekgoa]." Thus there is a pun embedded in this metaphor. More to the point, Segatlhe is asserting that Europeans are in some sense like pesky bugs: they are irritating, irksome, but really inconsequential. They can be swatted and killed quite effortlessly, but only if one (i.e., as a Tswana) has proper protection or strength. In this case, the power to reduce powerful and awesome Europeans to the condition of pesky insects lies in Segatlhe's medicine. These lines, then, refer to Europeans from the standpoint of a person who is competent and well armed. They ask us, the hearers, to join Segatlhe in seeing Europeans as pesky bugs and to share his pride and satisfaction in the efficacy of his medicine to put them in their place. In giving expression to these perceptions as objects of meaning for himself and for his hearers, Segatlhe is creating an object of experience. He has made a determinate experience out of an event which could certainly be invested with many different meanings.

There remains the question: "But does he really believe all he's saying?" Might he not be asserting something that will be contradicted and rendered absurd by other perceptions, both his own and those of Europeans? The answer is, of course, that this is possible. Only much fuller knowledge of this person could suggest a definitive answer. But even if these assertions do represent merely a feigning, a pretense, even a momentary reverie, they still present an object of experience that affects the individual in some way.

For hearer and speaker metaphor is unusually rich in references in comparison to ordinary linguistic signs. Segatlhe has predicated the full reference of his metaphoric lines on himself. He is the hero of the experiences created by the poem, the semantic and logical subject of the discourse. The intentional standpoint created by the lines is that of

Segatlhe looking at himself and simultaneously it is an appeal to others
to see him from that standpoint—that is, to appropriate his experience
as their own and by empathy to appreciate the valorization he is providing for himself.

If these claims concerning the implications of the self-predication of
metaphor are correct, the use of metaphor in self-naming or praising
should profoundly affect the development and maintenance of self-
idenity.

To appreciate how the power of metaphor is brought into play, we
must first understand the actual use of metaphor in this "heroic" self-
praising. Throughout the last two chapters I have quoted Tswana who
in effect assert that the negation of evil is the heroic. The hero personi-
fies and performs the good. Many commentaries I collected on the
topic of the heroic verify this. I put the following set of questions to
almost every respondent with whom I worked closely: "I would like
you to help me understand the Setswana idea of hero [*monna wa
bonatla*]. In particular, what characterizes such a person's behavior,
thoughts, and his life generally? Are such people described in proverbs,
stories, praises, etc.? Are such people to be found in this community?
If so, who are they?"

In Kgaphamadi three people were cited as heroes by many of the
twenty-seven respondents. One of them, Montsho, happened to be in my
sample. He mentioned his own status as a hero:

"There are very few heroes in life, but I am a hero. A hero is one
who is working very hard in this life, among his fellow men. He is
industrious and patient in his obligations. Modern chiefs, who
formerly were often heroes, are no longer. Olden chiefs used to do
great works for their people; they served people's needs—for example,
by making rain. They also lived among their people, so they could
understand their needs. Today the modern chiefs ride about in lorries;
they never feel hot sand on their feet or the sun beating down on
their heads. They simply travel on their buttocks [a reference to
sitting in a car]. A hero is one who contributes to the community
life through his works. A hero faces life as it is and works to overcome
its obstacles and frustrations, and in doing so, makes a contribution
to the nation."

Commenting on Montsho's heroism, another Kgaphamadi respondent
said:

"Certainly Montsho is a hero. He is renowned as a builder of dams.
Back in the days when Maneer Malan [an Afrikaner settler in
Botswana] owned all this land [now Content Farm], he hired a

number of us to dig dams for irrigation. When the rest of us were exhausted from heat and the heavy work, Montsho kept right on digging all day and all night. By the next morning he had finished the dam himself. He has dug dams and wells all over this area. These dams are monuments to his performance as a worker-with-hands."

Yet another Kgaphamadi respondent, Magano, commented:

"I have not met a true hero in my life, but in the olden days Dingane [a Zulu leader] was certainly a hero in his wars fought against the Boers. [Several other respondents cited Dingane as a hero and also Mzilikazi of the Ndebele.] In one particular battle, Dingane was in danger of being defeated by the Boers, so he sued for peace. Feigning to surrender, he told the Boers to come to a feast to celebrate the truce. But secretly he instructed his soldiers to bring their spears with them. When the Boers assembled, the warriors sprang upon them and slew them all."

Another Kgaphamadi resident told of a hero, Sebele, who defended the Kwena capital from an attack by the Boers.

"The Boers had surrounded the capital and held it in siege. Sebele ordered that his soldiers put his royal headpiece on a staff and place it in full view of the attackers. The Boers opened fire. Soon their ammunition was spent. Thereafter, Sebele led his soldiers in an attack on the Boers in which every Boer was killed and not one of the Kwena lost his life. . . . There are many kinds of heroes. But they all contribute to the whole nation. There are heroes of war, heroes of rule (governance), heroes of words (speakers), and heroes of doing (work). Each kind of hero uses his reasoning and his skill to overcome his own problems and contribute to the nation."

Another respondent said: "Seretse Khama [the president of Botswana] is a hero. He put an end to chiefs' despotism. A hero is one who serves the whole nation. Chiefs were fighting among themselves for their own ends. They were spoiling people [*ba ne ba sotlhe batho*]. A hero is one like Seretse who, when saving himself, saves the nation." (This is actually an allusion to Seretse's own expulsion from his tribe for his marriage to a European woman. Later Seretse returned to Botswana and became a prominent national figure and, in 1966, its first president.) Most Tswana echoed this opinion that a hero is one whose works, while benefiting the individual, redound to the common weal of the nation.

An elder from Gaborone, states this point directly:

"Heroism means industry, courage, and determination. A hero is one who can do things for himself, yet whose deeds benefit everyone.

A hero works so hard as to become an example to others. Heroes typically reap the rewards of their hard work by progressing from poverty to wealth. Heroes are men of words. They are people who hold fast to what they believe. They are able to defend their actions before the counsels of the people. They can persuade. The two roads to heroism are hands and words. Chief Isang [of the Kgatla] was a true hero. [Several respondents said this.] He brought education to his people. He organized the people to build a school for themselves."

These ideas of what it is to be a hero I found to be more or less common to all of the age cohorts and communities of Tswana. However there was one thing that distinguished all of the young from most of the elder in every community. The young in every case stated that they had never met, nor did they know of, any living heroes. They knew stories of heroes—usually chiefs of long ago whom elders had told them about. These were the same figures cited by the elders (e.g., Dingane, Mzilikazi, Isang, Sebele, Lentswe I). None of the young, however, cited the first president of Botswana, Seretse Khama, as a hero. Furthermore, unlike the elders, who almost invariably could point to one or two people whom they personally knew to be heroes, the young tended to think that the idea of hero was mainly legendary—referring to people in the past. One key to this difference between young and old was the claim of the young that a "hero is one who achieves all of his purposes in life." Several of the young in Gaborone suggested that they could not point to any living heroes because they were living in town. The implication here is that town life is inimical to heroism. When I pursued this inference, they simply suggested that in town the best one could expect of life was to survive and make a little money—hardly the works of a hero. Yet in rural life one might merely survive and yet become a hero. I told these urban respondents about how many people had described Montsho as a hero. They conceded this was possible because his works affect the life of the community (i.e., the dams create a water supply), but in town "the little money one makes only helps to feed oneself and a few others."

While formal schooling in the art of praising is no longer given, the reciting and appreciation of poetic self-praises or praise names is still widely found. The respondents claimed explicitly that what "hero" essentially means is best stated in the literature of Setswana—in particular, in praise names and animal fables. For purposes of illustration only, I have translated a typical Tswana praise name found in Schapera's compilation. This will be sufficient to demonstrate how what I said above about Segatlhe's impromptu praise applies to the established praise poems of history.

The following is a fragment of a praise poem composed for Chief Motswasele I, who died in about 1785 (cf. Schapera 1965, p. 123). The poem ostensibly deals with important events in Motswasele's life—his wanderings by himself before becoming chief of the Kwena; his leading the Kwena twice to new settlement areas; his stern rule, which led a section of the Kwena, the Ngwato, to secede from the tribe and form their own chieftaincy farther south; and a second, later secession of another part of the tribe which joined the Ngwato. Motswasele attacked these separated groups in battle, driving them farther south. None of these events is unusual in Tswana culture, for tribal fission is routine and internecine war commonplace. The events alone would not make a hero; it is the poem that creates him, by endowing the events with heroic significance.

Motswasele I
(d. ca. 1785)

Yellow-brown animal of the "bathing place of elephants,"	1
Red one of the River Metsemotlhaba,	
I was the River Metsemotlhaba.	
It was when I was still	
Provisioning (my) arroyos,	5
Rockfilled and craggy,	
That they took from me thriving cattle.	
He who disturbs the forests at Tlajwane,	
Not only did he disturb the forests	
He seized the forests and destroyed them all.	10
Fierce refuser.	
White quill of a porcupine, traveler of the Kwena.	
Refuser; bustard, shake yourself wildly	
That your dark feathers may grow.	
A thin resilient man is strong	15
And can suppress young tender ones.	

An interpretation of the ostensive reference of each line of the poem is given below:

Line 1: refers to Motswasele's complexion, his undisciplined manner, and probably his birthplace (north of Molepolole).

Line 2: refers to his complexion and to the area in which he lived much of his early life.

Line 3: allegory begins; note shift to first person, direct quotation.

Line 5: "provisioning" means making family and home; "arroyos" alludes to this also.

Line 6: description of arroyos refers to the course and quality of Motswasele's life.

Line 7: refers to either attack by enemy during peaceful time or to secession and removal of cattle by part of tribe during a peaceful time; "thriving cattle" implies peaceful times.

Lines 8-10: refer to place where some enemy probably lived and to Motswasele's revenge.

Line 11: refers to Motswasele's reputation: stubborn, uncompliant.

Line 12: refers to personality: tough, rigid, prickly; also refers to his reputation as a traveler.

Lines 12-13: refer to personality; admonition to act (out) so that he may grow properly to maturity; shaking of birds to dislodge first growth of downy feathers is necessary to gain adult plumage.

Line 15: another reference to personality by analogy with the porcupine quill.

Line 16: another allusion to personality and its role in his stern rule as a chief who dealt severely with those who challenged him.

This praise of Motswasele, like the praise of Segatlhe, contains not one literal utterance. While not particularly flattering, the poem creates a heroic archetype of the chief, who appears larger than life in an unambiguous cultural setting. The poem deepens the mere historical events into experiences for the hearer. Like all praises, the poem is a reflection, a meditation that retrospectively invests past events with metaphoric significance.

Most Tswana today still actively practice the art of "conversation," retrospectively investing events with meaning by placing them in the context of a tale, a narrative, a poem, or whatever. When a Tswana has done something, he wants to give the "news [*dikgang*]" to the world. But this news is not a simple objective description. It is—indeed must be—a fabulous creation that transcends the bounds of the natural attitude and the everyday. This transcending of the bounds of the everyday is strikingly revealed in another literary genre—the fables of animals and their adventures.

Tswana Animal Fables: The Trickster as Hero
Tswana animal tales directly illustrate an aspect of the heroic that is only implicit in heroic poetry—the vindication of acts that are otherwise

repugnant. These fables also express a universal quality of human being
—the desire to reach beyond the limitations and givenness of the conventional, to be more than what one is, to seize pure possibility, to
exert the will—including its moments of ecstacy and irrationality—
against an intractable environment.

Convention, law, the harsh environment, the rudimentary technology,
and society's need for predictable cooperation create for the Tswana a
world in which the individual must suppress or deny a considerable
portion of his species competence and power, his imagination, yearning,
and drive to self-actualization. The Tswana world is one where most
individuals from earliest childhood are "held by the law." It is not a
world of dionysian exploits and journeys, but one of rational and
decorous participation. The survival of the Tswana under harsh material
conditions testifies to the adaptedness of their culture and its genius
for organizing individual diversity into a collective life. But the mind
does not become one with the circumscribed behavior of the body. The
hero is testimony to the hiatus between mere events and their meaning.
This is clear in the case of the *trickster*, the hero of animal fables.

Evans-Pritchard's characterization of the spider in Azande lore is
equally apt as a description of the Tswana tricksters Rabbit and Hyena:

> Ture (spider) is a monster of depravity; liar, cheat, lecher, murderer,
> vain, greedy, treacherous, ungrateful, a poltroon, a braggart. . . . There
> is another side to his character . . . his whimsical foolishness, reckless-
> ness, impetuosity, puckish irresponsibility, his childish desire to show
> how clever he is . . . his flouting of every convention. . . . When his
> cocksuredness gets him into trouble, when he overreaches himself
> and sheds frustrated tears, then he is pathetic. He is indomitable. In
> spite of every failure, misfortune and humiliation, he perseveres.
> [Evans-Pritchard 1967, pp. 28–29]

How could such a character attain the status of hero? Despite his
seeming outlandishness, the trickster and his exploits have come in
recent times to have many correspondences in the everyday world.
According to many of my Tswana respondents, the animal fables are an
apt commentary on the fabric of daily life, especially in town and in
the mines. In the next chapter, I ask the old man Segalthe: "What
reflections or thoughts come to mind when you think back on your
life among white people in South Africa?" His response is the well-
known African story of the jackal, the hyena, and the Boer. This
story comprises a metaphoric, heroic discourse in which Segalthe

situates himself as trickster vis-à-vis the world of the European.

But these animal tales are more than amusing metaphors of the modern world; they are rooted in human universals that have existed for all of recorded time. From Africa to ancient Greece, from northern Europe to the American Great Plains, we find fantastic stories about supernatural animals, about masqueraderers, fools, and jesters. These creatures are fast-talking, fleet of foot, sly but blundering, unselfconscious, voracious, amoral, and libidinous. They go about committing absurd, even heinous, acts of self-aggrandizement against the interests of all and sundry. Children and grannies alike delight in hearing these seemingly innocuous tales of what could not possibly happen in real life. The same story, say that of Br'er Rabbit and the Tar Baby, will persist and travel throughout Africa and the New World, and it will retain its basic form despite millions of retellings and thousands of miles of travel. People laugh at and think cute characters which commit acts of incest, murder, fraud, and theft. These stories are told and retold so often that everyone in every society knows almost all of them. Even we, in our allegedly advanced state of cultural development, recite for our children Aesop's fables; we delight in the pranks of Bugs Bunny and Br'er Rabbit. We ourselves can be arrested by the ad man and his mythical creations: slinky blondes selling cars, leopards gracing home furnishings, one-dimensional cowboys and private eyes selling cigarettes and coffee or triumphing over evil the way James Bond does. We delight in the amoral universe of the big con getting his way in a world that only fantasy can create. The trickster is as libidinous as he is brazen: Hermes (Mercury) the messenger is at once the god of commerce, the fleet-footed, and fast-talking con.

How does one account for the universality of the trickster? Kerenyi (1956, pp. 173–91) suggests that this figure is the celebration of disorder and pure possibility in a world that is inexorably and oppressively ordered. The mind can imagine many lives, including one of impulse gratification, self-assertion, and potent affirmation of basic sexual power. We can imagine worlds in which every law and convention can be flouted and stood on its head. Indeed, to affirm order implies that we can be conscious of its antithesis. In a world that demands patience, conformity, sharing, self-denial, and planning, we can imagine acts motivated by impetuosity and desire. We can experience nonrational moments of awareness: hate, love, ecstasy, and passion. The trickster is a manifestation of the desire to affirm asocial individuality and possibility.

Jung (1956, pp. 195-211) has a less flattering view of the trickster than Kerenyi. Simplistically, Jung sees mythological characters or roles as projections—overt manifestations—of inner, psychic functions. These projections of the trickster and related creatures such as ghosts, goblins, and witches, as well as other "tricks that mind plays on us," are examples of a psychoneurotic acting-out which bears witness to inner psychic experiences that have characterized mankind throughout its history.

The trickster, says Jung, is part god and part animal. But he (or it) is amoral, not evil—he is mankind in a state of uncontrolled asociality. The trickster is the manifestation of an innate idea—called by Jung an archetype—that represents the sedimentation of species' experience going back to the dawn of man. The trickster is part of our "shadow"— the dark, impulsive animality in our nature. We have suppressed this awareness as best we can, but in dreams, fantasies, and the tales of the trickster vicariously "we get away with it"; we act out our shadow. We *need* to tell trickster tales because we delight in the hedonic tone of this part of our shadow—the sexual animality that civil society absolutely stifles and suppresses.

The accounts provided by Jung and Kerenyi, while not mutually contradictory, are certainly very different. Yet both may be right. The trickster may be a manifestation of amoral individuality—a part of our species' shadow. And he may be a celebration of possibility which we as humans delight in both for its own sake and as a protest against the conformity and fracturing of the self that society, with its division of labor, necessitates.

Rather than attempting to formulate an account of the meaning of the trickster, I will let the Tswana speak for themselves:

> "These stories are told to children. They are just for their amusement. But when we live in town, we sometimes have to act just like Mr. Rabbit. We Tswana are small; we are hunted by everyone; sometimes *ditrikinyana* [literally 'little tricks'] are our only means of survival. We tell our children to behave in town. But they must often become rogues just to eat. Among the Europeans people are spoiled. There's no humanity, just as with Rabbit and his friends."
> [Elder from Gaborone]

> "If we are to be heroes in our work in the mines, we must be as clever as Mr. Rabbit. That is to say, we are 'little' people. We have to make up somehow for this. Cleverness is the only way." [Kgaphamadi youth, aged twenty-two]

"When I was in town, I lived just like a jackal. . . . I moved through the streets like a hyena." [Kgaphamadi elder]

What these and other Tswana respondents are saying is that the world of town and wage labor—the heart of darkness—demands special means of coping which call forth the trickster in every man. The trickster may once have been merely the projection of our species' unconscious, but for the Tswana he has become an explicit literary model of European life as it involves them. "We are like the Rabbit in this modern life; everyone hunts us, but we can delude our predators" (Kalahari elder).

This conscious, retrospective explication of the meaning of personal experience under colonial institutions constitutes a symbolic mainte- nance of self-identity vis-à-vis the norms and expectations of European society. As such, these trickster tales comprise one of the most revealing indications of how the Tswana experience—that is to say, invest with meaning—the world of the Europeans. Just as important, these tales are models of a life-style—actual behavior deemed appropriate for cop- ing with the world.

It is when the Tswana are explicating the relationship between the trickster and their own coping with the modern world that they come closest to articulating the Western concept of alienation. This sense of alienation from the world of the European varies with age and ecologic niche (for details see the next chapter). But there is a common meaning of alienation shared by all Tswana, and it is this sense that the trickster tales aptly represent.

From the standpoint of the Tswana—all Tswana—the modern indus- trial world is amoral and utilitarian. It is there to exploit black people. There is no *botho* (humanity) to be found there. This world has its uses for the Tswana who in varying degrees consider the products of indus- trialization important enough to be gained at great sacrifice. A Tswana feels that modern life "takes him away from himself," "destroys his power to think constructively," "makes everyone to fight with and dis- like everyone else," "spoils humanity," "ruins cultural living," "takes away from us the fruits of our work," "makes coercion, rather than love, the root of life." These refrains I heard over and over again from Tswana of all ages and economic conditions. Consistent with this evalu- ation of the colonial political economy is the recipe knowledge used to cope with and minimize the frustration of living in this world. A com- mon recipe for success in town (discussed at length in the next chapter) is "superficial conformity and docility, as a mask for cunning and care- ful, strategic thinking." Now a world where *amoral social forces,*

*opportunities, and risks are met by cunning and opportunism is precisely
the world of the animal fables and their hero the trickster.* In these tales
the hearer encounters a life in which the one-dimensional characters
owe each other nothing. Life is a battle of wits. It is a game of survival
in which the boundary conditions of the game and its rules are amoral
and hedonistic, physical and absolute. This dark world of the West was,
quite coincidentally, adumbrated in the animal stories which predated
it by untold hundreds of years. There at the periphery of the culture
lay a blueprint of a world the Tswana would never have believed
possible until it came into being in the last third of the nineteenth
century.

To be sure, these trickster tales may reflect precontact societal forces
and (to take Kerenyi and Jung at their word) may express the universal
human drive to affirm being to the fullest, despite the suppressive
effects of civil society. But with the advent of the colonial political
economy the amoral hedonism of the animal fables ceased to be simply
an entertaining externalization of a "shadow" in human species consciousness; it became also an apt representation of actual life in the
colonial world.

Perhaps the single most important aspect of Tswana resilience and
indomitability in the heart of darkness is the capacity, exemplified by
the animal tricksters, to present many faces and act out many strata-
gems. The Tswana can play a given character (jackal, rabbit, hyena)
without becoming one with that character. The mask worn is a function
of the situation, not a function of the deepest layers of identity. This
acting can keep the straw boss or the police ignorant of one's intentions and feelings. Face-work has always been an important interpersonal skill for the Tswana in the context of their traditional communal
life. With the advent of industrial colonialism, the range of faces or
characters that one needed to master to perform competently had to be
expanded beyond what was required in life at home. By reflecting the
new reality, the trickster fables provided quite by chance a model for
the kind of social action that might guarantee survival in the harsh
world that Europe imposed on southern Africa one hundred years
ago.

Below I present a translation of one of the most popular Tswana
animal fables, "Mr. Hare and the Other Animals." Note in reading four
themes: "ripping off," "lightening the load," "urge to self-praise," and
"acting innocent." These are themes found in Tswana discussions of
industrial work—its burdens and opportunities (see chapter 8).

(MR.) HARE AND THE ANIMALS

"People say that long ago the animals lived together in the world. It happened on a certain day that they were very, very hungry, so they went in search of food. Going along, they came across a *Motsotsobyane* tree, which had become ripe with fruit. They ate of them.

"As it was nearing sundown, they broke off branches of the tree (to provide sleeping mats). The sun set. And they lay down; before going to sleep, they said, 'Should anyone think that because we are asleep he can get up and eat the food, beware; when he wakes up in the morning, we will kill him.'

"In the middle of the night Mr. Hare got up and ate (the remaining fruit). After he had eaten, he was reminded of (recalled) a certain plan, by means of which he could avoid being caught. He took a leaf (of the tree) and stuck it in the anus of a little animal called Red Hare. Then Mr. Hare went back to sleep.

"In the morning when all of the animals got up, they found that all of the *Motsotsobyane* fruit had been eaten. They questioned one another (concerning the eating of the fruit). Mr. Hare knowing full well what had happened, said, 'Let us bend over and see in whose rear end leaves may be found. In this way we can discover who has eaten all the food this night.' Now all the animals stooped and the leafy twig was found in the anus of Red Hare. Upon seeing it, the animals questioned him, but he denied eating any fruit that night. But the evidence was clear and visible for all to see. So they seized him and killed him.

"After they killed him, they were once again hungry. So instead of throwing him away, they skinned him to eat (him). Having skinned him, they divided him up and apportioned various parts among the animals. They then moved on. Mr. Hare was given a hind thigh to carry.

"As they were still going along, Mr. Hare lagged behind and sang out, 'I ate it, that *Motsotsobyane* (fruit), fruit eaten by chiefs, and at that place Red Hare [i.e., species] was killed.' One among the animals heard this song and asked him, 'What did you say? Huh, Mr. Hare?' The hare replied, 'I am weighed down by this red hare thigh.' The big animals took the thigh and gave him the lungs to carry. Then they went along. Further on, he lagged behind and sang out his song. Again, one other of the animals heard him and questioned him. Again Mr. Hare said he was weighed down, this time by the lungs. So they cut the lungs in two and then continued on. As they were going, he stopped a third time and sang his song.

"Now since he had not received a heavy load at all, they expected that he was lying. They questioned him, and he replied, 'I am being weighed down.' They reduced his load once more. They went on. Again Mr. Hare lagged behind. Just as he did this, the animals spoke to the tortoise. They asked him to go behind and hide, waiting to hear what Mr. Hare sang. Having hidden himself, the hare came along and spotted him. He said to the tortoise, 'It is often said that you tortoise people try to hide from us hare-folks. I see you.' So the tortoise went along to join the others. He told the others, 'He spotted me.'

"The animals went along; again the hare lagged behind. This time the lizard was instructed to lie in wait (for Mr. Hare). As Mr. Hare came along, he was singing, and the lizard heard him to say, 'I ate it, that *Motsotsobyane*, that tree eaten by chiefs, and there it was that Red Hare was killed.' The lizard hurried past, went to the animals, and told the big animals what he had heard. They all sat down on the ground. When Mr. Hare came, he was suspicious, so he did not sit near the others. They called him to come over and sit near them, but he refused. A certain animal left and went behind him to outflank him. But Mr. Hare became frightened and fled. They chased him, but he outran them.

"He fled and came upon an owl which was in a cave. He called out to the owl. When the owl finally acknowledged, Mr. Hare said to him, 'People are coming to kill you.' The owl left the cave; when he had done so, the hare went inside. When the animals came, they passed the cave, and they called out. He answered. They asked if he had seen the hare. He answered that he hadn't yet seen him. So they passed on. Further on, they came across the owl and asked him if he had not yet seen the hare. The owl answered, 'You see me here because it happened that the hare came along and told me that people were coming to kill me, so I left the cave.'

"The hare, realizing what would happen (because of what he had said), left the cave and hid himself a little distance away. When the animals returned, he heard the owl to say, 'Ah, perhaps he is inside.' They crowded around the cave, but inside they found owl's children only. They questioned them. the children told them what had happened.

"So they left. As they were going, they saw him. They gave chase, but he got away."

A crucial question implicit in this discussion of the heroic is whether the contradictory images of the hero that exist for the Tswana constitute psychic conflicts—conflicts at the level of self-identity. Does, for example, the traditional hero of works and words found in eulogistic poetry conflict with the hero of cunning found in the animal fables? Does the ideal of a life based on wanting-to-do and the attainment of the status of a hero of hard work conflict with the image of the hero as one who "gets" through dirty tricks? At the institutional level, does behavior exacted from the Tswana on the basis of material reward and punishment conflict with behavior that flows from desire-to-do? Is one alienating vis-à-vis the other? In the next chapter we will look at the colonial institutions of town and mine in terms of these and other possible meanings they may have for the actors in the situation.

8 WAGE LABOR AND TOWN LIFE: PROJECTS OF ACTION

Introduction

All phenomena, including towns and gold mines, are ambiguous and can therefore be invested with manifold meanings. Which meaning is given to an event—that is to say, what experience will arise from its perception—depends in large measure on how the event fits into an individual's overall project, or, in other words, how the event is relevant to him in terms of his motives and goals in pursuing a course of action. While wage labor, deep-shaft mines, and industrial towns are constituted by objective, material conditions, they in no way comprise a determinate set of experiences. Experience depends on "where you are coming from" and "where you are going." The goal of this chapter is to illustrate the variety of experiences the Tswana have in conjunction with mine labor, town life, and dealings with Europeans generally. The variations in experience are based on the varied projects within which different Tswana place the objects they perceive, both retrospectively and prospectively.

This task in understanding follows the admonition of Alfred Schutz (1962, p. 85):

We cannot understand social phenomena apart from their placement within the scheme of human motives, human means and ends, human planning—in short, within the categories of human action. . . . The social scientist must . . . always be in the position to ask what happens in the mind of an individual actor whose act has led to the phenomenon in question.

215

The Experience of Mine Labor

   Conflicts between societies or institutions which comprehend the
individual can give rise to what Peter Berger (1974, pp. 139–58) calls
the "collision of images." In the life-world of the Tswana, for example,
we can say that the world of industrial or mining employment "col-
lides" with the world of rural subsistence. But more than this, the
conflicts created by institutions give rise to collisions of various images
of these institutions in the minds of individual Tswana.
   For all Tswana I interviewed, the meaning of mine labor was derived
in part from the meaning of home. I will begin the discussion of mining
and industrial labor by looking briefly at the way several Tswana compared them with life at home:

                     My Village

   You were small and sad
   When I was still young
   Those were the dark ages
   Through which you lived

   You were as dark as they were
   (I remember the young men
   Who used to leave you behind
   To go to the mines in Johannesburg.)
   I remember what they used to say
   When they returned

   You produced young and strong men
   But when they returned,
   They seemed to have lost their senses
   They had lost all the respect
   They used to show.

   They laughed when they told stories
   Of the bad things they did.
   They boasted about their evil deeds.
   They thought they were civilized
   They despised you and said
   You were not worth living in.
   There was not even a school
   Built upon your whitish-pink soil.

But when I grew up you became bigger and famous.
Light started to shine upon your grey buildings
And in the dark memories of your inhabitants

. . . .

Now you are still growing
You have many teachers, children,
And many buildings in your school
Your name is sweet and meaningful

. . . .

You are my greatest and last hope
You capture the minds of people
You turn strangers into your inhabitants
Even the big road passes through you
To the copper and nickel mines of Selebi-Pikwe[1]

This poem embraces many of our concerns in this chapter: culture shame, departure, exile, return, celebration of the imperial culture, conspicuous emulation, pride in the symbols of jerry-built modernity. In this poem the educated author speaks in part of a world he knows from the words of others. The mines for him, and the handful like him, are places about which swaggering, brash, ill-mannered young men tell stories—grizzly or heroic. For those who stay behind in Botswana, "development" becomes the image, the myth, upon which young men fix their gaze. Tar roads, schools, jobs, even a mine; all these become extensions of self, the building blocks of pride.

Villages[2] are small in Botswana, ranging from a few hundred to twenty-thousand souls. The first tar road in Botswana was built last year. Dust from trails, tracks, and paths still shows how the Tswana move. Since the 1930s pummeled lorries grace a shop or two. In the village a person knows everyone. Every house is home. The village itself is home. Life in the village is "life at home." No lights; only stars

1. This poem (by Belinah Masheleng of Lobatse, 1973) was submitted to a national poetry contest sponsored by the Ministry of Education and was kindly made available to me by Mr. Reginald Salisbury, head of educational broadcasting at Radio Botswana.

2. In the following passages dealing with the contrasts between life at home and life in the mines and cities, I have intentionally used turns of phrase that young migrants especially used in their discussions with me on the topic of labor migration.

festoon the dry and cloudless nights. The moon casts shadows as long
as those of day. The people live close to the earth and the rhythms of
nature. One lives continuously among kin and friends. "Stranger" is a
special term used on those rare occasions when one sees an unfamiliar
face. A stranger or visitor at home means hospitality and the taking of
the news.

The house contains one's things, all of which, save perhaps the oxen's
yoke, can be placed in a single bag. Among those goods are a few
treasured iron pots, tools, perhaps a bicycle. The Tswana revere the
secret of making iron.

The world of nature—animals, plants, rocks, soil, rain, and drought—
is a major content of consciousness. Time itself is made up of events,
both God-made and man-made. Sunrise, the time for fetching water,
the time to take the goats from the kraal, the time for children to rise,
to wash and dress, the time for men to eat; the sun has pierced the sky—
midday; the sun returning to the ground, the corralling of animals, the
time for dinner, sunset, darkness, sleep. No mathematical divisions partition day, season, or lifetime.

Tasks are apportioned throughout one's life on the basis of sex, kinship, and age. A person finds his station as soon as he can walk. Life is
led among fellows from cradle to grave. The bulk of life is a quest for
physical security: the production and distribution of a food supply.
Conversation, stories, fables, even myth, revolve about famine, food,
hunger, and satiety. Wealth is what facilitates the quest for food.

Knowledge for the Tswana is knowledge of the world as it is given,
and it is accumulated slowly throughout life. Age and wisdom are one.
Throughout a lifetime, one achieves a greater and greater certainty concerning the life, customs, and wisdom of one's way.

Life on the Other Side

Within this quiet, certain world, young men face a challenge: the time
to leave, the quest for "life on the other side." Between the ages of
fifteen and seventeen, young men leave the scene I have described for
the first time. They have heard the stories from the older boys. They
know the lamentations of the older men who were boys before these
young men were born. But never mind. The older brother is a hero. He
knows of money that is to be made at the place-of-gold.

Let us follow a young man who leaves village life and takes up a
contract on the mines. Perhaps he has seen a train. He knows about the
truck that comes twice a week to pick up his kin and friends. They

have jumped on and disappeared into the dust. Some have not yet returned; a few never will. He has heard about the iron snake.[3]

The train is a central fact in lives that are lived in isolated worlds. It must have awed our young man as he boarded it for the first time.

"This thing [the train] came in, I tell you, with face turned upwards as if it were conscious of its own renown. I'm telling you the thing twisted its waist, gliding gently as it entered Bloemfontein Station. It did so with such self-esteem and so effortlessly. . . ."[4]

As the train enters Johannesburg, the young Tswana is filled with

---

3. Tjhu-tjhu-humakgala [an ideophonic representation of a train sound]
Beautiful things of White Man.
Madman, wearing a Towane-grass hat,
You make fog when skies are clear,
You churn clouds when winds are still,
You cover us in blackness.
Smoke billows; sparks fly,
As a bonfire fed on reeds.

Its speed (this bringer-of-sorrow)
Creates a storm of wind.
It shakes all things that are still.
Grasses and trees flap madly back and forth,
As if simulating flight.
. . . .
This black train is a spiteful one.
It took my brother away.
Now he's gone forever.
My heart was sore;
Tears welled up in my eyes
And flowed like rivers down my cheeks.
I stood there, crying out in grief.

Millipede-of-fields; dark brown one,
Whose feet are thousands;
Puny though they are,
You draw yourself in haste and keep abreast of time.

[B. M. Khaketla]

This poem is taken from a collection published by D. Kunene in his book *Heroic Poetry of the Basotho* (Oxford: Clarendon Press, 1971), p. 149. I have completely retranslated and reduced it to capture in English some of the stylistic and semantic impact it has in SeSotho. The morpheme-by-morpheme translation of Kunene causes most of the poetic character to be lost.

4. This is a quote excerpted from the words of Chieftainess 'Mantšebo Seeiso and quoted by Kunene, *Heroic Poetry of the Basotho*, p. 146.

nervous expectation. He anticipates fulfillment of his adolescent imagining. Train is iron; train is snake; train spits fire; train takes away its
prey. But what about a mine? What awaits him there? Let me describe
the young migrants' first experience of the mine by paraphrasing and
collating materials provided by several young men.

At the mine the young man finds his place of work: an inverted
anthill that tunnels down instead of up. He arrives and is shunted to
his room in the compound. Nine thousand Africans live there. Ten
languages are spoken there. Life is run like the regiments that his
grandfather told about. The compound boss is a chief. Failure or
disobedience brings punishment that is harsh and swift. He learns
about the White Man's fist; tough, sun-parched, hairy fist, protruding
from a khaki sleeve.

He learns to work on his back in a tunnel, picking at the gold that
falls and stings his eyes and nose. Hours and hours on one's back,
jagged rocks cutting flesh, falling rocks crushing limbs.

But at the mine, he eats; at the mine, he drinks; at the mine, he
becomes a man, with clothes. The sacraments of manhood: flare-
legged trousers from Johannesburg are found on Kalahari men, chic
in style but quickly torn by thorns and horns of stubborn goats. Jam
in tins and a radio. All these he'll get to prove that he's become a
man, with clothes.

He gets beaten at the mine, but he also gets beaten at home, and he
doesn't get paid to be beaten at home. So, better to be beaten at the
mine. The welts from home beatings meld with those of the compound boss.

Machinery: technology; trucks with twelve axles; towers three
hundred feet tall; cages with men inside that go down a mile into the
ground. Machines shoot water with such force that they knock down
mountains. Machines with limbs, like a praying mantis, gouge out a
ton of rock and pull it on to a traveling mat.

Next day, five hundred men stand nude against a wall. Hot water
pours over their bodies and disappears down a drain. Water going
down the drain. More water than he has seen in his entire life; enough
to grow a field of maize. Iron inserted in his rectum, in his mouth, in
his ears, in his nose; they press his chest against the iron. Iron needles
in his arm; lights put in his eye.

For him the world seems mad. Third day. Marching, yelling, hats
with lights, rope tying; he learns to put trees under ground, to hold
up the underside of the top of the world. This world *is* mad. Noise,
crushing, ear-splitting noise, drilling, TNT explodes; eye-stinging dust
in every pore. It's midnight; work begins. It's cold at night, standing
in the cage that takes him down below. Now it's hot. What makes the
ground so hot? The noise? Jagged rocks beat the hat-with-the-light.

Work until the muscles ache, and longer. Come up to the top of the
world, and then, he eats; he eats all he wants. He does not eat after

old men are done; he eats right away. Meat, mealies, greens—a thousand men eat together. He drinks beer from giant paper gourds— four giant gourds before dinner. Movies after dinner, something from the land of cowboys, where people hunt people, rather than game for winter meat.

Some Tswana say men lose their senses at the mine. They throw away their power to reason. Why?

White Man and the White Man's world: money, cars, trains, planes, guns, horses, megaphones, offices, books, papers, banging iron machines that write. Numbers, signs, paper everywhere; that thing that goes around and points the "number-time" all the time; that pointer-of-time never stops. Fights, fights, dice, money, cards. Strike! Police baton charge! Quick! Run, lock yourself in your room and hide!

A telex comes from mother. Money is needed at home. Sister is sick and must go to hospital in Gaborone. An *induna* comes and gets his thumb print; he'll send the money through the wire. (How can money go through wires? There's no hole in wire.)

The weekend. A pass to go to town. Look at the shops, the cars, the highways, the lights, Black people dressed in white folks' clothes, windows filled, "TJ" on every car; people pushing, rushing; everyone is late. No one talks. Who brings the news? No houses. Where do people live? Buildings with clouds around the tops. Everything is square. Everything's for sale. Money gets all that he can see. Nothing belongs to anyone. Everything's for sale.

Nine months later, his contract expires. Our young Tswana returns home. He detrains in Botswana and rides a truck to the west where he gets off and walks five, ten, or twenty miles to his village. Thorns and shrubs everywhere. A steenbok jumps at his approach. A few children dressed in loin cloths tumble in the sand. The huts seem hidden to everyone but a home boy's eye. Quiet is everywhere. A young man, weaned from his village breast, has come home. The things he has to tell! Wait 'til his kin have heard the news! Those who stayed, those sitting there where he left them, wait 'til they see, wait 'til they hear, wait 'til they taste his food and see how he has eaten!

In the previous paragraphs I have tried to provide a basis for an empathetic understanding of the experiences of a young migrant who leaves his home for the first time. Almost all of the language I have used was distilled from actual interviews with young migrants from Botswana. I have not tried to paraphrase even the curious turns of phrase used by young Tswana to refer to European material goods. I have tried to give an impression of what it means to speak of the "collision of images." I have in mind Peter Berger's goal (1974, p. 126) of "analyzing the manner in which particular individuals or groups relate to the modernizing carriers" (e.g., wage labor, industrial towns, European customs). None of these are simply objectivities in the world—though they may be treated as such. More important is their status as constituents of consciousness.

Community and Cohort Contrasts

In chapter 4 I outlined the basic material facts about mining, both technical and organizational. There I made some suggestions as to how the Tswana perceive and cope with the requirements of the mine and its organization. *Coping*—an aspect of any miner's project—is a key to understanding the standpoint from which the miner invests his labor with meaning. Its complement—retrospective interpretation—alters the worker's standpoint and thus endows the experience with new meanings long after the contract has ended. The materials I make use of in this chapter focus upon the latter—the mine worker's retrospective interpretations of his experience in the mines. The way in which the Tswana cope on the spot with the physical requirements of mine labor, how they act and what attitudes they assume, varies within rather narrow limits, as was suggested in chapter 4. But how the Tswana reinterpret the meaning and significance of work done there when they cast a retrospective gaze on the experience varies markedly among the clusters of Tswana I have already identified.

The elder Tswana both of Gaborone and Kgaphamadi and some of the young from Kgaphamadi describe mine work in terms of the theme: "the mines destroy humanity." In chapter 5 I showed that it was the elders who held and expressed most articulately a philosophy of human nature. Most younger Tswana of Kgaphamadi describe the mines in terms of crushing hardship and physical pain. The Kalahari Tswana and the young Tswana from Gaborone, while acknowledging the hardship and suffering, invest in mine labor many very positive attributes that are seldom cited by anyone in the other two clusters.

Older Tswana of Gaborone and Kgaphamadi

How the different clusters of Tswana experience mine labor can best be described by the Tswana themselves. I opened discussion of this topic with my respondents by asking each the following question, suitably modified stylistically to reflect the experience and "age" of the particular individual being interviewed: "You have spent many years living and working in South Africa. Most/much of that time you were working in the mines. Naturally you remember many things that you did there and what happened to you there. Now, I would like you to tell

me about the 'history' of your experiences both in the mines and in
South Africa generally." While I had prepared a list of guide and probe
questions to use during the course of the subject's reply, I found that
most interviewees gave detailed answers with little structuring from
me.[5] These answers showed the concordance described above, quite
independent of any suggestions I might have made, the only contribution from me being the opening question itself.

There is not room here to record all the interviews in their entirety.
Therefore I will present excerpts from a sample of the interviews collected from respondents in each cluster. I have included those remarks
which, while common to most or all of the members of a given culture
in content, are poignantly and compellingly expressed only by some.
Taken together, the set of interview extracts I cite for each cluster aptly
typifies the responses of the cluster as a whole.

"I started working at the mines in 1936. We earned one and six per
day. That was too little money for the hard work, so after ten months,
I returned home. The only advantage to mine work was the chance to
buy clothes. For £1 10s. you could get all the clothes you needed.
Back then, when I was young, clothes were important. They were the
basis for prestige. Good clothes, loose collar shirts, were the things to
have so when I met 'sisters' [chicks] on the street, they would know
that I am somebody [nna ke nna].

"I returned home in October and stayed three months. During this
time I was busy ploughing and fixing up the homestead. I soon heard
people were getting lots of money in their hats [an allusion to the
way miners used to be paid—holding out their hats and having money
dumped into them by the paymaster]. So I ran off to Crown Mines.
In those days it was easier to hold on to your earnings because everyone was farming then. There was no famine, so we just kept our
earnings for ourselves. [Q: If you didn't need the money for food,
why did you return to the mines?] I don't think at the time I realized
why I chose to return. I realized the dangers of mining and the hard
work there. Youthful blood is a real pressure on the mind. When at
home working for the elders I would daydream about the easy life in
the compound where there was no work to be done. When I was in
fact in the compound, life was smooth as I imagined it to be from at
home. But when I was down in the mine itself, I would think of the
easy life at home.

5. While some of the probe or guide questions appear to be "leading the witness," it should be borne in mind that most of the questions followed previous
discussions in which the respondent had clearly indicated his opinions on matters
pertaining to the question. I was often accused of asking "obvious questions," just
when westerners might suggest I was asking leading or provocative ones.

"When a person is young, the difference between labor at home and labor in the mine is very small. As a person grows older, the difference between the kind of work done in the mine and that done at home persists, but the way a person feels about those two kinds of tasks changes. As a person grows older, he soon sees that the work he does at home is a pursuit of his own wants and interests. The work done at the mines or in town simply furthers someone else's interests. The money is really too little to equal the suffering that takes place when you know that your work is making someone else progress in in life. . . .

"My third contract to the mines had a very definite purpose. I had to escape from home and hide abroad. My father had died, and three of my sisters died soon afterward, all on the same day. I ran away to avoid being bewitched. On this contract I was very unhappy at the mine. My purpose was hiding, not working, so the work was unbearably heavy. I found myself at loggerheads with the BBs [boss-boys] and the white underground foreman.

"Soon I was dismissed from my work contract. I refused to be pulled around by the nose. [Q: Were protests about work the only reason for your dismissal? Did anything happen in the compounds?] I don't deny that life was rough and wild in the compounds. And I don't say that I slid through compound life smoothly. Still, I avoided gambling, drinking, fighting, and girl friends. Also, I kept my mouth shut. Words start wars. I am not an aggressive person [ample observation on my part confirmed this claim], but I believe I have leadership abilities. I took on responsibility in the mines and proved my capability in most cases. I was not the kind of person who just wandered around after work. I stayed in my quarters and learned to sew with a sewing machine. I made extra money doing tailoring for other workers. . . .

"[Q: Tell me more about the work at the mine in comparison to work at home.] Work in the mines is very hard, but you get paid for it. At least, that's the way I felt as a young man. On the farms, you can plan carefully to lead a productive life, but you can create enemies. There is too much jealousy in Tswana villages. At the mines people also make enemies. People then go to the playgrounds to fight out their grievances. They sometimes wind up using axes on one another. But there still is not much jealousy [of the kind that 'bewitches' people]. Myself, I never got into those fights. I kept busy with tailoring just to stay out of trouble. I earned money as well."

Between 1940 and 1950 Solomon worked in Johannesburg. In 1950 he returned to Botswana. In 1954 he went back to South Africa to work in industry. In 1957 he took out a final contract to the mines.

"[Q: Why at this time did you take out a mine contract?] Things had changed in South Africa. You couldn't easily get a pass except for mine work. I stayed there for one year and a month, earning two

and six a day. This was much too little for the work I was doing, as a
fireman on a locomotive.

"To supplement my earnings, I got clothes from wholesalers in
Johannesburg and sold them at the mine. I was caught and arrested
for lacking a license to sell. They charged me with selling stolen goods.
But I had receipts to show where I'd gotten the clothes, so they dismissed me with a reprimand.

"This made me think of my life at home [1958]. By this time I had
been away from my children for a long time. They needed my help in
the ploughing season. I was now herding *my own* cattle, and ploughing my own fields. So I returned home.

"[*Q:* You seem not to have developed any real dislike for mine work;
was the work not that hard to take?] At the time when one first goes
to the mines, one sees nothing but confusion and coercion. Beatings
by the bosses underground. Daily fights among workers above ground.
Accidents are numerous, though I haven't seen any actually take
place. Escaping from accidents and not seeing any probably made me
able to tolerate work there without great effort. But the most important thing is that mine life destroys a person's humanity. There is no
freedom there. There is no civility. The Boers are very uncultured
people. You may think the boss-boys are themselves the cruelest lot.
But this is not so; the whole system of rules makes them to act the
way they do. You may think that the miners misbehave and that this
causes the BBs to be cruel. In fact, the misbehavior of the miners is
caused by the cruel and unfair treatment by the mine itself. [*Q:* Do
miners ever band together collectively to protest unfair treatment?]
Yes, of course. [*Q:* Do people of different nations [tribes] band
together in common efforts to protest unfairness?] Different tribal
groupings are unnoticeable below ground. But we live in tribally
segregated compounds, and there are many rivalries among the tribes.
But when it comes to protesting something concerning the mine as a
whole, complete mobilization of the whole workforce is required. You
must forget ethnic differences. . . .

"[*Q:* I can see many young people coming back from the mines
and they seem to act like conquering heroes. Why is that?] I know
very well that young boys from the mines walk around like heroes,
but they are insane from mine conditions. At the mines people do
not think. All things are completely ordered and arranged. The miner
never makes any decisions or choices. People are turned into
machines. This causes a person to become half-minded. These
youngsters have insulted elders at the mines with impunity. They
arrive home and think they have the right to do that. They have a
lump of money in their pocket; when they get home, they madly
spend it. The mines are not a place of normal human beings. To
survive there, you must not reason or think about anything. If you
do, you'll go crazy. But when a person doesn't think, he gets a false
(untruthful) impression of himself. That's why these young boys
think they're heroes.

"If I thought now that I would have to go to the mines again, I would vomit my lungs out. I don't even like to think about going. If I had to go, if I had no choice, I would go, of course, because I know how to deal with the situation." [Gaborone elder]

"Life at the mines is extremely heavy. There is no enjoyment at all. People only go there to get money. Contracts keep people from running away. [Q: Don't some people renew their contracts?] Yes, they are like soldiers. They get used to the conditions and forget what normal life is like. The boss-boys are given orders to treat the miners like creatures with no power to reason. They control miners like a span of oxen. . . .

"I worked in the mines for a number of years. During my stay there, I worked in almost all of the positions, even up to compound manager. I left the mines only because of home problems. Had they not arisen, I might have become trapped there myself.

"To be a boss-boy is no great achievement. [This person was a boss-boy of the highest rank.] You are expected to lead the workers into the stopes and check for fractures and for gas. Often it is the boss-boys who run the greatest risks of accident. But worst, boss-boys are often caught between people who are fighting, as in a strike.

"[Q: Could you explain something about strikes.] In 1925 I witnessed a very bloody strike in one of the compounds. The mine manager had instigated the Shangaans [a tribal group from eastern Transvaal and Moçambique] to fight all the other groups, especially the Tswana and the Sotho. It was started merely because the Tswana and Sotho had demanded to have Tswana and Sotho as members of the compound police force. [N.B., it is sometimes the case that Shangaan are selected by management for police duties more frequently than one might expect by chance.] We were searched and even our kitchen utensils were confiscated. The next day we were attacked by the Shangaan, but we really fought back. Many people were killed in that fight. Actually, the mine manager was found to be responsible for that fight. He was arrested. . . .

"Usually, strikes are against the mine, not one group against the other. In the compound the ethnic groups are housed separately; despite this, when there is a protest against the mine officials, all the groups band together and put aside their differences. . . .

"[Q: Do the young people returning from the mine feel they have become proper men from their rough experiences?] Definitely. They have returned from very heavy work and very harsh treatment. Surviving these makes them believe they are very brave. They feel they have conquered the world. But that is a completely false conception of what has happened to them. [Q: How do you feel about the mines now?] Mine work is like any other work, just as here in Botswana. What you will experience depends on the position you occupy in the organization. I have no hate for the mines. The thing I dislike is the violence of strikes. Strikes are foolishness, because many people lose their lives. Others are jailed. No one benefits. The mine is dangerous because of accidents. Tswana go there only because they have to. Once they get there, some forget who they are and just stay." [Gaborone elder]

"There is no life at all at the mines. Only suffering. The work is painful. The conditions most uncomfortable. You expect death any minute. You can grow thin and haggard because of the back-breaking work. Life in the compounds is bad too. You are constantly standing in lines, like ants. Fights are very common. When we are dismissed from work, we have to wait in endless lines to be lifted out of the ground while the Europeans come and go as they wish."

"[Q: Is there anything you can do about these grievances?] We are oppressed at the mines. Our cheap labor produces money for the Europeans. We are told the Europeans need so much money because they buy expensive food. We can strike—usually over wages and food. But these strikes are costly. Once the police came on horses with guns. People were killed just like sheep. The mines today are improving just because of African strikes. Still, you can lose your understanding in the mine. I would never go back to the mines." [Gaborone elder]

"The worst period in my life was in the South African mines. We worked hard all day long, on our backs. Yet we were kicked constantly. Despite beatings and hard work, there is no money. I took two contracts at the mines and then returned to Botswana for good. Go to the mine compound, and you will find people packed into shelf-like rooms, like tinned fish. We are awakened early in the morning, and all day long we are pushed and shoved around like goats. No one pays any attention to anyone else. You get so you don't notice anything. Conditions are unnatural in the mines. There is no sun, but only electricity. Farming at home is a natural undertaking. At the mines everyone becomes cruel. The whites are harsh, but that is because they purposefully want achievement in work. The Africans are worse. They become harsh and cruel for no reason at all. Boss-boys are the worst. They gain nothing for their cruelty. When people go to a place simply to eat, you cannot expect them to behave like human beings. People will remain civil only when they know they are making progress in life—aiming at a future. There is no future in a mine. There isn't even a language all can understand. They make us work together but not understand one another. The only way to survive in the mine is to remember why you went there—to earn money. But the oppression makes you weak and creates hatred among fellow workers. Hating one another makes you forget why you came to the mine. Your reason for being there becomes lost, so you find fights erupting frequently.

"Only dire poverty would force me to go to the mines again. [Q: Why then do some young people act like heroes when they return and describe the mine in such favorable words?] These people who have just come from the mines are fools. They think they are better

than the rest because they have on sharp-pointed shoes and because
they have entered showers naked with their elders. Cash jingling in
their pockets makes them behave so bizarrely. But that is a false
life. . . .

"I started hating the mines after I got home. When I think of how I
was kicked around while working so hard, I am filled with disgust."
[Kgaphamadi elder]

"When I was young, I thought the mines were a decent enough
place. It was a good place when I was a boss-boy. . . . But in comparing life in the mine with life at home, I would say the mines are a
place you go to only out of desperation. But when you are young,
you do not see it this way. You don't compare life in the mines with
life at home. When you go to the mines as a youngster, you do it out
of envy of the returning migrants. Then, later, you do it only because
you are determined to earn some money there, as no money can be
made locally." [Kgaphamadi elder]

"Life at the mines is very heavy (hard). Working in the grave is most
uncomfortable. You expect death to occur at any time, in your daily
work routine. In the compounds you may be stabbed because there
is so much ethnic hostility and rivalry.

"[Q: What was it like when you first went to the mines?] I had a
tough time adjusting to the mine conditions. Newcomers are particularly ill treated. The whole thing seems like confusion. You don't
understand the language; you don't know how to do the various
tasks. You are kicked and reprimanded continuously, no matter what
you do. The administration of the mine is the direct cause of the
unbearable conditions there. The foremen, whether white or black,
are very harsh and cruel. They tell you that whatever pain you suffer
there you have chosen to suffer voluntarily because you signed a
contract.

"[Q: How do you cope with this harassment and terror?] The only
way to achieve your ends is determination to do the work. Finish the
contract and leave. You don't dare think of anything else. You go
there with a purpose, and if you lose track of that purpose, you will
be eaten by the mine." [Kgaphamadi elder]

"Life at the mines is horrible. People just go there because of starvation and lack of local employment. Family problems [e.g., witchcraft]
can force you to go to the mines. I went because of the example I saw
among my age-mates. But when we get there the conditions are so
horrible that we do not consider one another as brothers, but only as
laborers. [Q: What are the bosses like?] The bosses are harsh, but that
is necessary to get the work done. A father here may be harsh on his
son so that he may get much work done. The son will think his father
is harsh and cruel. The main problem with the mine is accidents and
ethnic hostilities. Life is totally uncivil there." [Kgaphamadi young]

"I went to the mines because there were no jobs locally. When I got there, things were quite all right. Food and water were available. While we paid for these, the money was deducted from our salaries, so I didn't mind as much because I never saw the money in the first place. The most annoying aspects of mine work were that money was held for us until the end of the contract and that we were prisoners of the mine. Even if there is an emergency call from home, you can't leave." [Kgaphamadi young]

"The work at the mine is a risk. When working underground, any minute a rock can fall, crushing you to death. At the compounds death is also common. People of different ethnic groups are constantly fighting. Killings take place over very tiny issues. Pay is very poor. If you are injured, compensation is merely enough to make you not complain. It is very unhealthy. TB is everywhere. The distance to the mine forces a person to be absent a long period of time.

"My first contract was miserable. They made me stand and work in a smoky [steam-filled] room to get used to heat and dampness. Newcomers are ill treated underground, especially by boss-boys. They justify this behavior by saying they want you to learn fast. Whites are less cruel than blacks. The whites will kick you after several warnings, but the boss-boys kick you every time you go wrong. The blacks are cruel to us just so they can ingratiate themselves with their white bosses. They're trying to impress their own bosses and make them happy. So the newcomer is the complete victim of this process. There is a mine slogan [in *Fanakalo*] which the boss-boys say when they kick you mercilessly; they say, 'I am not from your home. I do not hear your mother's roosters.' By this, they mean they owe you no consideration. . . .

"[*Q:* Have you seen any strikes?] Strikes are mostly over food. This is when ethnic rivalries surface—partiality and discrimination are apparent in unfair food distribution. People use food to start fights. I have protested myself against a white boss, but I was calm and cool, and the matter was resolved reasonably and in my favor. Most strikes are entirely unconstructive—people letting out their hostilities caused by mine conditions. . . .

"[*Q:* Why do so many young returning migrants feel so heroic?] This is specious heroism. They act like peacocks because they have a little money in their pockets. They have been treated like children at the mine. They come home and act as if they have conquered the world. But in fact that is self-deception. As soon as their money has run out, they begin to return to normal. When I look back at my mine experience, I am filled with disgust because I was controlled like a baby. No freedom for thinking or decision. We just behaved like machines." [Kgaphamadi young]

"I first went to the mines in 1960. I was pretty observant of things there. Also the second time. The most intriguing part about mine work is how their labor practices affect your understanding. They dehumanize you to the point that you don't know whether you are working or not. When you are working very hard, a foreman will come up and berate you for not working. You receive a kick when you are doing nothing *and* when you are working hard. This creates a confusion in your mind so that you eventually stop trying to understand what you are doing. You just become determined to finish your contract." [Kgaphamadi young]

"[Q: Could you compare life at home with life in the mines?] There is no comparison, only a contradiction. The conditions among the people there are terrible. This is caused by irresponsibility that comes from being treated like a helpless child. People forget that they live in groups. Each person loses his awareness of the existence of other people. You are made nonhuman. This comes from not having to do anything for which you are responsible to your fellow workers. You just wake up in the morning and rush to the kitchen to get food that someone else has prepared. You don't make your bed. You don't have to take any responsibility for yourself. You are turned into a child. You are not allowed to think. You are never allowed to argue or complain, so you lose your ability to reason.

"The Boers are insidious in their treatment of Africans. Their demands can make you look like a fool. You must quickly learn to understand, because if you act stupid, the boss-boys' cruelty will be something terrible. Once you learn to understand what is expected of you, the boss-boys leave you alone.

"The only time cooperation among people exists is during a protest or strike. Then you let your feelings out. Otherwise, the different tribes are constantly fighting one another.

"[Q: Does this childishness created by the mines cause returning migrants to feel like heroes?] The young people coming from the mines are proud—looking into the air. I cannot blame them. They have worked nine months in back-breaking work and have received almost no wages. They then get here and are paid their full salary all at once. They become delirious with excitement. That thrill lasts only until the money is spent. But remembering it may make you go back on another contract. But that is the world of a child. I would never ever consider going back to the mines." [Kgaphamadi young]

Kalahari and Young of Gaborone
"[Q: Tell me about your experiences in mine work.] We wake up at 2:30–3:00 A.M. and start working at 7:00. In this time we are preparing ourselves for work—eating, putting on work clothes. While awaiting time to begin work, we are taught *Sefanakalo* [mine pidgin]. When the white boss arrives, he checks our tickets for daily work. When the foreman and the white underground manager enter the tunnels, they check for weak parts and mark them to be attended to. After they check to see that it is safe to enter, the inside is washed with water and they check for unblasted dynamite, called 'sekeleme' (blasting caps?). While we are working on the face [of the tunnel], you can

just go crazy and kill yourself with this unblasted dynamite. The labor is forced out of you. This is to obtain great achievements in the work. "[*Q:* Have you come to hate the mines?] No, I don't hate the mine work. But there are many disadvantages—mainly, the mines are very far away." [Gaborone young]

"Well, life is quite nice at the mines. When I first went to the mines, I was taken to mine school to learn *Sefanakalo* and how to do the tasks of underground work. The boss-boys are said to be cruel, but in fact they take their orders from the Boers. All instructions come ultimately from the Boers. [*Q:* Do miners ever protest these instructions?] Yes, miners strike, sometimes all night. But these strikes are a waste. Both white and black can die in such strikes. [*Q:* Do miners band together with solidarity in such strikes?] Yes, during strikes, miners forget their ethnic differences. This is what happened just recently at Carltonville [a strike where several were killed].

"[*Q:* How do you feel about mine work now—as regards liking or disliking it?] I haven't developed any real hate for mine work. But it is not something I would undertake except out of dire need. You are away from your home for twelve months. I could go back, but I prefer to work here in Gaborone." [Gaborone young]

"My first reaction to a comparison of life at home and life in the mines is that the two are totally unlike. Yet in thinking about it, I realize there isn't that big a difference. The thing is, I knew perfectly well before I left home for the mine that work would be very hard there. I was prepared for that and was determined before going that I would succeed, no matter what happened. [*Q:* How does that make mine work like work at home?] The two kinds of work are alike for many reasons. First, they are both hard work. Second, they were both part of my plans to progress in life. Third, I got from both kinds of work the things I sought in them. It is people who go to the mines expecting nothing but a smooth time that cannot persist. The key to succeeding in the mines is the determination to do what you went there to do: earn money.

"[*Q:* Did you plan then very carefully your first trip to the mine?] Yes, I had been thinking for some time about going to the mine, but I was concerned that this would create opportunity for my jealous sisters. I was reluctant to leave my home. But some friends of mine encouraged me to join in an escape they had planned. We would all go together to the same mine. These friends said our other age-mates were still in children's clothes [*megatla ya dipudi*]. So we left [1939]. We had free access to food, all we wanted; water and coal. It was a pleasant experience. I enjoyed relatively good health, and was paid well for my kind of work. In 1940 I returned home. In 1941 I went back to the mines and stayed five years. I needed many things: to build myself a decent house and to buy cattle for *bogadi* [bride wealth]. I was working at this time in Randfontein Mine, no. 14 shaft. It was a pleasant experience. I was a *picanin* of a certain white miner.

I carried his food and lamp. The wages were £3 per month. I lived in the compound.

"[*Q:* What was life like in the compound?] We had our food prepared for us. We were housed according to tribal group in bunk houses. There were police to keep order in the compound. On the weekends we got passes to go into town.

"During these five years I became a *'chesa* boy.' He is one who ignites dynamite. I loved this job because of the 3p. per shift increment I got. I started at 8:00 A.M., long after the other workers had started. It was light work, and I had freedom of movement. We ignited the dynamite at 3:00 P.M. after everyone else had quit work. This dynamite work is dangerous. I had to take many precautions. But there weren't many accidents. I do remember one leakage on the rocks which caused it to rot. It turned green, fell, and crushed people working in the shaft.

"[*Q:* Are you contemplating ever going back to the mines?] No, mainly because of my health. I got tired of working in the mines. When you are down there, you are either exposed to cold and darkness or to intense heat. These conditions have a bad effect on your health. It blocks your air passages, weakens your lungs. I weighed the advantages of mine work against the loss of my health, and I decided to come back and farm as best I could. I had saved a lot of money and was able to buy stock and other things. From that time on I have worked in different parts of Botswana herding cattle.

"[*Q:* Would you want to see your children going to the mines?] I wouldn't recommend to my children that they work in the mines. I would suggest they try to work in factories where the pay is better and where accidents are fewer." [Kalahari elder]

"The mine is a decent enough place for human beings. I was a boss-boy and enjoyed taking care of the miners. Of course, the mine is not like home. It is a place you go out of desperation. But when you are lacking food, when you are starving, you get to the mine, and then you can eat. There is harshness and cruelty in the mines. Of course, we got beaten, but we also got beaten at home. At least a person gets paid for his pains at the mine. Now there is money at the mines. Much more than when I started. There is no way we could survive these times of no rain except for the mine. We no longer choose whether to go to the mine or not. We just go." [Kalahari elder]

"Life at the mines is very heavy. There is a lot of confusion when you first arrive there. You work very hard . . . indeed, like a machine. And you can lose your power of reasoning. There are no workers' unions. So all problems are handled by the mine management. The boss-boys are like headmen. They just do what they are told by the white bosses. You may think that they are harsh, but that is the way to get the work speeded up. . . .

"Everything is rough at the mines. Taking a contract means you have to yoke yourself to the task to endure it. [*Q:* Many young men

who endure these experiences come home quite proud of themselves.]
Yes, they are just like men back from regimental practice [*mophato*].
So they feel that they are brave and real men. They also become very
excited when they receive their pay; they just don't know what they
are doing. . . . I don't hate the mine. Its major disadvantage is it is very
far away and takes us away from home for such long periods."
[Kalahari young]

"Life at the mines is like life at home. . . . Well, people speak of
accidents in the mines, but accidents are found everywhere. . . .

"Of course, my first reaction to the mine was that the work is
much too heavy. It was so hard on me I even thought of my mother,
but after three months I got used to it. I just began to feel at home.
The boss-boys and big stomachs did not bother me. They were fine as
far as I am concerned. It's important to maintain strict authority and
hierarchy to maintain control. . . .

"[*Q:* Have you ever seen or been involved in a strike?] Strikes are
common. I was once involved in one over pay. The Tswana, Xhosa,
and Sotho joined together to protest the low wages. Before things got
out of hand, the big stomachs responded to our demands. Usually
though, you can't get people of different tribes and nations to
cooperate. There is continual ethnic conflict. . . .

"[*Q:* Why do young migrants feel so heroic when they return home?]
It's just the money that has made them lose their good sense. They
want to buy the girls everything just to impress them. I feel a bit
embarrassed myself, as I have been a returning miner. Despite my
position of poverty, I still go to the mine. I feel like leaving right
now . . ." [Kalahari elder]

"My first experience at the mine was seeing people losing parts of
their bodies in accidents. The roof of the mine falls in, killing and
maiming. The bosses, though, treated us very well. Even the boss-
boys were respectful and kind. . . . There are fights in the compound.
The 'Russians' [some clique or gang of miners] were killing last year
about Christmas time. They went about with axes and knives. But
basically the work is good. We work together. We go to the mines
together; we return home together. Best of all, we receive money
which we can save until we get home.

"[*Q:* You seem to have few complaints about mine life.] Some
bosses are cruel, but this is mainly because of ethnic rivalries. A boss
who is not of your own tribe may discriminate against you. But we
just quit at the end of the shift, go to the compound, wash up, and
then get to the bar and enjoy ourselves over beer. Life is nice at the
mines. Most fights and troubles in the compound are handled by
sebonta [*induna*, or compound boss, of mine workers]. Fights and
quarrels are dealt with by him. [*Q:* Is he fairly effective in preventing
or settling fights?] The main cause of fighting is getting drunk. I don't
know why there are so *many* fights at the mines. . . .

"Strikes are best organized by the Malawians. Tswana are not reliable

as strikers because they immediately become cowardly and intimi-
dated when a confrontation occurs. They will reveal the ringleader as
soon as they are threatened. The Malawians never do that. Malawians
have solidarity. They usually get a favorable settlement of their
grievances. I once witnessed the Malawians striking over pay. They
were beating the compound police, and their riot was only contained
by the arrival of town [South African] police. The town police were
throwing cans that smoked into the Malawians' midst. They then
rounded up the Malawians and sent them home.

"I felt very depressed that the Tswana would never have the courage
to become unified and attain solidarity like the Malawians.

"[Q: Nevertheless, when Tswana come home from the mines, they
seem to act as though they've been successful.] Yes, when miners get
home, they have succeeded. Having money in your pocket is a joy;
that's why you see young men walking around with new clothes and
with confidence. I was once like these young fellows who have just
returned from the mines. When you feel like you've been successful
in your work there, you feel like a conquerer. We are also relieved that
God has kept us from being crushed by the mine stones [cave-ins].
We're happy to have returned to friends and relatives whom we have
not seen for some time. Even if you haven't been successful in getting
all the money you wanted, when you get back to your home, you feel
quite content.

"[Q: You seem to have no complaints at all about mine labor.]
None at all. [Q: What about beatings by mine personnel?] I don't like
being kicked. What assures me is that it is against mine law to be
kicked. No one has a right to kick anybody. The law protects us. If
you are kicked, you can report that person to higher authorities.

"The only job I don't like is driving a winch. This machine uses
petrol and sucks your blood. I like the boss-boys all right. It's their
job to look out for us. It's they who assure that a recently blasted
tunnel is safe before we enter. . . . If I needed the cash, for example,
to pay government tax, I would go to the mine. The government [of
Botswana] usually makes you take a mine contract if you fail to pay
the tax.

"[Q: What reasons led you to take a mine contract for the first time,
when you were young?] I went to the mine the first time because I
was attracted by the appearance of the other young men who had
just returned. I envied those from the mine. When I first went, we
went to mine school to learn the mine language, first aid, and safety,
as well as how to do the many kinds of work underground. . . .
It's important to have proper medicine [magical charms] to protect
you from accidents and trouble. Sorcery is common at the mines.
Therefore, you need *toise* [variety of 'medicine']. Then the whites
will promote you in your work. The Malawians have powerful magic."
[Kalahari young]

Interviews on Mine Experience: A Comment

All of the individuals whose testimony is presented here have confronted nearly identical events—migration to and labor in the mines. Yet these interviews make a clear prima facie case that the *experience of mine labor* is quite variable, despite the almost complete similarity in the material and institutional facts encountered. The variations in experience correspond quite closely to variations in the Tswana's material independence of mine or other wage labor. Those most dependent on wage labor, the town young and the Kalahari, show little or no marked hatred for the mines. Those whose dependency on mine labor is intermittent or long past—the residents of Kgaphamadi and the elders of the towns—show both strong dislike of the mine and, depending on age, a more or less sophisticated awareness of how their own perceptions of mine experience have changed as a function of aging and retrospective interpretation.

Individual contracts or stints at the mines can, of course, represent different experiences for a single individual. He may be injured during one contract and not during the others. He may be treated relatively well on one contract and not on the others. As one Kalahari respondent stated: "When you go to visit your in-laws, never defecate in the path." When visiting in-laws, you do not really know what to expect. Sometimes they can be hospitable and cordial—if familial ties are in good repair. At other times they can be sullen and hostile, even to the point of throwing you out. When this happens, you must return home on the path. If you have defecated, you will have to step in it. Hence, as a precaution against possible hostile circumstances (the unpredictableness of the experience), you do not go to the in-laws—or to the mine—counting on receiving hospitality and a good experience. You go expecting the worst and plan accordingly.

A number of verbal formulas like this one describe the determination and resignation required to "make the most" of mine work. For example, ethnic rivalry and conflict, which forms for all Tswana a focus of revulsion, is most often brought to the fore by the burdens of food distribution and sharing. While there is no shortage of food at the mines, many individuals use their positions in the commissariat to discriminate against members of other ethnic groups by unequal apportioning of food rations. The Tswana are very conscious of this association between ethnic conflict and eating. I asked why people would go out of their way to make trouble over food distribution when there is no food shortage. Several respondents said: "To eat is not to be loved." This means that one cannot permit questions of affection to get in the way of using food distribution as a weapon in a conflict where a rival ethnic group is competing for food. One group does not accord another the right to determine something as crucial as food distribution. "One dog cannot give another dog a bone." "One clump of grass cannot tie another."

I have mentioned kicking and beating many times. One of the stock responses made to me (mostly by Kalahari) as to why Tswana tolerate this was: "The snake is strong (endures) because of its stomach." The snake can swallow (take) anything, because in any case it is food in its stomach. At the mines one earns money that is desperately needed; hence, one will take any amount of mistreatment.

Interwoven with these references to determination and resignation were the sophisticated insights expressed by many of the non-Kalahari Tswana into the infantilization process that the mines intentionally use to create a docile, submissive labor force. These Tswana have seen the relationship between forced dependency on the mine, terroristic labor practices, and the resultant "colonization" of the mine workers' self-awareness. This insight, gained most often through a retrospective interpretation of the mine experience, definitely colors the manner in which many non-Kalahari Tswana formulate their revulsion at the conditions in the mine, as we have seen. The absence of a retrospective insight into this infantilization process among the Kalahari, coupled with their clear determination to pursue mining and their affirmation of its material importance, suggests that these most dependent migrants have internalized certain beliefs about the self and about mine labor that were generated by the mines themselves.

Town Life: Cultural Idealizations

Most nonliterate Tswana have experienced the mines of South Africa, which are therefore a taken-for-granted, if horrendous, part of Tswana life. As I have shown, those who are geographically most removed from the mines and striving diligently to maintain their traditional life-style are in fact most fully incorporated into the colonial political economy as dependents of the migratory labor system.

The place of the town in the material and institutional life of the Tswana is quite different from that of the mines, but as *experiences* in the life-world the two have much in common. Traditionally the Tswana have lived in very large villages, some with thirty to forty thousand inhabitants. Gaborone, the capital of modern Botswana, is half that size. But it is not population (either by size or by density) that is the important feature distinguishing the modern town (*toropo*) from the traditional village (*motse*), but rather the differences between the institutional and the face-to-face life-styles.

The noneducated Tswana population of modern Botswana is quite varied with respect to its first-hand experience of town life. Until the mid-1950s Tswana living in Bechuanaland could cross the border into South Africa in search of work with few or no formalities. Up to that time many Tswana spent some time working in one or more of South Africa's cities and towns. After 1957 severe restrictions were placed on migration to South Africa. Entry was restricted to those on contract to the mines or other industries with compounds for housing migrant workers; they would then be repatriated to Bechuanaland (now Botswana) upon termination of the contract. Since Botswana until just recently had no towns of any size, this means that it is almost exclusively among the older Tswana that one finds individuals who have lived extensively in towns. Since 1960 or so there has been a growth of towns in Botswana in connection with industry, commerce, and administration (towns still very small and lacking the complex socioeconomic infrastructure of South African cities). Only recently, then, have younger Tswana had any opportunity to experience the rudiments of town life. The first generation of town-raised Botswana Tswana has just appeared in the past decade or so.

The advent of towns in Botswana has given rise in the past decade to a pattern of circular and one-way migration among Tswana of all ages which in conjunction with mine labor migration acts as both an opportunity and a trap. Some young people who might formerly have gone to the mines are now "choosing" to seek work in one of Botswana's modern towns, as are elder Tswana with work experience in South African towns or in the mines who before would have tried to make a living exclusively through agriculture. Town migration is still small-scale in comparison with mine migration. But the outlines of the similarities and differences between the former and the latter are already patently clear (some of these have been outlined above in chapter 4).

Despite profound differences in institutional structure, town and mine are quite alike in the experience of the Tswana. But there are "objective" differences in the *consequences* of experiencing these two institutions which appear in the actual verbal testimony and self-image of Tswana.

I began my inquiry into the town experience by asking all respondents (male and female) in each community a series of simple, straightforward questions about town life and the wage labor to be found there. The answers I obtained were startlingly uniform and unequivocal. This uniformity persisted independent of whether the individual had in fact ever set foot in a town or not. Four of these questions are presented here.

Question 1: "Which of the following would you prefer, if you had both enough money and otherwise complete freedom to choose: to live in town (Gaborone) and work in a congenial, good-paying, steady job and live in a nice town-house, *or* would you prefer to live here in (*X*) (or at respondent's home) and earn a living by agriculture and cattle husbandry?"

Out of seventy-four responses, one person said *she* would prefer to live and work in town. The following is in all important respects like the answers given by seventy-two others:

"Why do you ask me such a simple question? Of course, I would like to be able to settle at home. Town has no life at all. In fact, there is no choice; if there were, no Tswana would live in town. I would definitely settle at my home. Rents and taxes of town life are high. We don't like towns in Botswana. They are things of the Europeans. Even the Boers who live in town are screaming about the pains of town life. They want to go back to the farms. So, of course, the Tswana do." [This individual had lived six years in Johannesburg and had been working in Gaborone several years at the time I interviewed him.]

Question 2: "Do you believe that life in town can 'corrupt' or spoil [*go senya*] many Africans who move there (here) from rural areas? Why or why not?" Of seventy-four responses, sixty-two stated firmly and emphatically that town life definitely corrupts the individual. Six said that town life did not corrupt individuals at all. And six stated that what happens to a person in town depends on how he is reared before he goes to town. Five of the six stating town does not corrupt were living in town at the time of my interview, and four of these had had extensive experience living in towns. Two of the individuals stating that town's effects depend on character formation in childhood were living in town. Most of the "urban" respondents did say, nevertheless, that town life either corrupts or is itself corrupt. The following answers expand on my summary. Responses (a) and (e) were given by Gaborone residents, the rest by rural people.

a. "Life in town is bad and risky. Death is common. Town folks have lost their origins because they don't know how to plough and farm. They have lost their manners completely. . . ."

b. "Life in town corrupts most Africans. A good example is me. I grew up in a rural life, and after this at an early age I lived in town. When I returned to the cattle post, I became confused totally. I thought the cattle posts were terrible places. I wanted to return to town. Now I realize, of course, that the only real life is at home."

c. "I don't approve of town life because of rents and rates for everything. Towns are breeding pools of bad manners because people of different customs live together. These conflicting behaviors create confusion and bad manners, which is against Setswana law."

d. "To lack town experience is to maintain one's human dignity."

e. "There can be corruption in people from town life, but only among those who from their childhood have not been properly shaped."

f. "Africans in town are absolutely corrupt. They don't obey traditional law. Neither do they adopt European law. They just become wild animals. They're people in between two laws."

g. "It corrupts indeed. . . . If one is in town and asks simple directions, no one pays any attention. People in town look down on people who lead a natural (traditional) life. Towns are just robbery and killing."

h. "Life in town is the negation of Setswana culture. Rural life is the affirmation of humanity [*botho*]. Town life spawns *tsotsis* [young thugs]. In the rural areas conflicts in one generation are settled by those of the next higher generation. In town there is nothing but mayhem; fists and blood are town ways to settle misunderstandings."

Question 3: "To become a proper adult ready for marriage and fatherhood, do you believe it is necessary first to seek wage-paying work in town or the mines? Why or why not?"

Sixty-three of seventy-four respondents stated unequivocally that it is a good thing for a young man to have to go through the hardships of finding and holding a job in town as well as to amass a grubstake before marriage. Three people said that if at all possible it is best just to farm and forget about wage labor. The remaining eight stated that the strategy was optional—its benefit being dependent on individual circumstances. The following answers are typical.

a. "I believe that one should work very hard in a wage-paying job before marriage as this serves two purposes: first, it proves that the young person has attained adulthood; second, it provides the means with which a person can purchase necessities for the household. Another thing accomplished by wage work is demonstrating independence of the parents. To work doesn't mean a person is ready for marriage; it means the person has acquired knowledge which is necessary for a good marriage. It shows he knows how to solve problems."

b. "It is traditional that young boys seek work before marriage. Formerly this could only be done in the mines. Now there are some jobs in Botswana, so where one works is a matter of choice."

c. "It is important for children to work before marriage. Working in towns is better than working in the mines, provided they save the money for marriage payments. But this work in town must not lead the children to forget their relatives in the rural home."

d. "Of course, a boy should work first in preparation for marriage. . . . He should save a substantial amount of money with which to buy *bogadi* (*lobola*) cattle. This is evidence that he is capable of maintaining a family."

e. "I am completely opposed to the idea of working before you get married. The reason is this: when you work and accumulate wealth, you learn the value of that wealth because you have had to be industrious and prudent in earning it. Now, if you just come home and marry a woman who lacks the experience of seeing how you worked to earn it, she will be reckless with your wealth. If you remonstrate with her, she will accuse you of saying she is a dog—poor right from her family. So my suggestion is to live together and work together to earn the money necessary for maintaining the household and for paying *bogadi*. Then both will understand from the hardships more about how to use wealth." (This last answer came from a young man from Kgaphamadi who in many respects was unlike his Tswana brothers and to my mind had extraordinary intellect and powers of thought.)

Question 4: "What do you like most about town life? What do you dislike most about town life? What do you like most about home life? What do you dislike most about home life?"

As with the preceding questions, the answers to this set of questions were almost completely uniform. The question, "What do you like most about home life?" was somewhat anomalous, as I imagined it would be. The Tswana do not break down *botshelo jwa Setswana* [life (based on) Tswana culture] into a set of attributes. But the other three questions received definitive answers from nearly every respondent.

The only real value of town, claimed almost all Tswana, lies in the opportunity it provides for wage labor. (Below I will discuss some elaborations on this provided by respondents with urban experience.) The only things the people I interviewed disliked about rural life were the lack of a reliable water supply and *lefufa* (jealousy and witchcraft). The same dislikes came out in replies to the question concerning how towns spoil Africans.

Taken as a whole, these responses suggest that the idea of town acquires much of its meaning apart from actual experience and in relation to the horizon of traditional Tswana values and ways of life. For the majority of my respondents the opinions they expressed were based on suppositions and verbal reports, not on extensive experience in town. But their opinions were almost identical with those of Tswana who were very involved in town life. The obvious and radical difference between the actual experience of the town dweller and the secondhand knowledge of the rural dweller is obliterated in the sameness of this general affective response. Town means about the same thing to town dwellers as it does to rural dwellers: town is the source of the wage labor necessitated by deficiencies in agricultural production. Urban Tswana possess a lot of knowledge about town that distinguishes them from their rural counterparts, but this knowledge has little influence on the overall response elicited in questioning. To learn about the more subtle aspects of town experience that manifest themselves only in actual engagement with its social life we must turn to those respondents who have lived extensively in town. This includes most of my Gaborone sample and four or five older people (found by chance in the rural sample) who had lived in South African towns earlier in life.

The Meaning of Urban Life

While finding wage labor is the principal goal of most Tswana who come to town, it is not the only one. It is significant that the Tswana themselves—including many of those in my sample—often express "attitudes" to town that belie the simplicity and certitude of the summary judgments reported above. When, for example, one asks a Tswana "to compare life in town with life at home," these phrases usually call up a response that gives an idealized cultural stereotype of town and home. However, when one presses the respondent to describe his experiences in town or watches his behavior and conversation with others on topics relating to town life, one sees evidence of "contradictions," or at least context contingency, in his attitudes.

Personal acquaintance with the Tswana in the rural samples allowed me to confirm through observation and discussion the fundamental sincerity and accuracy of their characterizations of the meaning of urban life. While I worked with most of the people in my urban sample for over five months, I did not have the same degree of contact with them—sharing the daily round of life and following them in their various routines. Nevertheless, I was able to observe enough to know that for many urban Tswana the meaning of urban life, even in comparison to home life, is more variegated than the most complete answers to my initial questions would suggest.

This state of affairs has already been alluded to in the Tswana's discussions of how many young people "escape [go ngwepa]" to town, how many of them lose a taste for rural life (makgwelwa). In my Gaborone sample I had opportunities to observe town dwellers interacting with newly arrived escapees from the rural areas. In many instances the former would at least feign enjoyment of town life and lay claim to the heroic status that comes from successfully coping with it. This behavior parallels what I found among returning mine workers who parade their victory for kith and kin on returning home.

Few people who cope with the vicissitudes of urban living over a long period of time retain a simple, one-dimensional hatred of it. The experience arising from such coping behavior cannot be devoid of ambivalence and other complexities. This was certainly the case with most of the Tswana with whom I worked in Gaborone. The mine also gives rise to a great variety of experiences, but here contrasts manifest themselves only if one looks at certain groups of interpretations—those given by a person over the course of his life, for example, or those given by heterogeneous groups such as the Kalahari and the Kgaphamadi. In the case of town living, variegated or ambivalent experiences can exist at one time within an individual's consciousness.

These facts suggested to me that town living can constitute a challenge to fundamental definitions of the self, of the past, and of native culture that is at the same time more profound and more subtle than the challenge that arises from mine-labor migration. As we shall see, in many cases this collision of experiences has a positive effect on the way the individual evaluates himself in relation to the powerful image of action embodied in the European.

In chapter 4 I suggested that in town the Tswana can confront the institutional manifestations of a colonial political economy in ways not possible in the mine. In town a person can exercise his fundamental capacity to act, make choices, and plan—in short, to determine his own fate, albeit within narrow limits. *The willed manipulation of a world that resists—however limited the manipulations may be—constitutes an affirmation of human being.* In such a situation a person is not determined from without; he can overcome the "mystifying" effects of Western institutions and technology through the rational insight that accompanies a commonsense knowledge of how these parts of the political economy work. Both of these consequences of coping with town living have important implications for self-evaluation and hence for the formation of self-identity.

Fortunately for the Tswana—and, incidentally, for ethnographic research—the projects of coping with and interpreting town life are made explicit in the verbal formulations to which the Tswana are so given. In the previous chapter I showed how the process of name-(reputation-) making is linked to oral literature. In particular, I reported the close association the Tswana make between the literary formulation of the trickster figure and the adaptive problem faced by those who come to work in town. The irresistible, irrepressible urge to self-praise shown by the trickster figure is found among the Tswana themselves as they recount the successes and travails of town living.

This can be illustrated from the following autobiographies, given to me by Segatlhe and Solomon. Segatlhe's experiences of the European world show clearly that for him there is little or no "collision" between the two cultures. Most of his life, on the contrary, has consisted of the daily integration of the European and Tswana worlds into a single life. Again I present his language with very little attempt at paraphrase or explanation.

Two Worlds in a Single Mind

"It is I, Gustav Ernst Segatlhe. I was born in 1899 in the western Transvaal. We moved almost immediately to a dorp [small town] near Rustenburg. My mother died when I was but fourteen days old. I was taken to another woman, who had another baby boy. She nursed me, and she cared for me until I was about twelve years old. Then I returned to my father's place [*ga phiri*] to live there with him, my two sisters, and two brothers.

"Like any young boy of that age I began to learn of this life by beginning work as a herd boy. I tended my father's herd. At the same time I began school [at a German Lutheran mission] and kept alive by stealing from the fields. I was baptized a Lutheran and was confirmed. I am no heathen. I continued school until 1918. In 1919 I began to 'work cattle,' that is, to go to the farms of the Boers to tend their herds. I worked one year for Meneer [Afrikaans for 'Mr.'] Isaac Linberg. At the end of the year I received one cow as payment for my work.

"Thereafter I tended the herds of Meneer Cornelius Scholtz. In both cases I was treated well by my employers. I received no money but was well fed and did receive a beast for each year's general farm labor. As with any human beings, we often quarreled [I and my employers]. But I must say I lived well.

"Now you know that as Christians we never took notice of

initiation school or thought of going. But even as a youngster we couldn't help but think about our cultural background as we grew older and as we witnessed other young boys going to be circumcised. So one day I and others went to be initiated. A good thing it is to be a man among others.

"In 1919 I went to Potchefstroom and worked as a cook's helper at a military base. That was my first job, and it was good. In 1920 I decided to taste life in the big city. I went to Johannesburg. I moved through the townships like a fox. Indeed, I lived the life of a fox. Always on the move, living with different relatives. Leaving the farms, leaving my home and going to Johannesburg removed me from the bondage of poverty for sure. I fared well in town. In 1921 I went to Natal, where first I signed a contract to work in a coal mine. Open-pit. None of this underground work for me. What can you learn of life if you're buried alive half the day. I worked at the mine six months, living in the mine compound. Now no one gets anywhere working in the mines. So I went to Vryheid in search of better work. Really I was looking for lots of things at once. At that age the thorn of young love makes one's blood run hot. I was constantly chasing after girls. I landed a job as a plumber's apprentice. I worked with a certain Mr. Long. He taught me many things, or rather I learned much from him. As you know the white men don't go out of their way to teach, to enable you to understand what it is you're supposed to be doing. They just point at tools, or work; grunt, and bark orders, and yell and kick if you do something wrong. But I was a clever fox. I used to watch Mr. Long every minute; I followed him and watched what he did and how he did his work. I learned a lot that way. If I had just been able to get more schooling I'd be in America right now. I like to watch and learn to do things on my own. Now this plumbing work was heavy for a young boy like me. Besides I had other interests and wanted to move on, so I quit in 1923 and went to the cane fields near Durban. That was rough work. Ow! Those Indian foremen were a mean lot. They would beat you. And if you tried to beat them back you'd wind up in a hell of trouble. This was useless work. So I ran away. To hell with the contract. Went into the city [Durban]. Soon I found a job in an SAS [Suid Afrikaanse Spoorweg] refreshment hotel. There I had a job as second chef. That was relaxation and good food for me. I would wash pots, peel potatoes, watch the cooking food, clean fish. Pay was pretty good. I got £2 4s., with 4d. increment per month each three months. I worked there for two years.

"Now as you know, I was still a young man at the time. And I enjoyed going places, visiting people on my bike when work was slow. Why should I bust my ass for two pounds? When my boss queried me about where I was going, I told him he wasn't the only white [i.e., employer] in the world, so I left the place and sought work elsewhere. I knocked around Pietermaritzburg for a long time doing odd jobs. In fact I did everything imaginable except commit murder. In 1929 I got a job at Grace Hospital as an apprentice to an electrician, a Scottish

fellow named Mr. Helsey. I even used to go to his house and eat rice
and drink tea and savor all kinds of other delicacies of the white
people. At this time I was living in a location called 'Settlers.' This
guy, Helsey, used to have me do everything. He'd send me on errands
to buy groceries, go do things for his wife. And as payment he'd let
me buy things for myself. I particularly like a variety of food. Eating
like Europeans is nice indeed. Pork is my favorite. I ate well working
with this electrician. But suddenly my luck changed. I suspect to this
day I was bewitched, by a certain policeman named 'Cele.' He used to
earn £2 per month, and he was jealous of me in my position, being in
charge of the electricity throughout the hospital. Anyway I was
burned on the hand and fingers by an electrical wire. That's why I
can't use my hand to this day. I was hospitalized for some months
and received pay of £4 10s. and £36 workingman's compensation. But
I lost my fingers. I had to quit work late in 1929, and for one year I
was out of a job. I had to live off my wits. Planning all the time how
to get through the day, the week, the month. Finally I got a job
helping a fellow in his shoe repair business, Mr. Ntombela. He paid me
6d. per shoe for stitching the heel or sole. I learned the art of shoe
repair from him, and that proved to be another skill that was an
asset.

"In 1931 I decided to leave Natal and go back to Johannesburg
where I lived with my sister. I had no fixed job at that time, so I
decided to get to Jo'burg. But I had managed to accumulate close
to £300 [probably an exaggeration], not in a savings bank, but in the
house where I was living, buried in the ground. Now if you die, that
kind of money buried in your place becomes 'ghost money.' When
I got back to Johannesburg some friends and I once tried to go dig
up some ghost money we'd heard about. But do you think we got
anywhere? This was in Mayfair [suburb of Johannesburg]. We hadn't
even gotten into the place when the cops spied us. They were
mounted on horseback and pointing revolvers at us. There we stood
with our picks and shovels. Fortunately they just told us to beat it.

"I did a lot of things in Johannesburg. I was working as a peddler of
soft goods in cooperation with a certain Indian shop owner. He would
provide me with the wares with instructions about sales price. I would
go off, sell, and we divided the profits. That job got me into difficulty. The cops caught me, as I didn't have a hawker's license. Fortunately they simply levied a fine of 5s. which I could pay, so I was
released. Another time I was passing near a shop, when a Boer cop
yelled at me, 'Kom hier jy kaffir! [Come here you nigger!].' I had no
pass so I had to escape. I jumped on my bike and took off. Now the
roads were slippery, wet from recent rain. I was peddling like mad
with the Boer behind me on his horse. Off we went down the road,
cop on my tail. Bad luck got me. I crashed the bike, but I was far
enough ahead of the mounted policeman that I made it to a barbed
wire fence, slipped through and got away. Sometimes, if it's a matter
of survival you can do amazing things.

"By the end of 1932 I was established in a private business of selling intestines, heads, and hoofs of beasts. Hawking from my bicycle. This was not the best line of work, and so thereafter I got enough money to open a shoe repair place in Brixton, where I could take advantage of the Boer trade. What a pain having to deal with the Boers! One day a Dutch lady came into the shop and said to me (mind you, no greeting or anything), 'Hey Jim!' Now my blood boiled. 'How much do you charge to attach this heel to a lady's shoe?' I said, 'I'm not Jim. Jim's in the backyard. So if you don't know me, which you don't, then you'd better call me by the trade I'm in: Meneer Skoenmaaker.' So I took her shoe and threw it out the window. Hours later her husband pitches up, and he had with him the same bloody shoe. He was very polite, he called me Meneer Skoenmaaker. So I took the shoe and fixed it.

"Shortly after this incident I moved my shop to Sophiatown [an African township] where I had expanded business opportunities.

"Now in 1933 I decided I'd better get to Botswana, Kgaphamadi, to learn about witchcraft. Now I'll tell you why. Just before I left Natal, when I was staying in Pietermaritzburg, I had sought out a witch doctor who could help me to become a witch doctor myself. The 'accident' at Grace Hospital made me aware that if I was to succeed in this life I would have to learn to defend myself from the jealousy and envy of those with medical power. So I had begun my studies as a doctor. Now while I was running my shoe business in Sophiatown, I was practicing some novice medicine to help people on occasion. It was then I realized that I could make much more money as a witch doctor than I could as a shoe repairman. Also I was hit by a spate of misfortune which I was convinced could have been avoided completely if I had known how to take the proper medical precautions. For example, I was arrested for a pass offense. I had neglected to renew my day laborer's permit for two months. I was taken to Newlands police station, booked, and kept there one week. Again, I was once arrested for playing cards [gambling in the street] at night. This time I was fined and discharged. Now all this was unnecessary if I had known how to protect myself. So in 1933 I went to Kopong [in Botswana] to learn to become a powerful doctor, at the hands of a Mokgalagadi [a Tswana from the Kalahari Desert; see pp. 74ff.] who lived there. There I became a powerful doctor.

"I went back to Johannesburg, but I entertained the thought of going back to Botswana one day. During this time I tried a lot of things. Some friends of mine and I had heard about the diamonds down in Lesotho. So we walked down to Maseru to see if we would turn up some. We spent months looking for diamonds but had no luck. We were running short of provisions and money, so we had to do something in a hurry. We got into the business of delivering *dagga* [marijuana]. It is a good line of work, but risky. I never got caught, but it was good luck. A week after I quit OFS [Orange Free State] to come back to Johannesburg, all of my friends who had stayed to deliver *dagga* were arrested by the police.

"For the next ten years I did odd jobs in Johannesburg. I managed to get into the taxi business with my younger brother's car. I was driving all over Johannesburg. All went well 'til 1939 when I was arrested for not having a driver's license. Actually at that time I had hired a driver who had no license, and I had no business license, so we were both arrested and fined.

"This license business is hard to figure out. In 1936 I decided to try work in the gold mines, so I signed on a nine-month contract. I worked one day underground. It was horrible. You could easily lose your mind doing work like that. So I ran away. I was later found by the police and arrested for running away from the mine. I was fined £ 1 10s. and discharged.

"For the next few years I did odd jobs. Nothing big came along. I was growing tired of the fast life. My blood was beginning to cool. And in 1944 I decided to leave Johannesburg and move permanently to Botswana. I gathered together all my belongings and packed them in my wagon and moved here to Kgaphamadi. While I had been doing quite well in the preceding ten years in Johannesburg, I longed to try my hand at farming. Also, I could continue my medical career here at the lands. In fact my reputation as a witch doctor has continued to draw people out here to this very day.

"[*Q:* What are some of the highlights of your career as a *ngaka ya Setswana?* (traditional Tswana doctor)?]

"*Bongaka* [Tswana medical practice] helped me in many ways in my work both in Johannesburg and here. In Johannesburg people pay for your help in cash. They do not hesitate to pay, pay well and promptly. Here these people simply make vague references to a cow or a sheep some place or another. Most likely you'll never see it. And when you begin to press for payment the patient will seek out another doctor to have you killed.

"In any case I've had good fortune in medical practice. No one has ever died at my hands while under treatment. Many barren women whom I have given fertility once again often named children after me; they're testimony to my success. I have helped many who ran the risk of losing their jobs to keep their work by preparing medicine against their employers' wrath. Of course in Johannesburg many people are plagued by *tikoloshes* [a familiar, or medium, of a person with 'supernatural' powers]. I have very good herbs for exorcising these horrible creatures. Once in 1959 a colored man came all the way from Jo'burg to seek my help in getting rid of a *tikolosh*. This particular one was a male and had gotten into the habit of demanding sexual relations with his wife, as well as with its other victims. In this case I discovered that the *tikolosh* had been left in the man's house by the former occupants. When the city council ordered all the Africans to move from Western Native Township to Moroke and to Meadowlands, many people were against this forced move. So this one individual left behind his *tikolosh* to plague the new occupants. The woman grew pale and thin from continuous intercourse with this *tikolosh*. He also would trouble the husband by eating the food from his plate whenever the man sat down to eat. I gave the man herbs with which to doctor the house and the *tikolosh* went away.

"In another case I helped a Xhosa shebeen queen who had a *tikolosh*. She used to use him to help her brew beer, at home. Now this woman was unable to satisfy the *tikolosh*'s sexual demands, so he turned on her. He got hold of her young daughter. This girl was growing pale and thin. The woman called me in and I diagnosed the problem; I provided medicine that was so powerful that the *tikolosh* left the house in broad daylight.

"There are no *tikoloshes* out here in Botswana, but there are plenty of other *baloi* ['spirits'] as Modise [author] knows from being ridden at night by the witches. That's why he gets up so late in the morning tired out. He's got no medicine to protect himself with.

"In 1946 I bought a scrap van and used it to haul wood to Lobatse. But my heart lay in farming and so I got these fields, you see there, from the chief in Mogoditshane and bought cattle with my savings to start a herd. I became a very successful farmer. There are thirty morgen of cultivated field here [about thirty hectares].

"My only downfall in life has been women. You know my wife disgraced me and left me some time ago. Had I not gotten bitten by women I would be a very rich man today.

"[Q: What reflections or thoughts come to mind when you think back on the many years you lived among the whites, including the Boers?]

"Let me tell you a story:"

THE STORY OF THE JACKAL AND THE HYENA
(as told by Rre Segatlhe)
One day jackal saw a Boer trek past in an ox-wagon. Leading the wagon was a young Tswana fellow. Jackal hatched a plan. He lay sprawled in the middle of the road, pretending he was dead. As the wagon approached, jackal lay very still. The Tswana exclaimed, "Master, here is a jackal lying dead in the middle of the road!" The Boer replied, "What the devil do you think I would want to do with that?" The Tswana answered, "You can use its skin to make a kaross [cape]." To this the Boer replied, "That's a good idea! Come on, pick him up and throw him on the wagon." This the Tswana did. Now in the wagon were barrels containing butter. While the jackal lay in the back of the wagon, he rolled one barrel off the wagon on to the road. Further on, he rolled off a second, and then jumped off the wagon himself. He rolled the barrels back into the woods and hid them; and then, he went back to join his friend, the hyena, and tell him the good news.

Jackal wanted a way to enjoy the butter alone so he said to hyena,

"Brother, lend me your towel as I am going to my child's baptism."
This the hyena did. The jackal went to barrel number one and ate one-
sixth of the butter. He then returned to the hyena. The hyena asked
him, "Tell me, what did you name your child?" The jackal replied,
"Hoop-One!" [This is an oblique reference by the jackal to the fact
that he ate the butter down to the first hoop, there being six hoops on
a barrel.] The second day, jackal came with another excuse to visit
the barrel alone. He said to the hyena, "I'm going to see my brother's
five sons who have come to visit me. Could you please lend me your
hat for my trip?" On the jackal's return, the hyena asked him, "Tell
me, how did it go? What are your nephews' names?" Jackal answered,
"The first one is called Hoop-Two, and the last one is called Lick-the-
Bottom." And so the jackal succeeded in cheating the hyena out of
the barrel of butter and did likewise with the second. The hyena was
angry and starving, and desperate. He chased the jackal in hopes of
catching him and making a meal of him. The jackal ran with the hyena
in hot pursuit. The jackal soon came to a tree trunk where there was a
hive of bees. He went up to the tree trunk and peeked into the hole.
When the hyena came by, the jackal said, "Stop, don't kill me, put
your head in here and listen to God's children singing!" When the
hyena did that he got himself stung by bees and fled for dear life,
leaving the jackal in peace. The jackal was free once more. He went to
lie by the road to wait for his next victims. The same Boer and Tswana
with the ox-wagon came by. The Tswana called out, "Master, there's
a jackal lying dead in the middle of the road!" The Boer retorted, "I
am tired of those tricks. Get a whip and give him a few lashes and see
if he can stomach the pain." The Tswana did that, but the jackal did
not move. Then the Boer said, "Turn the whip around and beat the
bastard behind the neck." The pain was too much for the jackal so he
got up and ran for dear life into the bush. [End]

Segatlhe's autobiography makes poignantly clear how the image of
the trickster has informed and enriched the standpoint from which this
old man looks back on his career and reconstitutes it in a narrative.
Segatlhe's life history illustrates how one individual's consciousness
represents the stock of social knowledge and the institutions that constitute society in southern Africa. His life takes place in a single world.
His retrospective view permits him to explicate events to himself, and
this process reveals the meaning of events to him. Wage labor, town
life, the life of farming, and African-European relations acquire subjective meaning in his awareness, in his way of classifying and evaluating
them. These same ideas receive confirmation in Solomon's story. He,
like Segatlhe, spent some years in Johannesburg, thoroughly enmeshed
in its rough-and-tumble underlife, where survival requires both guts and
wits.

"[*Q:* Rra Solomon, looking back on your life in Johannesburg, what thoughts and feelings about those years come most often to your mind? Can you tell me of the things that still stand out in your recollections?]

"I'm an old man now, but I still look back with pleasure on my life, including my years in Jo'burg. I am pleased especially that the wisdom I had to plan my life carefully has paid off. For example, during my leisure hours [in Johannesburg], I used to go to the wholesalers and buy some goods and sell these at a profit in the townships. I was able to look after myself. God has really blessed me with good fortune. . . .

"In 1940 [after three mine contracts] I moved into a room in Newclare—69 Wanderers Street. I learned the tailoring trade from my uncles. I made a living sewing and selling trousers . . . to people working in the mines. I was very prosperous and was well known to all the local *tsotsis* [dapper street slicksters]. I used to go to the mine compounds all over the Reef and come back home late at night. But I was never assaulted by these *tsotsis*. This was because I was their friend. I altered their pants to that bottle-shape [knee breeches] so they wouldn't get tangled up in them when they run away from the police.

"During this time I was married to my present wife. Now a certain man came to visit us, and he put up at my place for the night. He had certain ideas about taking my wife from me. He was envious of me. He also loved my wife. He pulled out a big knife and began playing with it. He demonstrated with it how one day he was going to kill me. The knife, he said, was his 'inseparable friend.' I just played it cool during his talk. I didn't show any fear of his words. Well, he left. But he recruited some *tsotsis* to come and kill me. They came soon, feigning that he left something. I refused to open the door. Then suddenly they battered the door down with a big cinder block. Five of them rushed in. One had a revolver pointed at my head. At gunpoint they began asking me questions. I just sat there completely in shock. The 'gun' asked me whether I was 'aware of my own death.' I said yes. They just stood there. Then finally one of them said they were coming at 2:00 A.M. to kill me. Obviously, they were hoping I would run away. They then left. I ran immediately to a Mohurutse [member of a Tswana tribe, the Hurutse] friend of mine. He was a good fighter and had a revolver too. He waited with me, and at 2:00 exactly there was a knock at the door. The *tsotsis* stood outside the door grumbling and arguing about whether it was a mistake to have told me exactly when they were returning. Finally they got scared because of their own doubts and quietly dispersed.

"The next day I saw this 'friend' alone and told him of his plan to kill me. I told him that if I die, he would be responsible [i.e., he would become bewitched]. After that, he tried all possible means to kill me using witchcraft. But his witchcraft backfired on him. He got chronic diarrhea. He thought I had bewitched him. He came running to me begging me to undo the curse. He admitted trying to kill me by witchcraft, but that everything had failed. Now he was miserable because he could do nothing except crap."

Segatlhe's and Solomon's careers in town are filled with these close scrapes and conquests. There is every reason to believe that their stories are basically "true." Life in the black locations of Johannesburg is like this. But the heroic, almost transcendent standpoint from which these tales are told suggests the self-esteem and confidence that come with experience reconstituted in retrospection. A recognition of the role played by reflection is as important to understanding how a person copes with town and its effects as is knowledge of the day-to-day recipes at hand for dealing with town life. Reflection is no less experience than life as it is lived. The strength and genius of Tswana culture reveals itself in the way they continually recast past events into new narratives—new tales—reconstituting the meanings of these events in terms of the individual's ever-developing life-project.

Compared to the heroic mode of these relived town adventures, the recipes for town living that the older, more experienced Tswana give youngsters leaving for town are quite prosaic.

I opened my discussion of recipes for town life with the following vignette:

"Living in town brings you close to the world of the Europeans. You have a chance to see how the rich (white or black) live, work, and behave toward Africans like yourself and toward each other. Part of living in town is adapting [*tlhwaela*] to the customs and usages of European culture. Is this true? . . . Now with these thoughts in mind, I would like you to tell me what you would say or do in the following situation: If a young Tswana is planning to come to town (Gaborone) from the rural areas for the first time, what kind of advice would you give him so that he could best get along or succeed in town to attain his purposes?"

All but one of the twenty-one male Gaborone respondents agreed that the question's premise was correct and that they had given such advice to their juniors on one or more occasions. The one who demurred said that to give advice is risky, for if the person goes wrong he may blame the one who gave the advice and seek revenge by trying to bewitch him. I suspect this individual had in mind an actual personal experience.

One of the most intriguing replies given by most of the Tswana was something I had not expected at all. As one respondent stated it:

"The key to being successful in town is to avoid becoming dependent upon town life. [Q: What do you mean by 'dependent'?] I mean two things: you should maintain your home life so that you have a means of livelihood in case town work runs out, and second, I mean you should not grow to like [literally, 'drown in'] the things of town which eat up your earnings and cause you to aspire to a life you can never lead and make you forget your origins. You should come to town to earn money, but use that money to maintain life at your home. Europeans and others with money have a very high standard of living. There is no purpose served in a Tswana trying to emulate these big stomachs."

This response—like those given by twelve others—suggests immediately a conviction that many aspects of town life, while experienced, should not be incorporated into values or beliefs about oneself or the ideally good life. An aspect of the Tswana's recipe for coping with town living seems to be *a deliberate and sustained conviction that town living is irrelevant.* This "attitude" would seem to underlie the firm desire expressed by all Tswana to live at home in preference to town.

As the primary purpose of being in town is to earn wages, it is not surprising that most spontaneous discussion of how the hypothetical young Tswana from the cattle posts should cope with town life revolved around getting and holding a job. The recipes in the main derive from maxims that prescribe proper conduct between seniors and juniors in the traditional culture. The following interview excerpts illustrate this.

"To succeed in town work, this young Tswana must take very seriously every task he is given, including finding work itself. He should spend the first few days just getting acquainted with the layout of town, especially the location of firms that are hiring. Then he should go early in the morning to the firms that are hiring, arriving before the other workers do. He must then respectfully ask if there is employment available. Even if he is told no, he should not give up right away, but continue to return to that firm again and again asking for work. Openings can occur on short notice. So he must just keep trying. If he succeeds in getting a job, he must strive continually to try to impress his bosses that he is a good worker. This is done by working hard all the time, even when he is not under surveillance. He should be patient and courteous in his dealings with his fellow workers and with his bosses. He should not do anything unless he understands clearly what is to be done. He mustn't act until he has received instruction. If he doesn't understand the instructions, he must ask for further explanations. Learning the rules of a firm is very important. This young person should immediately make the acquain-

tance of people who have been working in this firm a long time, as
they can help him with advice. But he must beware that Tswana are
jealous people. They are not like Europeans. A Tswana can give another the wrong advice intentionally, hoping to make this newcomer
mess up and lose his job. He must develop acquaintants with people
who do not compete for the same work. He must be circumspect in
acting on advice. Most important, he must be industrious at all times.
If he has a complaint, he should only make it if it is very important,
because if you complain over every little thing, you will risk losing
your job. On the other hand, if you never complain or seek advice,
you may do something wrong or stupid and lose the job anyway."

"Tswana are jealous people. Therefore, I would only give advice to
my relative, not to a stranger. I would first caution him about the
expenses of town life. Life in town is a life of money. He must learn
to avoid spending money uselessly. Second, I would tell him that
respectful, tactful behavior is important at all times. When looking
for a job, he should ignore the signs on gates that say there is no work.
Europeans put those up there just to keep down the number of
inquiries. Often there is work. Once he gets a job and begins to earn
money, he must think wisely how to invest his money to make more.
He must not walk with his head down as at the lands, because there
are *tsotsis* in town. He must be on guard for thieves. Big stomachs,
especially Boers, treat Africans like slaves, but they can't do a thing
without the Africans, and they know that. If you are industrious and
a good worker, you don't have to take any rebuke from Europeans
that is not deserved. You must maintain your dignity. Just quietly
explain your position. In most cases the dispute will be reasonably
settled."

"In order to deal with the work situation, you must have patience.
Remember, you just came here to work. All that you do must help
you to achieve that purpose. If this Tswana gets into quarrels with his
co-workers, he can lose his job, whether he is at fault or not. Firms are
not for trying cases. Just forget arguments and trying to prove yourself in the right. Co-workers are often jealous; if you are late or do
something wrong, other workers will report you to the bosses just to
impress them. Therefore, you must be very punctual, exact, and
industrious in everything, so you won't give fellow workers a chance
to complain."

"In town this young man must get used to using clock time. Europeans have a lot of respect for time, and they expect their employees
to respect it. Now, if that European comes at midnight to your place
and rouses you out of bed, you can demand that he respect his own
time. African employers have no respect for time. They will work you
like a dog. They expect you to arrive at the proper clock time and
leave when they have finished with you. That is unfair."

"The first big problem this young man will face is the language. English is the language of town. But he will soon learn. Meanwhile, he must not say he understands things when he doesn't, otherwise he may get into a hell of a lot of trouble. Illiterates are the victims of town living. After the person gets a job, he must only do what he is told; nothing more. Many times employers lay traps to test your honesty. Madams (housewives) may leave a few shillings around like they are lost to see if you take them. Never touch anything that you have not been told to touch. Await instructions."

"The advice I would give this young Tswana is to maintain the respectful, decorous behavior that he was taught in his home. No one in town likes these rowdy manners of *tsotsis*. I would tell him not to be tempted by the different kinds of food in the grocery stores. This is best done by not traveling around town past all the shops. This person must not spend a lot of time looking for relatives and visiting with them. When he is out away from his home, his own things can be stolen from him. This may lead him to believe he can steal to recover those goods. . . . Employers you should treat as you do your parents. It is sometimes impossible to impress employers because they are at times demanding and unreasonable, just like parents. Take all instructions; only question what you don't understand. But if the employer is scolding you wrongly, you cannot just accept that for the sake of work, or you will lose your belief in yourself. You must just wait until the lecture is over, and then quietly show why you are in the right. Often it is good after being wrongly punished to just act happily until sometime later, when the boss has forgotten the whole issue. Then you approach him and really give him your opinion firmly. This will show you are a human being and not a dog. A dog only fights back when attacked. A human being can fight back by means of reason. Do not just say yes, yes for everything because you might commit yourself to something you don't want to do. Only say yes if you wish to brush aside a small matter or if you do really agree."

These six excerpts include almost all the points made by the twenty-one respondents. Clearly present is an emphasis on law (*molao*) as a principle for efficacious coping. In chapter 5 I mentioned the importance of "keeping law" in the values of Setswana, and how upholding this precept can in a context like town work make a person's behavior appear unimaginative and reticent. The principle that a person should do nothing he does not understand or suspend action until he knows the lawful course can lead to total immobility. Many Europeans have interpreted this behavior as evidence of stupidity or of a disspirited, insecure state of mind. But this is clearly not the basis for "Tswana-like" behavior in town.

Europeans and Their World:
The View from Below

Most Tswana have coped with wage labor and town living by interpreting these manifestations of the colonial political economy in a highly restricted way that serves limited goals. In other words, town is relevant to the central values of most Tswana only within a narrow horizon.

Although most Tswana claim that they choose town life and wage labor in response to the demands of subsistence, we have seen evidence of an "identification" with wage labor (in the mines, in the case of the Kalahari, and in town, in the case of those living there), and this suggests that the effects of these institutions are more pervasive than the Tswana concede. Certainly the rather heroic autobiographies, with their accounts of how the individual has coped, belie the claim that town is always and only a place to earn a grubstake.

It is in direct confrontations with Europeans and European institutions that the most significant "collisions" in motives, goals, and basic values take place. In these situations the Tswana is almost invariably in the role of the laborer and the European in the role of the owner, manager, or executor. The values of Setswana and the self-identity of the individual receive their greatest assault and challenge in the experience of European domination and the structured social inequality based upon a European control of the means of production which most nonliterate Tswana only partly understand.

The most intriguing question for me was how the acknowledged fact of European wealth and power is interpreted by the Tswana who see it from varying standpoints. What does this systemic inequality and domination do to the self-identity of the nonliterates who invariably occupy the lowest levels. How do they perceive the white minions of this world? And how do they perceive their own selfhood, including their cultural background, in view of this seemingly overwhelming gulf?

A part of the answer to this question has already been presented: the Tswana try to avoid making invidious comparisons. They have defined as relevant to their central projects of action only limited aspects of the colonial political economy. The white world does not assault the Tswana's consciousness as a structure upon which he is totally dependent nor as a monolith all of whose empirical manifestations he must equally attend to.

256

WAGE LABOR AND TOWN LIFE

Inequality and Power

The *experience* of inequality or domination is not the same thing as the institutional structure of inequality or domination. This necessary nonequivalence arises from the fact that a person has the power to invest the world of his experience with meaning. The possession of *existential power* is not contingent upon whether it has determinate behavioral effects in the world of others. To be sure, in much social science literature "power" is defined in purely behavioristic, material terms. For example, it is sometimes defined in terms of what one person, group, class, or nation (call it *A*) can get another such entity (*B*) to do that *B* would not otherwise do. *A*'s power over *B* is always and only that which *B* does or does with a higher probability in response to, or because of, some action *A* has undertaken. And accordingly the absence of this action of *A* is associated with the cessation or diminution of that which *B* does in light of or because of *A*'s initial action.

Unquestionably the phenomenon defined above does "exist," but it cannot be the basis for belief in one's fundamental power as a human being to bring meaning to the world. This behavioristic formulation of power is not a statement about how power is conceived in consciousness. In several biographical accounts we have seen instances where an individual Tswana believed in his power over town life, mine life, European bosses, and so forth, while an observer could find no significant reaction of the latter to the former. A Tswana may act toward his boss in a way that affirms *in his own consciousness* a genuine sense of power to overcome and conquer. An outside ethnographer, however, can discern no action on the part of the European that can be correlated with the power claimed by the Tswana. Hence the ethnographer may be tempted to conclude that the Tswana has no power but rather is afflicted with "false consciousness." But such a narrow, behavioristic view of power will hinder our understanding of the significance of an encounter with inequality for the Tswana who must invest this encounter with meaning. What a member of a superordinate class (capitalist or ethnographer) finds trivial might constitute for a member of a subordinate group a fundamental affirmation of his self-identity. As Simmel has said: "Even in the most oppressive and cruel cases of subordination there still is a considerable measure of personal freedom" (Wolff 1950, p. 182). If the subject of subordination, even under external powers, retains any spontaneity whatsoever, he can invest his own behavior and that of his superordinate with meanings which cannot be determined by the latter. As long as there is spontaneity, the subordinate has real power—power that can under certain circumstances lead to throwing off the beliefs and behavior of the oppressor. Only if the person is completely determined from without—made into an object— by the tyranny of the master does he lose this power of consciousness.

If asymmetries of overt, behavioral power have a subjective aspect which is not determined by any overt behavior, dominance and inequality must have objective and subjective components and there must be correspondences between them. Inequality presupposes (as Schutz has argued [1962, p. 227]) a notion of "domain of relevance"—that is to say, a set of actions within which inequality as a possibility is believed to exist by the actors themselves. Inequalities apart from such specifications of relevance domain are devoid of meaning to the actors themselves. For example, that children are not the legal equals of adults before the adjectival law of common law countries occasions no comments about inequality. That I, as an American citizen, am debarred from voting in British elections when I visit the U.K. does not elicit in me the feeling that I am "unequal" to the British.

The same applies to "discrimination." Discrimination is a fundamental presupposition of thinking. If we did not discriminate among objects of consciousness, biological survival would be impossible. It is only when inequalities are based on discrimination in domains within which *we ought not to recognize* differences (by agreement, entitlement, justice, morals, custom, or pretension) that we find "discrimination" in its evil sense, or "illegitimate" inequality.

Only phenomena in the same domain of relevance can be adjudged equal or unequal. Thus an adequate theory of equality, and a fortiori of discrimination in its evil sense, presupposes a satisfactory account of *domains of relevance.* In the case at hand, we must know how the Tswana individually or collectively define domains of relevance in terms of their criteria of equality. These can be compared to the domains of relevance where equality and inequality prevail in the colonial political economy. The two will, of course, be in conflict to some degree. The extent to which the European political economy forces upon the Tswana, against their will or belief, actions, social statuses, and domains of relevance within which inequality must prevail —however illegitimate this is in terms of Tswana precepts—is the extent of European discrimination and domination.

Schutz (1962, p. 240) has argued that whenever an outsider succeeds in imposing "typifications" and relevances on an insider against his will, this is bound to affect the self-definition and self-identity of the victim. Now the Tswana living or working in town or in the mines must necessarily *learn to act* in terms of definitions of the world and of people, especially of Europeans vis-à-vis Africans, which are made by the dominant class (mainly white) and forced upon the subordinate class (black) against its will. We examined some of these in chapter 4. Our question now is: do the subject people—the Tswana—internalize, or accept as personal beliefs, any of the definitions of social life and personal identity created by the colonial political economy in organizing the forces and relations of production?

To illustrate the point of this question with an example: one Tswana may equate the relations of bosses and workers in the mine to the relationship of parent and child. If he authentically believes this analogy, then the meaning he invests in this "inequality" will be different from that invested in it by a Tswana who defines the relationship in terms of a set of contractual exchanges made among people bound by the same set of general rights and duties. Whether the conduct of a boss toward a Tswana worker will be seen as illegitimately unequal, discriminatory, or oppressive depends upon the meanings the individual invests in the relevant work roles. The power the Tswana will think he has will not be defined in terms of what he can get the boss to do and vice versa, but rather in terms of how freely and effectively he can invest his experience with the meaning *he chooses*. In other words, his power is the inverse of the power of the boss to *determine* the meaning of that experience for him.

With these preliminaries in mind, we turn to the question of how the Tswana experience the European world and themselves in that world.

That the Europeans in southern Africa are a class with incredible wealth and power is a fact all Tswana acknowledge. It is confirmed in the sense experience of practically every Tswana from an early age. The meaning of this acknowledged wealth for them is for the most part a function of three issues: (1) how the Tswana explain it vis-à-vis their own relative poverty; (2) the extent to which they identify with (i.e., covet) the life-style that this wealth reflects and supports; and (3) the extent to which a "positive" identification with European wealth and life-style signals a rejection of the idealized conception of Setswana culture. Variations in the Tswana understanding of these experiences is closely associated with the two factors that have been discussed throughout this book: (1) the objective material dependency on European-dominated institutions; and (2) the degree of knowledge of how these institutions work. Within these experiences, we find what for the Tswana are the essential features of inequality.

How White People Got Their Wealth

I opened the discussion of this topic with the following question: "Everyone can see that Europeans in southern Africa (Botswana, Lesotho, Swaziland, Moçambique, Rhodesia, and South Africa) are generally much richer than the black Africans. Can you explain to me why this is so?" In the more than seventy-five extensive responses I obtained, three themes recurred with great frequency: (1) some Tswana claimed that the Europeans gained their wealth primarily by *exploitation* of African labor; (2) some Tswana explained this wealth differential by stating that European culture and technology developed earlier than that of the Africans and was used for appropriating vast mineral wealth; and (3) some Tswana explained the wealth by suggesting that Europeans had either innate or God-given talents and abilities exceeding those of the Tswana and specifically suited to the production of material wealth. Many respondents mentioned all of these points, but in every case one of the three arguments was prominently emphasized.

More interesting than the regular occurrence of these three themes is the fact that the "self-subsistent old" (Gaborone and Kgaphamadi) emphasized the theme of exploitation; the "self-subsistent young" (Gaborone and Kgaphamadi) emphasized the theme of cultural and technological superiority; and the Kalahari (whether young or old) emphasized the theme of innate gifts for accumulating wealth. (Note that by self-subsistent I mean not abjectly dependent on regular migration to the mines to avert starvation.)

How is this manifest in their verbal expression? As above, I shall illustrate my generalizations by presenting sufficient numbers of interview excerpts to illustrate all of the points made by the cluster as a whole.

Self-Subsistent Old (Gaborone and Kgaphamadi)

"The Europeans became wealthier than we here in southern Africa because they got and gained everything from on top of the backs of Africans. You will often hear fallacious arguments from literates that they gain more wealth because they work harder. This is nonsense. Everything is done by people like me who do not read and write. The Europeans came to Africa and found us unable to protect ourselves. They suppressed and oppressed us and treated us like dogs. From all this came their wealth. [*Q:* Some Europeans claim they get their

wealth because they have superior intelligence or a superior culture.]
These people are lying. Europeans are not more intelligent than Africans. They make our children fail at school because they fear if we
obtained equal education we would dominate them as they do us.
[*Q:* Would you personally want—if you could—to live like the Europeans, in town in fancy houses with electricity, running water,
servants, and fancy food?] If we had the chance, we would think
about what kind of life we would like to live. With wealth would
come choice. That's what is important." [Elder from Kgaphamadi]

"The secret of Europeans' wealth is this: The Boers came here with
the permission of the Queen of England. When the Boers arrived here,
they ignored the human origin of African people. They considered us
people of limited thoughts and ability to reason. They played a dirty
trick on us. They started to beguile us with European toys and other
things we had never seen. They immediately began to cheat us by
buying our cattle at low prices and selling them elsewhere for high
prices. They exploited our labor and cheated us of our wealth, which
is cattle. When the Africans realized they were being cheated by the
Boers, the Africans ran to the chiefs for protection. But the Boers
got there with money and bribed the chiefs to continue allowing
cattle dealing. Then the Boers not only cheated us of all our wealth,
they began to oppress us right here in the land of our birth. In an
African society, once you control the chief, you control the whole
community. That's what the Boers and later the English did. [*Q:*
Some Europeans explain their wealth and power by claiming they
have superior minds and talents for dealing with the modern world.]
This is a totally false conception. When the African child goes to
school, he is taught half what the Europeans are taught. As soon as
the African child understands the idea of schooling, the school fees
rise, and he has to drop out. European children go to school with a
full stomach. The parents at home read and write and can help the
children. They are exposed to reading and writing from rising to bed-
time. There is no such thing as a differing ability to absorb education.
People are people." [Elder from Kgaphamadi]

"When the Boers came to Africa, they too were poor. But they were
united in caring for one another. This was a time of wars all over
Africa. Everybody was fighting everybody else. The Boers were just
like the Africans of those days. They won most of the wars. They enslaved the Africans and put them to work on their farms and later in
the mines. But their wealth also comes from their control of technology [*sephiri sa tshipi,* secrets of iron]. They had plans and ideas
for accumulating wealth with these tools which we lacked. Although
they gained everything on the backs of Africans, they put tools on our
backs as well. [*Q:* Do you believe Europeans are born with any special
gifts for wealth-making?] No. European children right from early
childhood are brought up in the world of books. When a European
mother sends her child to school, she makes sure the child is clean,

well fed, and has all the required school supplies. At night when the child returns home, the parents look over the schoolwork and help the child to understand its lessons. Africans, who do not read and write, can't do this. [*Q:* If Africans acquired all the knowledge that Europeans have, how would this affect the way they live? Would you be living like the Europeans do now?] We all live the same even now; it's just the materials are different. As for material wealth, we Africans would rather do things for ourselves. We do not believe in servants. [*Q:* Many Africans in Gaborone have servants.] They are exceptional. They've been corrupted by town life." [Elder from Kgaphamadi]

"Without black labor all these Europeans would be poor just like us. They enriched themselves not only by inspanning us like oxen; they cheated us through tricks of buying and selling. They robbed us of everything that belonged to us. We were empty-handed and helpless. So, naturally, we became dependent on them in all respects. That is why Tswana today are an appendage of European society. We depend on money. We depend on all kinds of things of which we were traditionally ignorant. [*Q:* Some Europeans say they are wealthy because they are born clever or wise.] [Emotionally] Indeed they are . . . Because of this, they will dominate us forever." [Elder from Kgaphamadi]

"The tribal wars of Mzilikazi and Shaka were going on when the Boers arrived. Naturally, this was a situation they could exploit. They took advantage of hostilities among Africans to conquer everybody. They enslaved us. Took our land and cattle, and then paid us poverty wages. [*Q:* Do other groups exploit Africans beside the Boers?] Yes. People in England fetched wealth in Africa. After World War II America took over Botswana, Lesotho, and Swaziland. Now they are trying to invade this country by constructing cattle fences." [Elder from Gaborone]

"We enriched the European with the labor of our hands. They also deceived us in commerce and looted us. But they are born wise. A European, no matter how poor he starts out, will become wealthy. [*Q:* Are you saying Tswana do less well in skills such as are taught in school because they are born less wise than Europeans?] No. Education is in English, so naturally, the Europeans have an advantage. That's why they learn faster. [*Q:* Why do all Europeans get wealthy then and not all Tswana?] I don't fully know. They certainly aren't ever born dumb. . . . Once there was a young, very poor white boy who came to us at home; he asked for food and settled among us. He made himself useful by working to mend broken-down wagons. He settled by the railway line, making a few cents a day in his trade. Then he began collecting wood and sending it to Kimberley on the train. Soon he opened a shop, and then many shops. Today he is a very rich man." [Elder from Gaborone]

"The Europeans gained their wealth through clever planning.

Africans are industrious, hard-working, and yet born for poverty. The Europeans are born to make money. They have ideas that make for success. It is curious that we can read as Europeans do, write as Europeans do, yet we remain poor. They are naturally gifted. [Q: Are Europeans born more intelligent then than Africans?] No. Intelligence does not distinguish Tswana from European. The Europeans have secrets for making wealth that we have not learned. [Q: Would Tswana choose to live like Europeans if they had the wealth that Europeans do?] Yes, we would live in town, have holidays in hotels, and have servants too." [Elder from Gaborone]

Self-Subsistent Young

"Europeans have knowledge of wealth. They understand business and how to accumulate wealth. It must be borne in mind that without African cheap labor, they could gain nothing. But their secret lies in understanding how to use machines and how to make us use machines without our knowing what we are doing. Europeans are highly educated; this helps them become wealthy and able to dominate us. [Q: Can Africans acquire this knowledge of wealth as easily as can Europeans?] Yes, of course, the pace at which people learn is the same. It is just the opportunities to learn that are different." [Kgaphamadi young]

"The Europeans created an era in southern Africa in which they sat in luxury at the top of the mine waiting for the toiling African to bring him lumps of gold. European technology dominated our minds and our reasoning. The power of their technology blinded and awed us. It was a veil over our understanding. [Q: Do you believe the knowledge of this technology can be acquired by Africans as readily as by Europeans?] Yes. There is no truth in this belief of Europeans that we are people of limited intellect. The conditions of learning are what affect the learning. Africa has imprisoned the Tswana. We haven't become aware of this new knowledge until recently. But given an equal access, we can learn all that the Europeans have learned. [Q: If Tswana obtained this kind of wealth, would they choose to live the same kind of life as the Europeans?] I'm not sure, but I think the only important factor is money. If we had the wealth, we would live like Europeans." [Kgaphamadi young]

"The Europeans became wealthy through technology and through tricks. They did not enslave or oppress us. They deceived us and they used their knowledge of tools to exploit the mineral wealth of this region. They were rich anyway right from the beginning. They have many plans for making wealth, and we should learn from these plans. [Q: Can Africans acquire the education necessary to learning the secrets of wealth as easily as can the Europeans?] Yes. Intelligence is not the question. Books are a center of their culture. Tswana have long committed themselves to manual labor, while Europeans have committed themselves to the knowledge of books. That is why they all become so gifted in making wealth. [Q: If Tswana acquired these secrets of

wealth and the wealth itself, would they live exactly as Europeans do
now?] Yes. Like them, and independent of them." [Gaborone young]

"The main reason why the Europeans are wealthy is because they
have the technology to produce the wealth. They are trained in all
aspects of the utilization of this technology. They are highly educated.
They translate their knowledge into wealth. [Q: Some argue Europeans gained their wealth through oppression of black people.] That
is rubbish. They gained their wealth by sitting down and laying plans
to become rich. [Q: Some argue Europeans have special inborn gifts
of intelligence; do you believe this?] Yes, I think so. European children learn to ride bicycles much earlier than do Tswana children. They
are born with that intelligence. [Q: If Tswana had that wealth of Europeans, would they live the same kind of life as Europeans, in town,
with servants and fancy houses?] Yes. If we had the chance, we would
live exactly like them." [Gaborone young]

"We can't say that European wealth resulted from slavery [this followed an assertion to that effect]. Wars and enslaving were common
practice before the Europeans arrived here, and no wealth resulted.
Batswana have enslaved the Masarwa [Bushmen], but we got no
wealth from it. No, the Europeans knew of the mineral wealth of this
country, and we didn't. They took it, and flew it overseas, and sold it
at a high price. That is how they became wealthy. Yes, they enslaved
us, but their technology produced the wealth. [Q: Does European
technology result from their having special inborn intellectual gifts?]
No, they get a superior education, that is all." [Gaborone young]

"When the Europeans first came here, they had technological knowledge already. So right away, they began exploiting the mineral resources. They did, it is true, benefit from the cheap labor of Africans.
Africans were slow to learn about the European technology. This is
what accounts for the wealth differences. [Q: Some Europeans say
they have this technology because they are more gifted intellectually
than are the Africans.] They are lying. The major barrier to Tswana
learning is English. Schools are taught in English. The English children
have a head start at school, that is all there is to it." [Gaborone young]

Kalahari (Young and Old)
"The truth is Europeans are born intelligent, more intelligent than
the Tswana. The Tswana are blind. They are jealous. They can't cooperate. They are happy to sit and drink once they get a few cents in
their pockets. The Europeans plan for the future. They are cunning.
[Q: Some people say the wealth of the Europeans came from the cheap
labor provided by Africans whom they enslaved.] This is utter nonsense. Had the Europeans not come to southern Africa, we would all
be dead right now. The Europeans are born intelligent and wise. There
is no doubt. The Tswana can't even dig their own boreholes. They are
so stupid because they drink dirty stream water." [Kalahari elder]

"The Europeans were born intelligent and gifted in every aspect of life-work. The only reason they oppressed us was because of their superior intelligence, which we lack in Africa. Africans aren't dumb, but they are less intelligent than the Europeans. Through their cleverness and technology they overwhelmed us and took the wealth from the ground. Whenever we showed sparks of understanding, the Europeans oppressed us more, making us more dependent on them so they could control us better. This dependency on them affects our reasoning. The Europeans will continue to improve in life while we remain miserable. [*Q:* Do you believe European children do better at school than Africans?] Yes. [*Q:* Because Europeans are born more intelligent?] Not necessarily. Africans are new to schooling and books. This does not prove the Africans are less intelligent. [*Q:* If the Tswana were wealthy, would they acquire servants, town houses, etc.?] Yes. Wealth determines everything. If we had such wealth, we would have servants chained to us as well." [Kalahari elder]

"The Europeans arrived here with advanced technology; I have seen this for myself. They straightaway began to extract the wealth from the ground. They worked from morning until night. [*Q:* But they used cheap labor to get this wealth at low cost.] People who say the Europeans turned us into slaves are lying. The Europeans were seriously looking for wealth. They worked very hard. They are born intelligent. The Africans are born stupid; their kinky hair symbolizes their limited sense." [Kalahari elder]

"We were conquered and enslaved. But the Europeans did this with their superior intelligence and technology. The Europeans will remain above us for all time. God made them to dominate the world forever." [Kalahari elder]

"I don't think anything but minerals makes wealth. The Europeans knew where to find it. They got it, and that makes them wealthy. [*Q:* Do Europeans have any inborn talents that lead them to know so much about wealth-getting?] I don't know. [*Q:* Are Europeans more intelligent than Africans in any way?] No, they just work hard to become wealthy. That's what they want to do." [Kalahari young]

"Europeans gain wealth because they work together to make wealth. They are not jealous. They do not despise their own poor. There is a story that in the beginning there were two families. One was African, the other European. The African family was senior. One day God sent a wretched old man to the African family. He was poor, with tattered clothes, and lice all over his body. The African family chased him out. The old man was dejected. God sent another poor old man to the European family. He was taken in, clothed, bathed, and cared for. Since then, God has cursed the African family and its descendants and blessed the European family and its descendants. The Europeans have been given good fortune by God." [Kalahari young]

"The major reason why the Europeans became wealthy in the land of our birth is that they are born more intelligent than we. They came here with their tools to take the minerals from the ground. We went to them and asked for work. We can't say they made us into slaves because we sought them out. Europeans are born cooperative and united. They always help one another to gain wealth, while Tswana are jealous and prefer to see their brothers remain poor. Originally the Africans and the Europeans were created equal. But the Africans became jealous and selfish. This individualism is the cause of our poverty." [Kalahari elder]

These few interviews substantiate the points I made above. The Kalahari clearly seem ashamed of their own culture (with its jealousy, selfishness, and stupidity) and adulatory of the European. They are resigned to this difference, as indicated by their general belief that this state of affairs was created by God or is inborn. The origin of this belief can in my view be found in the brainwashing effects of the mine experience, coupled with the absence of any other significant contact with Europeans or their institutions, which would lead to a more balanced picture of European life. A high degree of dependency on European-dominated institutions is associated here with an absence of willingness to see these institutions as exploiters of African labor—exploiters of the labor migrants themselves.

The self-subsistent young identify with much of European technology and see in that technology a power sufficient to explain the wealth of Europeans. In the life-projects of most of these young lies the hope that some small part of that technology can be controlled by them and hence produce for them some wealth. That it brought wealth to the Europeans confirms that *knowledge of tools* is the route to success, not special European intellectual endowment.

The elders, especially the Kgaphamadi, are unequivocal in seeing exploitation as the basis for European wealth. They do not identify with European technology nor aspire to penny capitalism. Rather, they see the European presence not so much as a model which they can emulate, but as a reminder of the invasion that severed their culture from its traditional origins. The elders think that the Europeans gained wealth at cost to the Tswana: the loss of their culture and the alienation of the labor of their hands.

These differing views of European culture would suggest that the Tswana hold correspondingly varied views of their own culture, Setswana. In the last pages of this book I turn to the way the Tswana describe their identification with their own traditions, "suckled from their mother's breasts."

Setswana: Identification and Estrangement

To ask a person about his "culture" is to convert a complex abstraction into a supposedly determinate object. For example, the question "What do you think of your culture?" makes the concept culture appear as a thing about which one can have some global feeling. Throughout this book I have been discussing Setswana—that is, Setswana culture. Yet if I were out of the blue to ask a Tswana to describe his culture, I would probably get a blank stare. Necessarily, then, throughout these discussions I have been slowly building up a picture of Setswana more complete and coherent than any that has existed in the consciousness of an individual Tswana at any time. In the closing section of this book, I want to describe the perceptions of the Tswana about Setswana, which here means the concept of Setswana as I created it in a particular set of questions.

The view I elicited on culture was guided by the request that the individual think of the points of similarity and contrast between *Setswana* (culture) and *Sekgoa* (European culture). In particular I asked my respondents to think about their culture as a whole, as an idea. Then I asked them to tell me what aspects or parts of that culture were most important, most prominent, closest to its origin or essence. These aspects I wanted to tell people in America about, so they could learn of *ngwao ya Setswana* (the wisdom or tradition of Setswana). The responses I got brought me back full circle to the topics raised in chapters 5 and 6: exercise of power or will and "doing what one wants for oneself." This elegant coherence, this closure, both intrigued and delighted me: that I could in a single question elicit a summation of the results of months of often trial-and-error questioning, a process which only gradually led me to an understanding of the complex meanings I had been investigating. Equally interesting, variations in the responses to this question corresponded to variations on other topics I had explored. Notably, there was a definite congruity between the way a given cluster of Tswana described Europeans and their world and the way they described their own culture. Thus, for example, the "self-subsistent" old strongly affirm their belief in the value of Setswana traditions, despite the fact that they acknowledge that the modern world has severed these traditions from their origins. The old see the Europeans as having prospered by *appropriating something of value* that was formerly an aspect of traditional culture—the wealth of land and the labor of the Tswana. They speak as in a reverie of autonomy and farming. The self-subsistent young and the Kalahari—those whose horizons include many aspects of European knowledge and technology —do not reject traditional culture, but they acknowledge, often without any compunction, the *inevitability of its present or future irrelevance.* Many affirm the need to embrace European ways for their own sake or as a matter of survival. Again, the words of the Tswana themselves can most powerfully and compellingly convey these attitudes.

Self-Subsistent Old (Gaborone and Kgaphamadi)

"The pride of the Tswana people in their culture lies in the fact that we have absolute control over ourselves and our personal belongings. Freedom to move, freedom to choose what we can do, and independence of the control of others is the root of our culture and our pride." [Elder from Kgaphamadi]

"Our pride lies in the sufficiency of cattle and fields. From the beginning we have depended on these and survived in virtue of these. This is the source of pride in our culture." [Elder from Kgaphamadi]

"Our culture is represented in initiation. It is heartbreaking that the Europeans have put a stop to this. This country has become theirs, I guess. Initiation is our cultural school. Europeans would be appreciative of it if they could understand it. But you have to participate to understand. I know that the Indians at Ramoutswa are quite intrigued by the concept of initiation. The education received in initiation is beyond verbal explanation. So it is with Setswana." [Elder from Kgaphamadi]

"From the beginning, Tswana have honored their cultural roots by farming and raising stock. Cattle are the Tswana bank. We are also proud of our independence. We make everything we need from local resources. Self-sufficiency of the individual is a feeling beyond description [*tlhaloso*]." [Elder from Kgaphamadi]

"Tswana have nothing worthwhile in the way of culture. They have no knowledge at all. When they get enough sorghum to fill their stomachs, they just dance and sing. That's all. Initiation school is but a hollow ritual. We who went there became baboons. This experience has retarded our education and progress. It is nothing but a process of imitating sayings and proverbs and learning a few tricks which are useless in today's world." [Elder from Kgaphamadi, one of the very few elders to express such sentiments]

"When speaking of our culture and our pride in it, it is best to speak not so much of specific traditions, but of specific ideals. It is the great ideal of Tswana culture that all people of the community should strive for mutual understanding [kultwano] and cooperation. We should overcome enmity and jealousy, to help one another progress. We are well known for our decorous behavior and propriety. We are also people who believe in the use of hands to achieve self-sufficiency. The concept of lineage and ward is useless in today's world. Once the children are married, their life is their concern." [Elder from Gaborone]

"The great strength of Setswana is simplicity and self-sufficiency. Simple food, like bogobe [a sour porridge made from sorghum]. Producing all our necessary tools, food, housing, furniture, etc., from local resources which we control. This is our cultural pride." [Elder from Gaborone]

"The pride of Setswana is the family. We have strong family bonds which are cemented by bogadi. The man is the root of the house, and he earns the entitlement to this station by his payment of cattle to the wife's kin. European families are not so stable. You gather women like mushrooms." [Elder from Gaborone]

"The pride in our culture lies in our self-sufficiency. We make food from that which is readily available in nature itself. We know how to survive in a desert country. We dry melons and grind watermelon seeds and preserve these as provisions for a later time. If we walk a long distance, we have food for such distances. We take sorghum, fry it, and grind it. A few spoonfuls of this will last you all day. The life of the Tswana is symbolized by that of the white ant. They are very small. Yet they do great works. You can't understand how they get water. The Tswana depend a lot on local wild bulbs and roots. This is a great strength of our culture. We are not dependent on the shops and someone else's supplies. Although there has been much influence from modern life on Tswana people, when they fail to make progress in European ways [mo Sekgoeng], they will return to Tswana ways. We make many, many things from wood—almost every article imaginable: spoons, dishes, buckets. We also utilize clay. We are great potters. We make sledges from locally growing trees. Every Tswana has a sledge, even if his cattle are finished (dead). Another great part of Setswana which Europeans lack is the blood tie. Once a European boy is married, he is on his own, cut off from his family. In Setswana wards we organize life around blood relationships. This is symbolized in the distribution of meat from the slaughtered cow. For example, the kidneys go to the old people who lack teeth. The head is eaten at the kgotla [court] when the old men instruct the younger men in the law. There is also traditional schooling called initiation. At this school young men are taught how to become proper adults: how to raise cattle, how to treat their wives, how to endure pain and deprivation. They learn to sing the old praises. Young women are taught the same.

Adulthood has to be learned from people with experience. . . . Setswana is good because traditionally there was no loitering around. Each person had his place (home) and plenty to do. When people visited, they worked and helped; they ate a traditional porridge for old men and discussed the law." [Elder from Kgaphamadi]

Self-Subsistent Young and Kalahari
"As far as culture goes, I am too young to know much about it. Had I gone to initiation school, I would know something about it. But this initiation is finished. The modern world is our culture now. So there is very little I can say concerning Setswana." [Kgaphamadi young]

"The only aspect of Setswana worth mentioning is cattle. This is our source of livelihood. So that is all." [Kgaphamadi young]

"Our culture has very little that helps us with modern-day problems. This is because Tswana today despise their culture. The Europeans respect their culture and for this reason it thrives. There is nothing left of Setswana but plowing and raising cattle. But even this we gained from the Europeans. So the Europeans surpass us altogether. My conclusion is that we should welcome European culture. But we have nothing to offer them in return." [Kgaphamadi young]

"Our only cultural pride is farming. The rest is known only by the elders. Initiation is too strenuous. And *bongaka* [traditional medicine] is only in Setswana, so we can't teach that to Europeans." [Kgaphamadi young]

"I have little to say concerning Setswana culture. I was born during modern times. I can't understand the concept of culture myself, so how can I explain it to you? The only thing we have is plowing. Initiation I know nothing about. It scares me. So it would certainly scare the Europeans." [Kgaphamadi young]

"Our culture is farming. Every wise person seems to come from Europe. So I can only suggest that they would do well to raise cattle like us. They would do well at it. But we can learn from them. Most Tswana are blinded by initiation. They don't seek a formal education. Initiation is just dogma. If I ask old people about it, they just tell me the law says they can't say. So we can't have any clue of its possible benefits. If I ask you, Modise [me], about school, you tell me. You would explain without hesitation. Knowledge is not secrets. So we must just accept European knowledge." [Gaborone young]

"Cattle is the pride of Setswana, even if you do not have these new improved breeds. Even if your cattle die, you can still point with pride to the kraal where they were once kept; unlike money—which goes leaving no trace. But now we are becoming a world of money, so cattle must be sold to make money with which to buy things of the Europeans. Modern life has changed everything. Setswana does not exist as it used to. In fact, Setswana has diminished and died. There is

exist as it used to. In fact, Setswana has diminished and died. There is nothing left." [Gaborone young]

"The effects of civilization have robbed us of all the cultural pride we have had. Before modern times the Tswana were proud of ox-pulled wagons and donkey carts [all European imports]. Before the corruption of modern times we had strong social rules that guided conduct and compelled respectability—for example, *meila* [postpartum sexual taboo]. These practices prevent the death of young people. We had respect for elders. This dominance by elders was a unifying force in Tswana communities which is now lost. Life was much more harmonious back then." [Kalahari young]

"As far as culture is concerned, I am confused. I don't know what to make of Setswana in today's world. It is clear there is nothing of value in it. We live by money now." [Kalahari elder]

"Setswana cannot be described, because it has lost its roots. I cannot answer the question, though it is a reasonable one. We live by European customs now. I can't think of anything else to say." [Kalahari elder]

Testimony from the Tswana concerning their own and European culture reveals a province of meaning, an experience, quite different from the representation of culture outlined in chapters 5 through 7. In these earlier chapters the meanings of Setswana were shown to exist as at once rules of action, ideals, and values alive in the individual consciousness. In this chapter we witness the unmistakable global effects that colonial industrialism has had on Setswana. This can be most clearly seen when the Tswana describe their culture from the vantage point of a single retrospective gaze. To be sure, this viewpoint was encouraged by the questions I posed. But the consistency of the answers reflects an understanding that existed prior to my questions.

Despite the "collision," as Peter Berger calls it, that the meeting of Setswana and Sekgoa has brought about, the Tswana in the main affirm their existence in terms of values and an image of the self that parries and overcomes the denigration inherent in the colonial political economy of southern Africa. Only among the Kalahari do I detect that an "overdetermination from without" has occasioned a loss of the "sense of humanity" the Tswana so revere. Only the Kalahari seem to have translated their material dependence on the world of capitalist production into the belief that indeed they may be thing-like and passive appendages of the dominant culture.

But even this incipient trend among the Kalahari is, I am convinced, situational—a function of their dire poverty and dependency on mine labor, their experience of the gargantuan power of alien social formations and lack of any other experience of the European world. They do not have the opportunity to exercise their fundamental power to make choices, to invest events and encounters with their own meanings in a setting where Europeans are present, yet not able to stifle all spontaneity.

The Tswana of Gaborone and Kgaphamadi are in many cases as poor as those of the Kalahari; they experience dependency on the mines; they go to the mines, though not so regularly. These Tswana, whether young or old, have not drooped or died in the face of their own poverty, their dependency on mine labor, and the radical contrast between their position and universal white affluence and power. They have entered, often for extended sojourns, into the deep recesses of the white man's heart of darkness. They have entered seemingly without power. There they experience the alienation of their labor and the alienation of their bodies from their fundamental self-identity. They return home to toil in a "peasant's" life. But despite this alienation, despite the struggle that bare subsistence continually demands, most of these Tswana claim and affirm the values and identity of the unalienated consciousness: what they do much of the time is what they authentically want to do. Their means and their ends are in large measure a unity. They enrich and deepen the world of acquaintance and encounter with meanings of their own, thereby creating experience of their own. Facing every handicap and disability forced on them by colonial domination, still they form life-projects in which they aspire to levels they may not reach and in which they live a world of thought—belief, value, and desire—that melds with a world of deeds.

My study of the Tswana requires little recapitulation. The testimony of the Tswana themselves, with minimal aid from me, has provided a compelling answer to the question with which I began: how do social institutions affect an individual's beliefs about who and what he is. The evidence presented here fails to confirm the "scars-of-bondage" thesis—that the denigration inherent in modern colonialism colonizes the minds of those who occupy its lowlands, producing deep and lasting psychic scars. On the contrary, the Tswana in the main demonstrate the ennobling effects of belief in one's ability to understand and act on personal experience. These effects of the "will to believe" persist for most Tswana despite the often precarious and humiliating dependency on the institutions of a colonial political economy. The conditions of material autonomy and dependency do not determine the life-project. Instead the meanings of both Setswana culture and colonial industrialism derive in part from the individual's life as he intends it and makes of it a project of action.

9 CONCLUSIONS

The theme of this study and the central concept it brings to its subject matter is meaning-in-consciousness. While my primary aim has been to come to an understanding of one people at a particular moment in history, I have tried at the same time to suggest the universal human questions that form the horizon of the study and to whose understanding it hopefully contributes. A particular study, or even a science, fails not because of what it says but because of what it ignores or disregards. The main shortcoming of positivistic social science in this century has been its ignoring of the central place of consciousness or mind in human being and scientific understanding.

In the first chapter I proposed a number of attributes of consciousness which I said would prove relevant to this study, in particular its freedom, or power, which we call the will. In the concluding chapter I would like to return to these assertions about consciousness, the general propositions that situate the study. In doing this I will defend these assumptions and suggest directions for further research of the kind I have reported here. To do this fairly and constructively I must make very clear what I am saying about the nature of human consciousness, in particular the will.

Consciousness and the Will

In the human order of things, need, emotion, and habit only take on complete senses in relation to a will which they solicit, motivate and in general affect; while reciprocally, the will takes on these senses if only by its resignation. The will determines them by its choices, moves them by its effort, and adopts them by its consent. . . . Only the living interrelationship between the voluntary and the involuntary is intelligible. [Ricoeur 1967, pp. 217–18]

273

Willing transcends all "characterological" descriptions. It is genuinely free and creative. Willing is constitutive, in the sense that situation, circumstance, factuality, environment, knowledge, emotion, habit, and drive are *all* qualified in human existence by participation in the power called will. "I am that effort which opposes itself to a body that resists. I am that liberty which comes upon itself in an alien world of necessity" (Ricoeur 1967, p. 223). The sacrifice of need attests to the fact that need is ready to submit to general evaluation (I can decide to go on a hunger strike).

We often see the "weakness of the will" brought forward as an argument against freedom.

[Yet] . . . pain and fatigue can never be regarded as causes which "act" upon my liberty. . . . They do not have their origin outside me, but always have a significance [because of me] and express my attitude towards the world. Pain makes me give way, and say what I ought to have kept to myself, fatigue makes me break my journey. . . . We all know the moment at which we decide no longer to endure pain or fatigue and when simultaneously they become intolerable in fact. My own fatigue brings me to a halt because I dislike it, because I have chosen my manner of being in the world. [Merleau-Ponty, 1962, p. 441]

. . . All explanations of my conduct in terms of my past, my temperament, my environment are true provided that they be regarded not as separable contributions but as moments of my total being, the significance of which I am entitled to make in various ways, without its ever being possible to say whether I confer their meaning on them or receive it from them. . . . The fact remains that I am free, not in spite of, or on the hither side of, these motivations, but by means of them. For this significant life, this certain significance of nature and history which I am, does not limit my access to the world, but, on the contrary, is my means of entering into communication with it. It is by being unrestrictedly and unreservedly what I am at present that I have a chance of moving forward; by living my time I am able to understand other times, by plunging into the present and the world, by taking on deliberately what I am *fortuitously*, by willing what I will and doing what I do, that I can go further. Nothing determines me from the outside, not because nothing acts on me, but on the contrary, because I am from the start outside myself [i.e., conscious of myself being conscious] and open to the world. We need have no fear that our choices or actions restrict our liberty, since choice and action alone cut us loose from our anchorage. [Merleau-Ponty 1962, pp. 455–56]

Ricoeur and Merleau-Ponty suggest what for much of modern social science is a heresy: that human thought and action are not simply process, not just the discharge of forces. They are not simple events or factualities, and to the extent they are not, they are free. Says Gramsci: "It can be excluded that economic crises directly produce fundamental events; they can only create more favourable ground for the propagation of certain ways of thinking . . . [and] the decisive element in every situation is the force . . . which can be advanced when one judges the situation favourable. . . . Therefore the essential task is that of paying systematic attention . . . to forming and developing this force, consciousness of itself" (Meszaros 1972, p. 85).

This power of consciousness to transcend givenness and factuality by positing new factualities, new existence, means that every human act or event is not simply an actual reality but is also the potential reality it seeks to bring into being. The dialectic of society and history, its possibilities and contingencies, is *unintelligible* outside the contribution made to it by human freedom.

These thoughts are at once the theme and perspective of this book. As such, the text is necessarily both a theory and a set of observations. There exist no conscious observations of the world which are independent of beliefs or theories about the world. There is no rational demarcation between observation and theory. As Marx has wryly observed: every sense organ is a theoretician. The rawest perception is a highly abstract process in consciousness. What exists apart from consciousness is unknowable, for whatever is perceived has already been placed within a theoretical framework; it makes sense because its very way of signifying is embedded in the manner in which it is known. What appears to be *given* in the world (as the theoretical physicist Margenau has asserted) is never simply given, but is in part a product of *habit*—our invariant mode of perception at a given moment in history. We are doomed to live in a world of meanings. Even when we are most certain that we have grasped the "facts," the "things-in-themselves," we have grasped meanings-for-us. This is our relationship to the world, which we call understanding.

This is what I have sought to suggest in my discussion of the Tswana. In doing so I have consciously tried to avoid the pretense—the vain fiction—that my observations simply represent a world of facts. Instead I have attempted to present the Tswana, not as they are in themselves, but as I saw them. The Tswana in this text are my interpretation—my quest for meaning which, thanks to universal features of language and mind, I can communicate to you faithfully. The reader, through language, is the *witness* of my quest for meaning: value and self-identity among the Tswana. Hopefully I have, by means of language, communicated the methods of this quest with sufficient clarity to allow any reader to undertake a study of his own that might falsify what I have claimed to be true for us and true for the Tswana. The question arises whether, if my interpretation is accepted, this has implications for falsifying others' claims about the Tswana (or other peoples in similar situations)? I think it does, for the very important reason that many other interpretations of human social behavior deny or ignore consciousness and will, especially in their attempts to understand nonindustrial peoples. The supposition that people and society can be made *objects*—can be made thing-like—to render them fit for the investigations of science, destroys the phenomenon of consciousness before inquiry has begun.

A direct consequence of the ignoring of consciousness or claiming that it lacks will or freedom has been the "finding" in social science and psychology that peoples who undergo poverty, crushing oppression, or the onslaught of industrial forces and relations of production incur profound psychological scars.[1] When they become objects in the lowlands of these colonial systems, they are "found" to be objects-for-themselves. In my view this "finding" flows not from what the victims of these arrangements think and do, but from the conviction held by scientists of behavior that these consequences do, theoretically, follow. This conviction *creates the observations* that are then called findings. These convictions, as I have tried to argue, are in error. They are false.

An important and related problem raised by the study of the "culture of the poor" in empiricist social science is the biases that flow from the vested interests of the political classes that produce or sponsor social research among colonized minorities. As Marx has observed, human behavior reeks with class interest. Behavioral and social science has done little to contradict this claim.

1. I do not want to take time here to review and critically appraise the vast literature I have in mind. Below I list some important examples of it, which illustrate how an empiricist conceptualization of human behavior has occasioned the "scars of bondage" thesis, reference to which was made in chapter 1.

Many writers on the societies of the colonized world take that colonial context for granted, that is, they ignore it. Hence events are interpreted in terms of a crude behaviorist synchrony. No sense of history informs the putative facts, which are allowed to speak for themselves. Studies of acculturation or social change, for example, simply assume the movement of Western usages and norms. Change is seen as movement from one "equilibrium" to another, the new one being simply a modus vivendi on terms dictated by world capitalist interests. In this research individuals become the unit of analysis (in fact only "components" of individuals are analyzed). People become bundles of features deemed critical by the analyst. The colonial social structure is seldom described as the overwhelmingly important part of the social and cultural ecology it is in most societies subjected to colonial control. Writers often assume that the meaning of any social fact can be discovered in the mere description of what is directly experienced. No conceptions of class, of exploitation, of history, of the unseen substrata of memory or consciousness that precede lived experience are called upon to inform interpretation in much of empiricist social science.

Modernization and Consciousness

Peter Berger has proposed the perspective on culture and change that I have in broad principle adopted here. There are some differences in perspective and the degree of familiarity with the peoples and cultures most dramatically affected by colonial industrialism. As my research among the Tswana bears centrally on many of Berger's ideas, some comment is in order.

Berger's thesis, very briefly, is this. There is a general correspondence between the institutional fabric of society and the conscious meaning of that society for the individual. In particular, says Berger, "each phase in the establishment of modern economic institutions has its correlate on the level of consciousness (1974, p. 125). Sometimes the establishing of a new correlate in consciousness by the individual's incorporation into alien social formations can be traumatic. Berger claims this effect for migratory mine labor in southern Africa.

It has attracted [?] large masses of African labor. . . . Streams of migrants move toward [mining centers]. The immediate consequence is the weakening of village life and its traditional cultural patterns. . . .

While such migration often has serious effects on the communities left behind by the migrants, *the effects on the migrants themselves are probably much more devastating.* . . . In such a situation the structures of modernity . . . must necessarily appear to the individual as an alien powerful and, in the main, coercive force. . . . In such a situation there is little if any direct identification with modernity. . . . Such identification begins to grow with the length of time that an individual is exposed to the new situation. [1974, pp. 121–22, emphasis mine]

We have seen clearly in the case of the Tswana that the effects of colonialism on consciousness have not been as severe nor as irremediable as have been its effects on rural institutional life. Nor does the degree of identification with the structures of modernity increase simply as a function of propinquity and the passage of time. While variations in identification do occur, they cannot be explained in terms of a contrast between a simple internalization or appropriation of Western values and the casting off of traditional values. Processes of change involve, among other things, aging in a *cultural sense,* material dependency, and urban work experience.

Berger is quite correct to argue that "it is necessary to analyze the manner in which particular individuals or groups relate to the modernizing carriers. . . . Each such relationship (hypothetically) has its own specific correlate on the level of consciousness" (1974, p. 126). This is what I have sought to do in this inquiry. However, I have done more than simply define the relationship between individuals and "modernizing carriers" in terms of *institutional niches;* I have also tried to describe these relationships in terms of the actual *plans and projects of the individuals* involved. In other words, I have attempted to study the manner in which individuals are articulated to modern institutions in terms of their own conscious, deeply felt beliefs, plans, and goals, and their motivations for incorporating these institutions into their intended action. The meaning of their incorporation into the modernizing carriers cannot be specified apart from the plans and goals they, the Tswana, consciously formulate and the projects they undertake in relation to these carriers. There can be no causal explanation of the impact of modern institutions on consciousness that does not take account of the projects of the actor who experiences these institutions.

Berger states that "through education, mass communication, and also through face-to-face contact with individual agents of the primary modernization carriers, the individual becomes conscious of a world

beyond the confines of his everyday experience. Inevitably he begins
to compare his own situation with that world. Almost inevitably the
comparison is depressing in so far as the new horizon includes information and imagery about advanced industrial societies" (1974, p. 135).
As applied to the Tswana, this claim is erroneous. But more important,
the result of a conscious comparison of life at home and life "on the
other side" is far more than a utilitarian preference along with subsequent dejection that one lives with the second choice, not the first.
This characterization is simplistic and fails to take into account the
cohort and group differences relevant to the comparison—differences
that can be traced to the disparate projects that characterize the various
cohorts and groupings (as we have seen among the Tswana, for example). Specifically, Berger's claim that "the images of modernity inevitably collide with the images of tradition" (1974, p. 141) is true, but
only in very limited sense. Certainly the young mine-labor migrant
experiences a collision—one I have tried to describe. Yet he does not
simply live with the initial collision and continue to suffer dissonance
and dislocation. Almost immediately he begins to cope in consciousness.
He begins to articulate these formerly unconnected provinces of meaning in retrospective explication and organize them into a larger rational
structure—a set of plans, goals, and interpretations of his own past.
Segatlhe and Solomon illustrate quite poignantly that what began as a
collision can achieve a state of coherent integration.

Berger continues by saying that "as modernization proceeds there is a
transformation both in the organization of knowledge and in cognitive
style, in what is known and how it is known." "Most important the
specific form of rationality associated with modern science, technology,
and . . . economy imposes itself as an alien force in most traditional
societies" (1974, pp. 144, 147). The institutional "force" is certainly
there, but the *experience* of these institutions on the part of the Tswana
is hardly a simple analogue of our definitions of modern science, technology, and economy. These institutions are in the main *leviathans*.
They incorporate labor in a way that is a world removed from the way
they incorporate us, who are their executors and beneficiaries. The
force of these institutions for the Tswana lies in the appropriation of
labor and the *attempt* to appropriate the self-identity. Berger argues
correctly that they are an alien and indeed alienating force, which potentially could lead to a radical alteration in the way a person defines
his very identity. Nevertheless, colonial industrialism does not usually
succeed in radically altering the consciousness of labor by forcing the

latter to "internalize" its own assumptions about human nature. While it does alter self-identity, the actors—the Tswana in this case—play a creative and independent role in working out that altered identity. The Tswana have not become the "print-out" of industrial automata. While the Tswana incorporate elements of modernity into their self-identity (as Berger suggests), *the synthesis is a novel creation*. The change in identity is as much the result of meanings the Tswana invest in their changed material conditions as it is the result of meanings that the institutions of colonial industrialism seek to impose.

This fact alone leads me to agree with Berger that "people will be able to liberate themselves from social and political oppression only if they first liberate themselves from the patterns of thought imposed by the oppressors" (1974, p. 176). I presume Berger means that this is a necessary condition for liberation, in which case it has been achieved by most of the Tswana I worked with: the uneducated (the bourgeoisie are another matter altogether). As Eric Hoffer has said somewhere: discontent alone does not produce the desire for change; there must exist a sense of power. Power means to make one's own meanings in the world. This is the beginning of freedom's liberation from him who would oppress it.

SELECTED BIBLIOGRAPHY

Allport, Gordon W. 1958. *The nature of prejudice.* Garden City: Doubleday (Anchor Books).

Alverson, Hoyt. 1977. Peace Corps volunteers in rural Botswana. *Human Organization,* vol. 36, no. 3, pp. 274–81.

———. In press. The scars of bondage: imago of the black American in behavioral sciences research. *Phylon* (in press).

Berger, Peter, et al. 1974. *The homeless mind: modernization and consciousness.* New York: Random House (Vintage Books).

Biccard-Jeppe, Carl Wilhelm. 1946. *Gold mining on the Witwatersrand.* Johannesburg: Transvaal Chamber of Mines.

Biesheuvel, Simon. 1952. The study of African ability. *African Studies,* vol. 11, no. 2, pp. 45–58.

———. n.d. *The occupational abilities of Africans.* Pretoria: Offprint of the (South African) Council on Scientific and Industrial Research.

Botswana, Government of. 1970. *National development plan 1970–75.* Gaborone: Government Printer.

———. 1971. Ministry of Development Planning. *Statistical abstract.* Gaborone: Government Printer.

———. 1972a. Central Statistics Office. *Report on the population census of 1971.* Gaborone: Government printer.

———. 1972b. Ministry of Agriculture. *Kweneng resource survey.* Gaborone: Government Printer.

———. 1973. Central Statistics Office. *Guide to the villages of Botswana.* Gaborone: Government Printer.

Clark, Kenneth B. and Mamie P. 1958. Racial identification and preference in Negro children. In Eleanor Maccoby et al., ed., *Readings in social psychology* (3d ed.). New York: Holt, Rinehart & Winston.

Dai, Bingham. 1961. Minority group membership and personality development. In Jitsuichi Masuoka and Preston Valien, eds., *Race relations.* Chapel Hill: Univ. North Carolina Press.

Davis, Allison, and Dollard, John. 1940. *Children of bondage: the personality development of Negro youth in the urban South.* Washington, D.C.: American Council on Education.

Douglas, Mary. 1966. *Purity and danger: an analysis of concepts of pollution and taboo.* New York: Praeger.

Doxey, G. V. 1961. *The industrial colour bar in South Africa.* Cape Town: Oxford Univ. Press.

Dubb, Allie. 1974. The impact of the city. In W. D. Hammond-Tooke, ed., *The Bantu-speaking peoples of southern Africa.* London: Routledge & Kegan Paul.

Eding, D. F. et al., eds. 1972. *Report on village studies.* Gaborone: Government Printer.

Elkins, Stanley M. 1959. *Slavery: a problem in American institutional and intellectual life.* Chicago: Univ. Chicago Press.

Erasmus, Charles J. 1967. Upper limits of peasantry and agrarian reform: Bolivia, Venezuela, and Mexico compared. *Ethnology* 6(4).

——. 1968. Community development and the encogido syndrome. *Human Organization* 27(1).

——. 1970. Comments (on Gerrit Huizer, Resistance to change and radical peasant mobilization). *Human Organization* 29(4).

Evans-Pritchard, E. E., ed. 1967. *The Zande trickster.* Oxford: Clarendon Press.

Fanon, Frantz. 1970. *Black skin, white masks* (trans. Charles Lam Markmann). London: Paladin.

Foster, George M. 1967a. Introduction: peasant character and personality. In Potter et al., eds.

——. 1967b. Peasant society and the image of the limited good. In Potter et al., eds.

Fromm, Erich. 1970. *Social character in a Mexican village: a sociopsychoanalytic study.* Englewood Cliffs: Prentice-Hall.

Goffman, Erving. 1961. *Asylums: essays on the social situation of mental patients and other inmates.* Garden City: Doubleday (Anchor Books).

Gurevich, A. J. 1976. Time as a problem of cultural history. In UNESCO, *Cultures and time.* Paris.

Halpern, Jack. 1965. *South Africa's hostages.* Middlesex: Penguin Books (Penguin African Library).

Inskeep, R. R. 1969. The archaeological background. In Wilson and Thompson, eds.

Institute of Race Relations (annual). *Survey of race relations.* Johannesburg.

Jung, Carl. 1956. On the psychology of the trickster figure. In Paul Radin, *The trickster: a study in American Indian mythology.* New York: American Philosophical Library.

Kagame, Alex. 1976. Empirical apperception of time and conception of history in Bantu thought. In UNESCO, *Cultures and time.* Paris.

Kardiner, Abram, and Ovesey, Lionel. 1951. *The mark of oppression: a psychosocial study of the American Negro.* New York: Norton.

Katzen, M. F. 1969. White settlers and the origin of a new society, 1652–1778. In Wilson and Thompson, eds.

Kerenyi, Karl. 1956. The trickster in relation to Greek mythology. In Paul Radin, *The trickster: a study in American Indian mythology.* New York: American Philosophical Library.

Leacock, Eleanor Burke, ed. 1971. *The culture of poverty: a critique.* New York: Simon & Schuster.

Lewis, Oscar. 1965. *La Vida: a Puerto Rican family in the culture of poverty.* New York: Random House.

Merleau-Ponty, Maurice. 1962. *The phenomenology of perception* (trans. Colin Smith). New York: Humanities Press.

Meszaros, Istvan. 1972. Contingent and necessary class consciousness. In Istvan Meszaros, ed., *Aspects of history and class consciousness.* New York: Herder and Herder.

Miller, Delbert, and Form, William. 1964. *Industrial sociology.* New York: Harper & Row.

Mine Labour Organization. 1974. Statistics collected by author at Kaale, Botswana office.

Mischel, Walter. 1961. Father absence and the delay of gratification. J. Abnormal and Social Psychology 63.

Morel, E. D. 1969. *The black man's burden.* New York: Monthly Review Press.

Morland, Kenneth J. 1963. The development of racial bias in young children. *Theory Into Practice* 2.

Moynihan, Daniel P. 1968. The professors and the poor. In Daniel P. Moynihan, ed., *On Understanding Poverty.* New York: Basic Books.

Pelc, Jerzy. 1971. Semiotic functions as applied to the analysis of the concept of metaphor. In *Studies in functional logical semiotics of natural language.* The Hague: Mouton.

Pettigrew, Thomas P. 1964. *A profile of the Negro American.* Princeton: Van Nostrand.

Potter, Jack M. et al., eds. 1967. *Peasant society: a reader.* Boston: Little, Brown.

Rex, John. 1973. *Race, colonialism, and the city.* London: Routledge & Kegan Paul.

Ricoeur, Paul. 1967. *Husserl: an analysis of his phenomenology* (trans. Edward G. Ballard and Lester E. Embree). Evanston: Northwestern Univ. Press.

Rohrer, John H., and Edmonson, Munro S., eds. 1960. *The eighth generation: cultures and personalities of New Orleans Negroes.* New York: Harper.

Schapera, Isaac. 1940. *Married life in an African tribe.* London: Faber and Faber.

——. 1947. *Migrant labor and tribal life.* London: Oxford Univ. Press.

——. 1965. *Praise poems of Tswana chiefs.* Oxford: Clarendon Press.

Schutz, Alfred. 1962–66. *Collected Papers* (vol. 2, *Studies in Social Theory*, ed. Maurice Natanson). The Hague: Martinus Nijhoff.

Smit, P. 1970. *Botswana: resources and development.* Pretoria: African Institute.

Strauss, Robert. 1969. The problem of conceptualizing poverty. In Thomas Weaver and Alvin Magid, eds., *Poverty: New Interdisciplinary Perspectives.* San Francisco: Chandler.

Thompson, Leonard. 1969a. Cooperation and conflict: the Zulu kingdom and Natal. In Wilson and Thompson, eds.

——. 1969b. Cooperation and conflict: the high veld. In Wilson and Thompson, eds.

UNESCO. 1976. *Cultures and time.* Paris: UNESCO Press.

Valentine, Charles. 1968. *Culture and poverty: critique and counter-proposals.* Chicago: Univ. Chicago Press.

van der Horst, Sheila. 1971. *Native labour in South Africa.* London: Frank Cass.

Wilson, Francis. 1971. Farming, 1866–1966. In Wilson and Thompson, eds.

——. 1972. *Labour in the South African gold mines 1911–1969.* Cambridge: Univ. Press.

Wilson, Monica. 1971. The growth of peasant communities. In Wilson and Thompson, eds.

Wilson, Monica, and Thompson, Leonard, eds. 1969–71. *The Oxford history of South Africa.* 2 vols. New York: Oxford Univ. Press.

Wolff, Kurt, ed. 1950. *The Sociology of Georg Simmel.* Glencoe: Free Press.

Wright, Richard. 1964. *White man, listen.* Garden City: Doubleday (Anchor Books).

INDEX

Absenteeism. *See* Villages and village life

Achievement. *See* Success

Africans. *See* Black Africans; Tribes, Tswana; Tswana people

Afrikaners (Boers), 142; vs. African peoples, 17, 19, 21-28, 30, 72, 203, 230-31, 245-46, 253, 260-61; British vs., 19, 21-25, 29; labor practices of, 22-23, 231, 243; as labor source, 16, 26; migration and expansion of, 16-19, 21-24, 55, 260, 261; republics of, 22, 23, 25; Tswana view of, 225, 238, 260, 261. *See also* Black-white relationships; Europeans

Age: and age-sets (ranking by age), 11, 13, 19, 142; cultural vs. natal, 48-49, 145, 154, 170-71, 278; division of labor by, 12; and employment, 70, 71, 76, 77, 88-89, 116-17, 150, 218; and expectations of future, 176-78, 179-82, 183, 184-85; and "hero" idea, 204; and knowledge or wisdom, 170-71, 218; and opinions on education, 162, 176; and opinions on European wealth, 259-63, 265; prerogatives of and respect for, 68, 132, 270; ratios, in population, 38, 52-53, 57, 88; and self-identity concept, 49, 111, 116, 145; as social category, 12, 13, 19, 142; and "success," 123-24, 157-58; and values, 128, 155, 180; and views of rural elders, 179-82; and violence, 153; and "wants," 116, 124, 145-46, 150-51, 154-64, 224. *See also* Time

Agriculture and husbandry: chief crops, 11, 22, 51, 54, 268; crop failures, 36, 51, 55, 57, 76, 123, 148, 154; of European settlers (Afrikaners), 17, 19, 21, 22, 23, 25-26, 55; and fencing, 159-60, 261; "finished," 75, 147-48, 151-52; "progressive" vs. traditional, 158-60, 177-78, 180, 181; and surplus, 60, 64, 122-23, 158, 173-74; wage labor vs., 41, 116-17, 118, 136, 158, 178, 180, 238, 239, (labor recruitment and) 26, 33, (dependency on) 48, 75-77, 88, 123, 241, 255; as "want-to-do," 122-29, 133, 145, 154. *See also* Botswana, Government of; Cattle and livestock; Climate; Food; Labor; Land; Rainfall; Rural society; Villages and village life; Water

Alienation, 134, 136, 210, 265, 271; from home (*magkwelwa*), 71, 161; of land, 41. *See also* Coping; Villages and village life

America, 111, 261, 266

Animal fables, 195, 196, 204, 206-13, 248-51. *See also* Literature, oral

Animals. *See* Agriculture and husbandry; Cattle and livestock

Bantu-speaking people, 10, 13, 17, 49, 167; European "knowledge" of, 99-100; migrations of, 9, 16. *See also* Language; Tswana people

"Bantustans" (South African native reserves), 36. *See also* Land

Basutoland, 24

Community *(continued)*
of, 46; cash vs. traditional reciprocities in, 62, 63, 141, 160, 161; and charity, 40, 149; development programs, 42, 64; "face work" in, 140; ideally good, 137–38; lack of confidence in, 133, 149, 151–52; political, 13; social sentiments and relations of (hospitality, peace, law), 122, 138–44, 158, 159–60; Tswana definition of, 137; and "wants," 122, 145–64 (passim). *See also* Chiefs and chiefdom; "Face work" (face-to-face contact); Family, the; Social relationships; Villages and village life
"Compound system." *See* Mines and mining
Congo, the (Zaire), 30
Consciousness. *See* Mind or consciousness
Content Farm (government research), 159, 180, 202. *See also* Botswana, Government of
Conversation. *See* Language
Coping, 3, 130, 165, 174, 279; and doing-for-oneself, 120, 135–36, 156; with European/Western world, 45, 58, 178, 210; vs. fear and depression, 184; mine workers and, 222, 228; with town life, 242, 243, 251, 252–54, 255. *See also* Culture; Hero, the; Success; Survival
Cottage industry, 37, 149, 181; and crafts, craftsmen, 58, 61, 62, 64. *See also* Industrialism
Court (of law), village, 14. *See also* Laws
Crafts and craftsmen. *See* Cottage industry
Culture: beliefs questioned, 172–75, 265; and cultural vs. natal age, 48–49, 145, 154, 170–71, 278; and culture shock/conflict ("collision of images"), 27, 158, 177–79, 216, 221, 242–43, 258, 270, 279 (*see also* loss of Setswana, *below*); and doing-for-oneself, 133–37, 148–49, 155–57; European (*Sekgoa*), 266, 270;

influence of Western, 74, 85, 86, 133, 251, 252, 265, 268, 278; and initiation rites, 194, 244, 267–69 (passim); knowledge-in, and explication, 186; and life-projects, life-worlds, 8, 145, 154–58 (passim), 163–64, 265, 271–72; loss of Setswana, 67, 72, 86, 138, 140, 147, 158, 179, 184, 258, 265–70 (passim), 277–78; and "nature" of Black Africans, 90, 96, 98; "of poverty," 2, 276; "presenting," 91; pride in, 47, 134, 267–70; transmission of (handing down), 111, 152–54; "treasures" of, 125–29, 134, 195; Tswana view of, summarized, 266–72. *See also* Animal fables; Coping; Education; Europeans; Hero, the; Language; Laws; Poetry; West, the

Death, 270; expectation of, (in mines) 227, 228, 229, 231, 234, (in towns) 239; infant mortality rate, 39; mine mortality rate, 95; Tswana idea of, 15, 113, 127
Demography. *See* Population
Desert, 10, 46, 48, 50. *See also* Rainfall; Water
Diamonds and diamond mines, 22, 24, 26, 27, 28, 37, 55, 246. *See also* Mines and mining
Diet. *See* Food
Difaqane. See "Time of great troubles" (*difaqane*)
Dingane (Zulu chief), 21, 203, 204
"Discrimination," 2, 257. *See also* Social relationships
"Doing-for-oneself." *See* Success; "Wanting-to-do" (of Tswana people)
Douglas, Mary, 188
Doxey, G. V., 26, 27
Drinking habits: and beer, 11, 59–62 (passim), 76, 83, 107; in mines, 93, 104, 106–07, 233
Dubb, Allie, 32
Dutch, the: Africans as peons of, 21, 22; amalgamate with Khoikhoi, 16; British vs., 19; and East India Com-

250, 264, 265; and missionaries, 21, 23, 24. *See also* Belief(s)

Republic of South Africa. *See* South Africa

Reservations, reserves. *See* Land

Responsibility, 100, 188, 191, 224, 230; "failure" and, 120

Rex, John, 34

Rhodes, Cecil, 28, 29

Rhodesia. *See* Zimbabwe

Ricoeur, Paul, 273–74, 275

Rift Valley, 9

Rural society: of Afrikaners, 29; Botswana as, 38, 40, 42, 79; endangered, 29, 30, 157; "escape" from, 48, 84; and poverty, 33, 75–77, 83, 164; relationships in, 14, 54, 85–86, 137–38, 159–60; and views of rural people, 72, 179–82; and wage labor, 46, 47, 50. *See also* Agriculture and husbandry; Urbanism; Villages and village life

Sand River Convention (1852), 23

San peoples, 16, 17. *See also* "Bushmen"

Savanna or veld, 10, 46. *See also* Platteland (highveld)

"Scars of bondage" thesis. *See* Colonialism

Schapera, Isaac, 55, 58, 66, 67, 70, 196–97, 204, 205

Schutz, Alfred, 215, 257

Sebele (Kwena chief), 203, 204

Sechele (Kwena chief), 24, 28

Segatlhe, Gustav Ernst, 75–77 (passim), 197–98, 201–02, 205–07 (passim), 279; autobiography of, 243–49, 251

Sekgoa (European culture), 266, 270. *See also* Culture

Self-concept, self-evaluation. *See* Self-identity

Self-esteem, 181, 251

Self-identity: age and, 49, 111, 116, 145; beliefs about (as indicators of), 1, 7–8, 45, 48, 92, 111–16, 145, 210, 271; child-rearing and, 65–71, 115;

defined, 3–4, 6, 110, 115; empiricist vs. rationalist views of, 4–5; "human" nature" and, 110–11, 112–15, 222; inequality and, 46, 85–89, 255–59; institutional control of behavior and, 46, 90, 92, 278–80; name and, 194; oral literature and, 193–94; religion and, 74; sexual differences in, 50; Tswana view of, 111–16, 187, 192–94

Self-praise. *See* Poetry

Self-sufficiency. *See* Economy

Seretse Khama (president of Botswana), 184, 203, 204

Senwelo (Kgatla chief), 126

Setswana. *See* Culture; Language

Sex ratios, 38–39, 52–53, 57, 88. *See also* Women

Sexual play, 68, 87

Shaka (Zulu chief), 18, 261

"Shame orientation," 189. *See also* Guilt and shame

Shangaan tribe, 226. *See also* Tribes, Tswana

Simmel, Georg, 256

Slavery: under Boers/Europeans, 259–65 (passim); British Empire abolishes, 21; effect of, on African personality, 2; and hybrid population, 16; and indentured servitude, 17, 21; and peonage or serfdom, 21, 22, 61–62. *See also* Labor

Smit, P., 35, 36, 41, 42

Smuts, Jan, 105

Social class. *See* Class, political and social

Social relationships: apprentice, 102; with "big-stomachs," 72, 73, 138, 176, 233, 252, 253; with "boss boys," 91–93, 97, 101–02, 108, 224–34 (passim); community, 122, 133, 137, 138–44, 151–52, 158, 159–60; "discrimination" in, 2, 257; father-son, 132–33; friendship, 87, 104, 129, 133–34, 139, 149; interethnic antagonisms, segregation and warfare, 18, 75, 77, 79, 93, 153, 203, 225–36 (passim), 253, 260, 261,